Recovering Subversion

Feminist Politics Beyond the Law

Recovering Subversion

Feminist Politics Beyond the Law

NIVEDITA MENON

PERMANENT BLACK

UNIVERSITY OF ILLINOIS PRESS URBANA, CHICAGO, AND SPRINGFIELD

Manufactured in the United States of America

∞ This book is printed on acid-free paper.

1 2 3 4 5 C P 6 5 4 3 2

Complete Cataloging-in-Publication data is available from the Library of Congress.

ISBN 978-0-252-07211-6 (pbk)
ISBN 978-0-252-02969-1 (cl)

Contents

Preface

This book makes an argument about law and feminist politics that I have been working out for several years now. I started thinking about what appeared to be an increasingly troubled relationship when I first began my doctoral dissertation in the early 1990s. Since then parts of my dissertation have been published as papers, critiques and responses to which have helped to refine my argument. In addition I have expanded the field of my inquiry, and thought through several knotty areas by considering fresh material on areas ranging from feminist initiatives on sexual harassment and debates on conversion in India to the parity movement in France. Over the last couple of years, several friends have insisted from time to time that I draw together the different scattered threads of my argument into a book. I would like to thank them for their encouragement, and Rukun Advani for the query that finally got me going—'Do you have a book lurking inside?'

It seems I did, and here it is.

The Introduction and Chapter 5 are previously unpublished, and the remaining chapters have been substantially reworked with fresh material. The genealogy of these is given below:

Chapter 1 is developed on the basis of two earlier papers in which I first started thinking along these lines: 'Rights, Bodies and the Law: Rethinking Feminist Politics of Justice' in *Gender and Politics in India*, ed. Nivedita Menon, Delhi, Oxford University Press, 1999, and 'Rights, Law and Feminist Politics: Rethinking Our Practice' in Swapna Mukhopadhyay, ed., *In the Name of Justice*, Delhi, Institute of Social Studies Trust, 1998.

Chapter 2 is an expanded and revised version of 'The Impossibility of Justice: Female Foeticide and the Feminist Discourse on Abortion' in Patricia Uberoi, ed., *Social Reform, Sexuality and the State*, Delhi, Sage Publications, 1996. (This volume was earlier an issue of *Contributions to Indian Sociology*, 29, 1&2, 1995.) The very first version of these ideas was published in a short article 'Abortion and the Law: Questions for Feminism', in the Canadian *Journal of Women and the Law*, vol. 6, no. 1, 1993.

Chapter Three takes off from 'Embodying the Self: Feminism, Sexual Violence and the Law' in Partha Chatterjee and Pradeep Jeganathan, eds, *Subaltern Studies XI*, Delhi, Permanent Black, 2000. It includes new work on sexual harassment law in India.

Chapter Four is an expanded and revised version of 'Elusive "Woman": Feminism and the Women's Reservation Bill', *Economic and Political Weekly*, 21–27 October/28 October–3 November 2000.

Acknowledgements

It is a pleasure to acknowledge here the friendships and solidarities, the welcome opportunities, the shared commitment and visions, out of which this book has emerged.

Friends who generously spared time from their own busy schedules to track down references and books, reports and news, or simply brought to my attention things that proved to be crucial for my understanding—Aisha Khan, Ashwini Sukhtankar, Deepak Mehta, Laxmi Moorthy, Meenu Gaur, Monobina Gupta, N. Harish, Nandini Sundar, Prakash Upadhyaya, Rajive Tiwari, Ritty Lukose.

The resources of Jagori Women's Resource Centre, and the Centre for Women's Development Studies, Delhi have been invaluable. The staff at the library of the Indian Institute of Law have been invariably good-humoured and knowledgeable, and of course the Nehru Memorial Museum and Library has been home for most of my adult life. Sujit Deb, Librarian at the Centre for the Study of Developing Societies is always enthusiastic and extraordinarily helpful. Friends at Saheli, particularly Laxmi Moorthy, have been patient with queries and prolix with replies—many thanks to all of you.

The core of this book is my doctoral dissertation from Delhi University, and I would like to thank Professor Manoranjan Mohanty for his encouragement and space-giving supervision. When I began to write my dissertation I did not have a computer, and Urvashi Butalia revolutionised its production by the loan of her laptop. Before that act of generosity, several very dear friends bore with fortitude my arrival on their doorstep with handwritten drafts and notes, resignedly laying an extra place at the table and organising an extra bed the moment my finger shrilled their doorbell. Madulika Banerjee (and the Banerjee family), Farida Khan (and Arif Ali and Abid) and Dilip Simeon will shudder reminiscently at this. The various bits and bobs in different programmes then had to be converted to one compatible with Urvashi's laptop—Nath, Sharada Nair's husband, did this for me with a sort of benign contempt for one so ill-equipped to cope even with what was still the late twentieth century. Years later, when this book was being printed out, KAQA Hilal and Himangshu Bhattacharya performed similar kind offices, for which I would like to record my gratitude.

Over the last six years, several fellowships have given me invaluable time away from the rigours of teaching, and enabled the luxury of research and solitude—an Indian Council of Social Science Research Fellowship to Maison des Sciences de l'Homme (Paris) under the Cultural Exchange Programme, a Charles Wallace Fellowship to the School of Oriental and African Studies (London), a Visiting Fellowship to the Centre for the Study of Developing Societies (Delhi), a Rockefeller Fellowship to the Chicago Humanities Centre, University of Chicago, and a Sawyer Fellowship to the Advanced Study Centre, University of Michigan, and a brief stint at the Nehru Memorial Museum and Library. I would like to thank here the individuals and institutions that made this possible, especially Arjun Appadurai, Nicholas Dirks, Valentine Daniel, Ashis Nandy, Jean-Luc Racine, Meenakshi Gopinath and O.P. Kejriwal.

My stay in Paris was made especially fruitful by Rada Ivecovic and Danielle Haase Dubosc, who went out of their way to help find references, fix appointments, translate whenever necessary, and who, simply by sparing the time for long conversations, enriched my understanding. Meeting the legendary Etienne Balibar and talking to him is a cherished memory. (I will confess naively that a little shiver ran down my spine as he said casually, 'I told Foucault' . . .) I would also like to thank all those activists and scholars in Paris who were kind enough to give me interviews—they are cited in the pages that follow, but I need hardly add that their incorporation in various ways into my argument should not implicate them in any way.

The four batches of students of my Women and Politics course at Lady Shri Ram College (LSR, Delhi University), many of whom continue to be good friends, contributed more than they might ever know, to my growth and understanding. I thank them for forcing me to clarity, for their enthusiasm and their youthful cynicism. Friends who formed my emotional, intellectual and political support group at LSR—Sarah Joseph, Vasudha Pande, Anuja Agrawal, Anjali Bhatia, Maya Joshi, Sharada Nair, Hephzibah Israel, Nilofer Kaul, Sumangala Damodaran, Ujjayini Ray, Mitali Mishra, Ira Singh—I miss the daily mutual affirmation! Mr S.C. Mittal has been valiant and gracious about acting as courier between LSR and Patparganj—for that and his other innumerable kindnesses over and above the call of duty, I am grateful.

Meenu Gaur, Sunalini Kumar and Bhrigupati Singh expended much creative energy in the final stages of this book, for which my love and thanks.

The intermittent meetings many years ago, of the feminist reading group composed of Mita Radhakrishnan, Kalpana Vishwanath, Maya, Janaki Abraham, Pratiksha Baxi, Geetanjali Gangoli and Kath were stimulating and enjoyable, and I learnt and rethought a great deal.

Ayisha Abraham, Satyajit Mayor, Aamir Mufti and Chandana Mathur made my first visit to New York a glorious adventure. Strangers turned family overnight, they made that crazy and beautiful city come alive for me—I can never thank them enough for their spontaneous warmth and generosity. All of them, with the addition of Saloni, Ishar, Dermot and Conall continue to be home for me, wherever they are.

Cherished friendships, some of which have survived the daunting distance of oceans, others the claustrophobic closeness of a flight of stairs—Akbar Zaidi, Ania Loomba, Greta Mathews, Hari Nayer, Harsh Sethi, Hartman de Souza, Jamal Kidwai, Janaki Abraham, Javeed Alam, Jinee Lokaneeta, Krishna Menon, Mahmood Mamdani, Malathi de Alwis, Mary John, M.S.S. Pandian, Narayan Gopalkrishnan, Pradeep Jeganathan, Priyamvada Gopal, Rachana Johri, Rada

Ivecovic, Rajeev Bhargava, Ranjana Padhi, Ranjani Mazumdar, Ravi Sundaram, Ravi Vasudevan, Sadia Khan, Sanjay Mishra, Satish Deshpande, Shahana Bhattacharya, Suvir Kaul, Tani Bhargava, Usha K.R., Uma Chakravarty, Vinitha Nayer, Vishwas Satgar, Yogendra Yadav.

Conversations, arguments, intellectual debts—Kian Tajbaksh, Partha Chatterjee, Rajeswari Sunder Rajan, K. Saradamoni, Sumit Sarkar, Tanika Sarkar, Zoya Hassan.

To the large circle—the many circles—of friends and fellow-travellers who have provided contexts for action from time to time, in some of which I have been directly involved, in others peripherally, and in yet others, through solidarity; but whose collective vision makes possible my world, its interpretation and its changing—Sampradayikta Virodhi Andolan, People's Movement for Secularism, Dilli Janwadi Adhikar Manch, Parmanu Bamb Virodhi Andolan, Movement in India for Nuclear Disarmament, Campaign for Lesbian Rights, Delhi University Forum for Democracy, Aman Ekta Manch, Yamunapaar Residents' Initiative, People's Union for Democratic Rights and Saheli—a warm salute.

Families—past and present, nuclear, unclear—

Gopi, G.K. Menon Sr., Lakshmi Menon, Arunima, Santwana Nigam, Aditi, Shankar, Rajindranath, Monobina, Lara.

Susheela Sharma, who keeps our home running like clockwork.

My brother Dilip and sister Pramada—exasperating, challenging, beloved.

Anirban Gupta Nigam—another world *is* possible, and I hope you help to build it.

Aditya Nigam—companion, comrade, fellow-dreamer.

My father B. Madhava Menon and mother Parakkat Devaki Kutty—who let us go, let us grow, and grew with us—to them I dedicate this book.

NIVEDITA MENON

List of Abbreviations

AIDWA	All India Democratic Women's Association
BJP	Bharatiya Janata Party
CLS	Critical Legal Studies
CPI	Communist Party of India
CPI (ML)	Communist Party of India (Marxist-Leninist)
CPI(M)	Communist Party of India (Marxist)
CSWI	Committee on the Status of Women in India
FASDSP	Forum Against Sex Determination and Sex Pre-selection
GSCASH	Gender Sensitisation Committee Against Sexual Harassment
IPC	Indian Penal Code
LCI	Law Commission of India
MTP Act	Medical Termination of Pregnancy Act
NCW	National Commission for Women
NGO	Non-Governmental Organisation
OBC	Other Backward Castes
PIL	Public Interest Litigation
PNDT Act	Pre-Natal Diagnostic Techniques Act
SD Tests	Sex Determination Tests
SMA	Shetkari Mahila Aghadi
WRB	Women's Reservation Bill

Introduction

Constitutionalism and the Feminist Subject

This book addresses a particular dilemma as I see it, for radical politics—in particular, feminist politics—in India. The dilemma has become visible over the last two decades, and arises at the interface of radical political practice with the logic of constitutionalism. By 'constitutionalism' I refer to a specific method adopted by modern democracies of safeguarding the autonomy of the individual self. In a classic formulation, Carl Friedrich in his study *Constitutional Government and Democracy* saw the core objective of constitutionalism as that of safeguarding each member of a political community.[1] It is now generally recognised however, that this objective is achieved by a process of enforcing universal norms that marginalise, render obsolete and de-legitimize contesting worldviews and value systems. This particular method of organising democracies has a specific history and arose in a particular geopolitical location—that is, in Europe in the seventeenth century. By historicising this method, we remind ourselves, to use Upendra Baxi's words, that 'much of the business of "modern" constitutionalism was transacted during the early halcyon days of colonialism/imperialism. That historical timespace marks a combined and uneven development of the world in the processes of early modernity . . . [C]onstitutionalism inherits the propensity for violent social exclusion from the "modern".'[2] Constitutionality is driven towards the erasure of any kind of normative ethic which differs from its own unitary central ethic—precisely in such a denial of subjective ethics and the assertion of 'objectivity' lay its emancipatory potential four centuries ago. That moment may have passed.

Four centuries later, the dilemma that faces radical politics is what I term the 'paradox of constitutionalism'—that is, the tension in which the need to assert various and differing moral visions comes up against the universalising drive of constitutionality and the language of universal rights. The language of rights and citizenship is thus no longer unproblematically available to an emancipatory politics—this is the heart of the argument I will unfold over the pages that follow.

Specifically in the context of feminist politics, it has become difficult to sustain 'woman' as the subject of such a politics, despite (or perhaps because of) the explosion of 'gender' as a category of analysis in official state and NGO discourse. Susie Tharu and Tejaswini Niranjana point to one aspect of the dilemma when they say:

> For all those who invoke gender . . . 'women' seems to stand in for the subject (agent, addressee, field of inquiry) of feminism itself. There is a sense therefore, in which the new visibility is an index of the success of the women's movement. But clearly this success is also problematic. A wide range of issues rendered critical by feminism are now being invested in and annexed by projects that contain and deflect that initiative. Possibilities of alliance with other subaltern forces (Dalits, for example) that are opening up in civil society are often blocked, and feminists find themselves drawn into disturbing configurations within the dominant culture.[3]

Here they refer to the phenomenon of the 1980s and 1990s, where the active presence of women in right-wing movements (against the Mandal Commission recommendations on reservations for Backward castes and in Hindu right-wing mobilisations), and the use of feminist slogans by these, forced feminists to rethink many old certainties.[4]

The French feminist Michele Le Doeuff highlights another aspect of what appears to be a global phenomenon when she uses the term 'state-organized feminism', which, she suggests, is replacing feminist politics on the ground in France and elsewhere: 'If people think that there is now a feminism from above, a kind of state-organized feminism, you may find the area you want already occupied.' This kind of feminism from above has happened before in history, Le Doeuff points out, citing the examples of Turkey under Ataturk and the Soviet Union. Nor is it to be rejected out of hand: '[I]ntroducing literacy for girls and abolishing polygamy are important steps. But it is never enough. Moreover, it has an important drawback. It discourages ordinary women from taking the initiative. In the long run culture is not altered without individual and collective action "from below".'[5]

We encounter another question altogether regarding the proper 'subject' of feminist politics, with the growing recognition that 'women' do not simply exist to be mobilised by feminism. The controversies over Shah Bano and the Muslim Women (Protection of Rights Upon Divorce) Act in the late 1980s, and over the Women's Reservation Bill in the late 1990s, have revealed the impossibility of appealing to 'women' as a category unmediated by other identities like religion and caste. Even in issues like femicide of foetuses and sexual violence, where the existence of the female body and its violation in different ways appears to be incontestable, I shall argue that the intersection of feminist notions of the body with legal discourse produces dilemmas of a nature that feminist politics has not fully confronted. The experience of feminist politics in the arena of law not only raises questions about the capacity of the law to act as a transformative instrument but more fundamentally, points to the possibility that functioning in a manner compatible with legal discourse can radically refract the ethical and emancipatory impulse of feminism itself.

Feminist Critiques of Law as Strategy

Feminist theories of laws have developed considerably over the last two decades. Early feminist work (from the 1960s onwards) saw laws in instrumental terms as the potential source of equal rights and the emancipation of women. Society being steeped in patriarchal values and practices, the law and the state were seen as the only agents with the power and the legitimacy to bring about egalitarian social transformation. Gradually, especially by the 1980s, the experience of women's movements all over the world has led to an increasingly critical engagement with legal discourse. Four interlinked strands of argument can be discerned in this engagement:

(a) Most legal systems have features which are actively discriminatory to women, denying them equal rights to property, to certain kinds of employment, and so on.[6]
(b) Even where there is *de jure* equality, law in its actual functioning discriminates against women because legal agents interpret laws in patriarchal ways.[7]
(c) Even when law treats men and women equally it is discriminatory to women because men and women are located in an unequal and hierarchical manner in cultural, social and economic formations. In other words, it is unjust to treat unequals equally.[8]
(d) The law and the state render invisible women's subjective experience of oppression since objectivity is installed as the norm. In this sense the law is essentially Male and can only ever partially comprehend the harms done to women.[9]

This kind of critical analysis of the law underlies feminist campaigns all over the world. The goals are to redress the discriminatory nature of particular laws, to create new laws in areas of 'judicial void',[10] that is, in the 'private' realm of the family, and consistently to expose the patriarchal bias in the interpretation and implementation of existing laws.

In India there has been over a decade of feminist engagement with the law on the issue of violence against women. Particularly in the 1980s the women's movement reacted to almost every instance of violence against women by demanding legislative action. These efforts have been successful in that every campaign resulted in legislative changes such as the Criminal Law Amendment Act 1983, Dowry Prohibition (Amendment) Act 1984, Indecent Representation of Women (Prohibition) Act 1986, Commission of Sati (Prevention) Act 1987.[11] This success however, raised a new set of questions: why did the implementation of these laws remain conservative and partial? In fact, as Flavia Agnes points out, since most of the new laws provide for more stringent punishment, there have been fewer convictions than before.[12]

The legal campaign as strategy has always been accompanied by debate within the Indian women's movement and the major lines of criticism that have emerged are:

(a) That the law is not enough. Nandita Gandhi and Nandita Shah for example, hold that no part of the women's movement is under any illusion that the law is a genuinely transformative instrument. At most, women's groups see legal campaigns as a broad strategy to achieve legitimacy, to create public awareness on specific issues and to secure some short-term legal redress. The struggle to transform the patriarchal nature of existing laws can only be part of a wider struggle. Similarly, Nandita Haksar urges the incorporation into legal practice of an understanding of the political and social basis for gender injustice. Without this, no law reform can be effective. She gives the example of a question in the Criminal Law examination when she was a student—an impotent man kills a prostitute who laughs at him for his infirmity. Can he take the defence of provocation? Haksar says that nearly all the women students held that he could not, and did badly in the examination.[13] The point that Haksar's account underscores is that law reform cannot be divorced from the more fundamental struggle to transform social values.

(b) That constant recourse to the law creates a series of new legislations which often mean the increase of state control, while implementation remains unsatisfactory. This misgiving has been consistently expressed by Madhu Kishwar, Ruth Vanita and Flavia Agnes.[14]

(c) Gail Omvedt holds that lobbying for legal reform by urban-based groups wastes energy without achieving much. Such a strategy offers little challenge in her opinion, to the social, systemic basis of increasing atrocities against women. The real challenge can only come from mass-based militant politics.[15]

In a recent significant essay Nandita Haksar considerably complicates her own earlier position. She focuses on the conflict between feminist and human rights ethics, on the basis of her experience as a lawyer in both fields, and presents a complex account of the contradictions involved in moving within both discourses simultaneously. Taking up the issues of obscenity/pornography, the rights of the accused in rape cases, and property rights within customary laws of tribal peoples, she comes to the deeply challenging conclusion that 'we should resort to the law only when the movement is strong enough to carry the law reform forward'. This is a statement that goes far beyond the familiar litany of 'the law is not enough'—rather, Haksar is clear that continual recourse to the law is 'a substitute for the other harder option of building a movement for an alternative vision'. She is particularly critical of feminist initiatives to press for property rights for tribal women, because she sees this as being predicated on 'classical human rights arguments' which are incapable of comprehending the complex practices which make up tribal jurisprudence. She urges the need for a struggle within tribal communities to evolve new customs which are more egalitarian—'a far more difficult task than filing a petition under Article 14[16] or getting the support of women who have no stakes in the survival of tribal societies'.[17]

Another notable recent intervention is an essay by Vina Mazumdar, one of the matriarchs of the women's movement in India, who charts her own and the movement's journey over the last five decades. The essay reflects the confidence and optimism that characterised social movements in the early years after independence, but is even more remarkable for its honesty and evident rethinking over the years. In a significant footnote, discussing the confidence that the new constitution gave women of her generation, she talks of her father, 'a self-confessed conservative', resolving her dilemma over the conflict between maternal and professional responsibilities. He introduced a missing 'third factor'—her responsibility not to waste the resources the country invested in her training. This sense of responsibility to the nation-state, and correspondingly, the expectation of progressive transformation through it, is characteristic of the generation which came of age through the anti-imperialist struggle. This confidence began to unravel after the Emergency years, and as Mazumdar tracks the changes, gradually the women's movement began to focus on economic issues, particularly from the 1980s. Thus a new identity was asserted by the movement, breaking out of dominant perceptions of women's issues as mainly social, not political and economic. What is notable is that this new identity was posited in opposition to the state, not in the spirit of partnership of the early years. In the course of this journey, says Mazumdar, 'I may have lost the sense of certainty which I shared with the earlier generations of the Indian women's movement . . . in viewing legislation as the major instrument for ushering in changes in social order.'[18] Later in the same essay she tries to limit her criticism to a particular moment, holding that the law's 'historical failure at a particular point of time should not be generalised . . . to an impossibility'.[19]

Thus the legal campaign as strategy has always been accompanied by doubts and questions among Indian feminists, all the more so in recent years. So it is untenable to hold as Archana Parasher does, that feminist critiques of law reforms only come from societies where women already have won formal equality in legal rights:

> Feminist writers who point to the drawbacks of law reforms all live in societies in which women have already gained formal equal legal rights . . . Their concerns shifted beyond law reform and equal rights only after they had virtually achieved legal equality with men.[20]

Parasher thus suggests a simple hierarchy—first, 'formal legal rights' for women which must historically precede 'demands for the autonomy to control their sexuality or the right to the inviolability of their bodies.'[21] Further, Parasher evidently sees this as a process which would proceed by similar stages in all societies, that is, legal equality followed by other kinds of transformation.

There are two problems with this argument. First, the disquiet about law reform among feminists in the West is not simply a matter of looking 'beyond law reform' after equal rights have been achieved, as Parasher sees it, but a realisation that law reform itself has worked against feminist interests.[22] A second, in my view more fundamental, problem is that in postcolonial societies such as ours where the law was a product of the exigencies of colonial administration, it cannot be granted the same emancipatory force it might have had in Europe during the transition from feudalism to capitalism. While some kind of notions of justice and rights did exist in pre-colonial Indian communities, 'rights' in the modern sense were produced by the colonial transformation of indigenous judicial discourse and administrative institutions. The fact that this encounter with modernity occurred through a political system that was at its core, violent, distinguishes 'our' modernity (to use Partha Chatterjee's evocative phrase)[23] from modernity as it emerged in Europe. The dislocation caused by modernity in Europe four centuries ago was equally brutal, but in Asia and Africa there was a double violence involved—the simultaneous disruption caused by modernity and colonialism. This is the encounter suggested by the term 'postcolonial' as I use it here. Postcolonialism thus begins from the very first moment of colonial contact. As one set of scholars puts it, 'It is the discourse of oppositionality which colonialism brings into being.'[24]

The emergence of this modern language of rights certainly empowered many subaltern sections against indigenous elites, but contrary to the claim of this language to universality, was not unambiguously emancipatory for all. Indeed, it had devastating consequences for many subaltern sections which were drastically marginalised and disciplined by the operation of modern codes of identity and governance.[25]

Despite misgivings, however, the women's movement, like other social movements in India, continues to retain the vision of the law as a transformative and emancipatory instrument, flawed and recalcitrant though it may be. Vina Mazumdar as we saw above, despite her rethinking over the decades, continues to retain faith in regenerating the law's transformative role. Further, the critiques that have emerged have yet to confront the full implications of a radical problematising of legal discourse. For example, what happens to notions of 'public' and 'private'—a distinction central to designing the legitimate scope of the law—in the course of feminist critique? The next section will point to some kinds of impasse that such critiques have reached.

The Public–Private Dichotomy

In liberal theory the distinction between 'public' and 'private' answers the question of the legitimate extent of the authority of the law. The public realm is understood in this context to be open to government regulation while the private realm is to be protected from such action—sexuality and the family being understood to be private. In Marxist theory too, this distinction is central, although from a different point of view. Engels argued that women are oppressed because 'the administration of the household lost its public character . . . It became a private service.'[26] The 'private' here is the arena of oppression and only when women emerge into the sphere of production will they become truly emancipated. Since, for Engels, the motor force of history is provided by changes in the relations of production (defined, in the context of capitalism, as the relations between capital and labour), housework is not 'work'. Women participate in history only to the extent that they emerge from the 'private' and enter the industrial workforce.

Feminist scholarship emerging from both liberal and Marxist traditions have contested this distinction as being conceptually flawed and politically oppressive. From within the liberal tradition comes the argument that the dichotomy assumed between 'public' (non-domestic) and 'private' (domestic) has enabled the family to be excluded from the values of 'justice' and 'equality' which have animated liberal thought since the seventeenth-century beginnings of liberalism. The 'individual' was the adult male head of the household, and thus his right to be free from interference by the State or Church included his rights over those in his control in the private realm—women, children, servants. Thus, oppression within the family was rendered invisible to political theory.[27]

In addition to sharing this view, socialist-feminists critique the public–private distinction in Marxist theory produced by the model of political economy based on 'production', defined as economic production for the capitalist market. This model, they argue, ignores the 'private' sphere of reproduction, where women are responsible for reproducing both humans and labour power. A very influential analysis has been that of Juliet Mitchell who uses the Althusserian notion of overdetermination to express the complexity of women's situation. She sees the key structures of women's situation as *Production, Reproduction, Sexuality* and *Socialisation of Children*, and rejects therefore, the idea that 'women's condition can be deduced derivatively from the economy' as Engels would have it.[28]

Another socialist-feminist, Michele Barrett, arguing against the view that women's oppression is located solely at the ideological level, says many of the categories which are called economic are in fact constituted historically in ideological terms—for example, the wage form in capitalism. Thus, the limitations of women's participation in wage labour are related to familial ideology; wage bargaining rests mostly on definitions of skill, which incorporate ideological assumptions, for example, the view that women's wages are secondary because of the ascription to all women of the destiny of wife and mother.[29] Similarly, Nancy Hartsock argues that to the extent that Marxism is grounded in men's activity in production and ignores women's activity in reproduction, Marxian categories themselves require critique.[30]

A more fundamental point is made by Linda Nicholson who establishes that the public–private distinction forms the very core of the Marxian understanding of production in so far as 'production' is understood to be conceptually different from 'reproduction'. This distinction historically evolves with capitalism since in pre-capitalist societies, child-rearing practices, sexual relations and 'productive' activities were organised conjointly through the medium of kinship. The Marxian model of political economy therefore, falsely universalises aspects peculiar to capitalism. Thus according to Nicholson, the Marxist theory of history is fundamentally flawed to the extent that it assumes class to be the primary basis of exploitation when the very distinction between class and gender is an aspect of capitalist relations of production alone.[31]

Clearly, feminists across the political spectrum are agreed that the public and the private are not two distinct and separate spheres, for the 'public' is enabled to maintain itself precisely by the construction of certain areas of experience as 'private'. As Gayatri Spivak puts it, the feminist reversal of the public–private hierarchy is more than a reversal—it is a displacement of the opposition itself. 'For if the fabric of the so-called public sector is woven of the so-called private, the definition of the private is marked by a public potential since it is the weave, or texture of public activity.'[32]

However, the consequences of this understanding for feminist practice are not so clear. From one kind of position it is possible then to argue that many claims important to feminists, from reproductive rights to protection against sexual harassment, are most effectively grounded on claims to privacy.[33] In fact the rhetoric of the individual's right to privacy has been used to secure some rights for women against the patriarchal family. For example in the USA, the landmark judgement on abortion in *Roe* v. *Wade* (1972) is based on the belief in the individual woman's right to privacy.[34] So was the judgement in 1965 that the right of married couples to use contraceptives is part of 'a right to privacy older than the Bill of Rights'.[35] Feminists who support privacy as a ground for securing rights for women, while they also challenge the traditional public–private dichotomy, make the argument that the virtues of privacy have not been available to women since they did not have the status of individuals in the public sphere. In this view therefore, the task of feminist practice is to transform the institutions and practices of gender so that a genuine sphere of privacy, free of governmental and legal intrusion, can be ensured for both men and women.[36]

Diametrically opposed to this is the position arising from the slogan 'the personal is political' which has brought into the public arena issues such as domestic violence against women, child abuse and marital rape. Adherents of this position do hold that the state is paternalistic and masculine, but they are confident that if a law is designed by feminists from the standpoint of women, it can be of advantage to women. The law should intervene therefore, in the recesses of the 'private' to ensure gender justice. From this point of view, the right to privacy is only a means to protect the existing structures of power and access to resources in the private sphere. For example, Catharine MacKinnon argues that by sanctioning abortion as a right of privacy, the state has ensured that the control women won out of this legislation has gone to men. She holds that when women get abortion as a 'private privilege', not a 'public right', in effect it is men—husbands, fathers—who end up controlling the decisions to abort. Further, when abortion is framed as a right of privacy, the state has no obligation to provide public funding for abortion.[37]

Feminists in India generally function from the second point of view, seeking legal intervention in more and more areas of 'judicial void'.[38] However, the focus on legislation is restricted to the realm of the 'private', that is, family and sexuality. There has been no nationwide feminist campaign for legislation comparable to this on any issues relating to the 'public' sphere, such as for the enforcement of the Equal Remuneration Act of 1976, or for crèche facilities at the workplace and so on. In effect, the only national-level feminist legal campaigns conducted have been on issues related to the family and sexuality. This is not surprising or unique to India. As Mary Fainsod

Katzenstein points out, 'body politics', that is, sexual/reproductive issues, reach the public agenda only when women's groups organise independently of the state. Government initiatives on gender issues are likely to be in the arena of economic issues because economic issues have always been 'public' in the sense of being accessible to reflection by society, and therefore very much on the agenda of the state, while sexual/reproductive issues have not. [39] Naturally, then, the feminist project has been to combat the privatisation of the latter.

However, 'to make public' can be understood in two senses, to use a distinction formulated by Seyla Benhabib—'making public' in the sense of questioning life forms and values that have been oppressive for women, making them accessible to reflection and revealing their socially constituted character, and 'making public' in the sense of making these issues subject to legislative and state action.[40] It seems to me that much of the experience of feminist politics all over the world has been that we have tended to conflate the two. That is, sexual/reproductive issues have been put on the public agenda *in the form of* demanding legislative action. In the Indian context Nandita Gandhi and Nandita Shah suggest that women have found it easier to fight against the state, or against social custom through the state, than to fight for their rights within the family or on 'personal' issues which 'bring us closer to the starkness of the inegalitarian and oppressive relationship between men and women'.[41] Is it precisely the intractability of the oppression at the level of 'the body' which leads feminist practice to attempt to comprehend and contain it in the discourse of coherence and uniformity offered by the law?

It is time to re-examine the relationship between legal discourse and the public–private distinction. Is 'the private' private because the law cannot intervene and influence it? But consider also that it is the law that constructs the private by refusing to intervene, by closing off that arena as inappropriate for its own intervention. Take, for instance, the judgement of the Delhi High Court, later upheld by the Supreme Court, that 'introduction of Constitutional law into the ordinary domestic relationship of husband and wife will strike at the very root of that relationship' and that 'in the privacy of the home and married life, neither Article 21 (right to Life) nor Article 14 (Right to Equality) has any place'.[42]

Evidently, the law sees the protection of 'the ordinary domestic relationship' as its business. Formulating the public–private distinction in this manner seems to resolve what Frances Olsen sees as the 'incoherence' of the language of intervention and non-intervention. Olsen's argument is that if 'the private' is defined as that unregulated by law, it is difficult to hold simultaneously that the private is in fact, indirectly regulated by law.[43] As the judgement mentioned above illustrates, the state's abdication of regulation is precisely a form of regulation.

If 'public' and 'private' have no existence prior to legal theory but are constructed by the functioning of legal discourse, what is the implication for feminist practice? Both strategies discussed—that of valorising the private as providing a sphere of individual freedom which has been denied to women, as well as that of opening up the oppression within the private to the public scrutiny of the law—fail to overcome and deconstruct the public–private dichotomy. The first reinscribes the separation of the two on the very site that this separation is being critiqued. It assumes that something called 'privacy' can be made to exist by using the law to limit its own jurisdiction, when the existence of 'privacy' is dependent on the same discourse which sets up 'the public' as the arena of political virtue. For example, Jean Cohen argues for the right to abortion in terms of 'new privacy rights', that reproductive rights are to be justified in terms of individual control over the symbolic interpretation of the body.[44] However, this argument assumes precisely what any project to radicalise reproductive freedom should confront, that is, that symbolic order which inscribes the body as body, as separate from other bodies, as gendered, as healthy/unhealthy, and so on. Cohen's argument for reproductive freedom in terms of individual rights assumes the individual to be the arbiter of what shall be understood as her 'own' body. However, 'the individual' does not simply occur in nature, as it were. Is not the very idea of individual as separate self, generated by the same discourse which legitimates privacy rights and which constructs the gendered and heterosexual body as the norm? Surely a feminist consideration of reproductive freedom should work to contest the production of this identity?

The second strategy sees liberatory potential in using the force of law to illuminate the darkest recesses of the private, in effect pushing the law to define with greater and greater exactitude the contours of legitimate and illegitimate modes of sexuality, the family and conceptions of the body. Does this effectively plug in the interstices in dominant discourses through which the intended meaning of 'the body' escapes, precisely those interstices in which subversive discourses like feminism operate to recuperate meaning? As Foucault points out, 'silence and secrecy are a shelter for power, anchoring its prohibitions; but they also loosen its holds and provide for relatively obscure areas of tolerance'.[45] For example the experience of feminists in Canada after rape law reforms has been that feminist proposals became part of a package of greater regulation over sexual behaviour deemed undesirable—such as homosexuality and under-age sex. So feminist legal reforms coincided with other demands for greater control over sexual behaviour, and the overall impact has been to tighten regulation by the state.[46]

The public–private divide is characteristic of modernity, as we saw in the argument of Linda Nicholson earlier in this section. In postcolonial societies like India therefore, there persist modes of social interaction which do not attempt to categorise in these terms. Simultaneously there is the continuous move by the arch instrument of modernity, the law, to render these alternate, more ambivalent modes of perception illegitimate. Upendra Baxi holds that as far as dispute settlement is concerned, in India there are two broad complexes of norms, institutions and processes—state legal systems and non-state legal systems. The first are marked by the quest for certainty and exactitude and are predicated upon the assumption of a clear demarcation between public and private. The second work on shared traditional perceptions of family honour, kinship ties and caste relations, and the public and private are not distinct categories in their understanding.[47]

In this context it is illuminating to consider studies of 'abducted' women and children in the Partition riots on the Indian subcontinent.[48] The governments of India and Pakistan set up administrative machineries to recover on behalf of their families, these women and children. However, in the Indian case, which these studies examine, many of the (now Pakistani) Muslim women who had been abducted by (Indian) Hindu and Sikh men had been absorbed into the families of their abductors. However, the government insisted on 'recovering' these women and repatriating them to Pakistan regardless of the pleas of their new families and of the women themselves that they be allowed to remain in India. As Veena Das insightfully comments, 'It was not the order of the family which was scandalized by the threats to purity that the presence of Muslim women posed, for the strategies of practical kinship knew how to absorb them within the family itself, but rather, the ideology of the nation that insisted upon this purification.' Das points to the variety of strategic practices within the family, which were flexible enough to accommodate a wide variety of behaviours, in contrast to the order of the state in which identity had to be firmly fixed. Let me emphasise the fact that both orders were repressive for women—this is not in question here. The point is that the entry of the state into a realm it prohibited to itself under 'normal' circumstances necessitated the freezing of identities into exact categories that were non-negotiable. For the state, the identity of the women could be cast only in terms of citizenship, whereas 'the exigencies of practical kinship' allowed for considerable flexibility under extraordinary conditions.[49]

The general argument I make in this book is that there is a contradiction generated by the mutual interaction of the language of rights and the law. This contradiction arises from the belief of social movements that they are articulating the universal values required by legal discourse when they use the language of rights, when in fact rights are constituted differently by the moral perspectives of different discourses. This opposition between the universality and uniformity required by the law on the one hand, and the multi-layeredness of rights on the other, becomes particularly problematic when feminist politics attempts to use the law, through the language of rights, to liberate 'women's bodies' from the oppression of patriarchal structures and institutions.

The Body and Law

Both mainstream (non-feminist) and feminist political theory see 'the body' as a natural object situated in the realm of the 'private', and the 'making public' of the body through legal discourse is assumed to be a transformative step. However, since 'rights over bodies' have their particular significance only within the specific discourses that generate them, the clarification and containment of 'the body' by legal discourse can run counter to the feminist vision. The body is not a simple physical object but rather, is constructed by and takes its meaning from its positioning within specific social, cultural and economic practices. The dominant discourses impose heterosexual and reproductive sexuality as the only morally sanctioned order. The assumption that bodies are naturally gendered and that the category of *sex* exists *a priori* imposes a duality and uniformity on bodies. This violence of categories is embodied in law through, for example, laws against homosexuality, laws regulating marriage and procreation and laws on what constitutes rape. Joan Scott points to the influence of law on perceptions of 'nature' when she argues that, 'By a kind of circular logic a presumed essence of men and women became the justification for laws and policies when in fact this "essence" (historically and contextually variable) was only the *effect* of those laws and policies.'[50]

Primarily for these reasons, feminist politics centring on the law may not have the liberatory potential intended. On the contrary, constant referral to the law to legislate on issues relating to 'the body' becomes in effect a revalidation of legal norms on what this body is, and on what it is that rights over 'our' bodies can be. The question will be asked—is everything 'only discourse' then? What about 'real' bodies? The point here is precisely that the multiplicity of 'real' bodies is rendered invisible or illegitimate through the functioning of hegemonic legal and cultural codes. To suggest only a few instances—infants born with no clear determining sexual characteristics, eunuchs, or men and women who have characteristics that are 'non-masculine' or 'non-feminine' respectively. All these have to be disciplined into normalcy (through methods ranging in severity from cosmetic to surgical intervention), or declared to be abnormal or illegal. Our very language, held implacably as it is in the grip of a bipolarity of gender, falters in attempting to refer to such bodies.

Take for instance, a revealing letter to the medical columns of a Sunday paper from 'A grieving mother', who seeks advice about her eighteen-year-old son whose sudden depression she traced to the fact that 'his nipples and breasts are bulging out, which disgust him'. The doctor's reassuring reply is that *nearly 30 per cent* of men have 'suffered' from what is termed 'gynecomastia' at some time or the other. In some cases, the cause could be tumours or malnutrition, but this is rare. *The most common cause* of 'gynecomastia', says this doctor, is simply this—'pubertal', due to the fact that breast tissue, normally dormant in boys, is 'super sensitive to the minuscule amount of circulating female hormones'. The doctor says that once the 'rare causes' have been ruled out by an endocrinologist, either the condition is self-limiting, or if it is not, *may require surgery.* In other words, nearly a third of the male population can have 'breasts', and if it is not due to rare endocrinological causes, the condition is perfectly normal. It seems to have no other ill effects than causing 'disgust', but nevertheless, it is pathologised ('gynecomastia'), and surgery is recommended when other serious illnesses are *ruled out.*[51]

The hormonal conception of the body is now one of the dominant modes of thinking about the root of sex differences. Nelly Oudshoorn points out that the hormonal conception of the body in fact allows for the possibility of breaking out of the tyranny of the binary sex-difference model. That is, if bodies can have both female and male hormones, then maleness and femaleness are not restricted to one kind of body alone. However, the biomedical sciences have preferred increasingly, to portray the female, but not the male, as a body completely controlled by hormones. In this process, a clear nexus has emerged between the medical profession and a huge, multi-billion dollar pharmaceutical industry. All sorts of 'disorders' in women—such as the ageing of the skin, depression, menstrual irregularities—are prescribed hormonal therapy.[52] This pathologisation clearly extends to male bodies that react to the 'minuscule amounts' (as the doctor in the letter above firmly qualifies) of female hormones circulating in them.

Or consider the startling study in the USA of intersexed infants (babies born with both ovarian and testicular tissue or in whom the sex organs were ambiguous) which showed that medical decisions to assign one sex or the other were made on cultural assumptions rather than on any existing biological features. Thus, a baby might be made into a female but then still require hormonal therapy all her life to make her stay 'female'.[53] Again, 'gender verification' tests for the Olympic games were suspended in 2000 after enough evidence had emerged that 'atypical chromosomal variations' are so common that it is impossible to judge 'femininity' and 'masculinity' on the basis of chromosomal pattern alone.[54] In other words, maleness and femaleness are not only culturally different, they are not even biologically stable features at all times.

Biomedical language is often adduced to buttress legal discourse in order to produce the body as a natural given object that has to be one or the other in a series of binary oppositions—male/female, juvenile/adult, healthy/diseased, heterosexual/homosexual. On the other hand, the experience of self and the body validated by feminism as 'real' acquires meaning precisely through an interplay of contexts, a movement that is halted by the rigid codifications required by legal discourse. It would seem that the juxtaposition of rights as understood to be discursively constituted (hence ambiguous, flexible in significance) and the law (which demands certainty and exactitude) is especially problematic for feminist practice in the realm of the 'private' where the body is located.

Two caveats before we proceed further. One, I must emphasise that the focus of this book is squarely on the law and the state as engaged with by feminist practices. The non-state domain of dispute settlement—which is vast and powerful—remains unexplored here. It is also a realm that feminist politics has not taken seriously except to criticise as embodying patriarchy and traditional power relations. Whether that domain offers any emancipatory potential at all is a question that remains to be asked.

Two, a note on my use of the idea of 'emancipation'. I understand emancipation as a process without closure, it is not a goal that we can reach. Each victory becomes the site of a fresh cooptation, but conversely too, each defeat releases new potential to resist oppression. To move away from legal and state-centred conceptions of political practice is to recognise political practice as the perpetual *attempt* to eliminate oppression rather than the *achievement* of this elimination. Nevertheless 'emancipation' remains a horizon that should drive our political practice.[55]

I explore the implications of these arguments in the light of the experience of the women's movement in India particularly since the 1980s. The focus is specifically on three issues: (a) abortion and femicide of foetuses; (b) sexual violence; and (c) the campaign for reservations for women in Parliament. All three issues illustrate the central question raised by this book: Who is the subject of feminist politics? It seems to me that we have tended to assume this subject to be already existing, in a body that is self-evident. But whether it is Woman as choosing to abort a female foetus, as resisting/surviving sexual violation, or as seeking political representation, the experience of feminist politics shows up the gaps in the constitution of this Subject. In this work I suggest that the creation of 'women' as subject should be understood to be the *goal* of feminist politics, not its starting point. If this is so however, appeals to the law, necessarily based on the assumption of an already existing subject—'Women'—about whom the law shall speak, are bound to produce disjunctures between feminist ethics and legal transformations.

In the process of engaging with these specific issues I expect to reveal a more fundamental set of questions about the issues of citizenship, representation, and the subject of radical politics in general, for I do not suggest by any means, that only Woman is problematic to constitute as Subject. These are questions I will attempt to take forward, if not precisely to answer, by the last chapter of this book.

NOTES

1. Carl Friedrich, *Constitutional Government and Democracy,* Boston, Ginn, 1950.
2. Upendra Baxi, 'Constitutionalism as a Site of State Formative Practices', *Cardozo Law Review,* vol. 21, no. 4, February 2000, pp. 1184–5.
3. Susie Tharu and Tejaswini Niranjana, 'Problems for a Contemporary Theory of Gender', in Nivedita Menon, ed., *Gender and Politics in India* Delhi, Oxford University Press, 1999, p. 495.
4. Gabriele Dietrich addresses this phenomenon in 'Women and Religious Identities in India After Ayodhya', in Kamla Bhasin, Ritu Menon, and Nighat Said Khan, eds, *Against All Odds: Essays on Women, Religion and Development from India and Pakistan,* New Delhi, Kali for Women, 1994.
5. Michele Le Doeuff, 'Feminism is Back in France—Or is it?', *Hypatia* 15.4 (2000).
6. Nandita Haksar, *Demystifying the Law for Women,* New Delhi, Lancer Press, 1986; Vasudha Dhagamwar, *Law, Power and Justice,* New Delhi, Sage, 1992; Archana Parasher, *Women and Family Law Reform in India,* New Delhi, Sage, 1992.
7. A. Sachs and J.H. Wilson, *Sexism and the Law: A Study of Male Beliefs and Judicial Bias,* Oxford, Martin Robertson, 1978; Lina Gonsalves, *Women and the Law,* New Delhi, Lancer Paperbacks, 1993.
8. Ratna Kapur and Brenda Cossman, 'On Women, Equality and the Constitution: Through the Looking Glass of Feminism', *National Law*

School Journal, vol. 1, 1993. (Also available in Nivedita Menon, ed., *Gender and Politics in India*, Delhi, Oxford University Press, 1999.)

9. Catharine MacKinnon, 'Feminism, Marxism, Method and the State: Towards Feminist Jurisprudence', *Signs*, vol. 8, no. 4, Summer, 1983; Carol Smart, *Feminism and the Power of Law*, London and New York, Routledge, 1989.
10. Tove Stang Dahl, *Women's Law: An Introduction to Feminist Jurisprudence*, Oslo, Norwegian University Press, 1987, p. 75.
11. Nandita Gandhi and Nandita Shah, *The Issues at Stake*, New Delhi, Kali for Women, 1992, pp. 213–72.
12. Flavia Agnes, 'Protecting Women Against Violence? Review of a Decade of Legislation 1980–9', *Economic and Political Weekly*, 25 April 1992.
13. Nandita Haksar, 'Dominance, Suppression and the Law', in Lotika Sarkar and B. Sivaramayya, eds, *Women and the Law: Contemporary Problems*, New Delhi, Vikas Publishing House, 1994.
14. Flavia Agnes, 'A Critical Review of Enactments on Violence Against Women', in Maithreyi Krishna Raj, ed., *Women and Violence: A Country Report*, Bombay, SNDT University, 1991; also, 'Protecting Women Against Violence?'; Madhu Kishwar and Ruth Vanita, 'Why Can't We Report to Each Other?', *Manushi*, no. 37, 1980–1; 'Using Women as a Pretext for Repression: The Indecent Representation of Women (Prohibition) Bill', *Manushi*, no. 37, 1986.
15. Gail Omvedt, *Violence Against Women: New Movements and New Theories in India*, New Delhi, Kali for Women, 1990, pp. 39–40.
16. Article 14 of the Indian Constitution guarantees the Fundamental Right to Equality.
17. Nandita Haksar, 'Human Rights Layering: A Feminist Perspective', in Amita Dhanda and Archana Parasher, eds, *Engendering Law: Essays in Honour of Lotika Sarkar*, Lucknow, Eastern Book Company, 1999, pp. 71–88.
18. Vina Mazumdar, 'Political Ideology of the Women's Movement's Engagement With Law', in Amita Dhanda and Archana Parasher, eds, *Engendering Law*, pp. 339–74.
19. Ibid., p. 351.
20. Archana Parasher, *Women and Family Law Reform in India*, p. 34.
21. Ibid.
22. The critique made by western feminists is discussed at length in Chapter One. See also Carol Smart; I. Snider, 'Legal Reform and Social Control: The Dangers of Abolishing Rape', *International Journal of the Sociology*

of Law 13(4), 1985; Judy Fudge, 'The Public/Private Distinction: The Possibilities and Limits to the Use of *Charter* Litigation to Further Feminist Struggles', *Osgoode Law Journal*, 25 (3), 1987.

23. From the title of Chapter 11 of *A Possible India: Essays in Political Criticism*, Delhi, Oxford University Press, 1997.
24. Editorial note by Bill Ashcroft, Gareth Griffiths and Helen Tiffin in *The Post-colonial Studies Reader*, London, Routledge, 1999, p. 117.
25. I explore this idea at length in the first chapter.
26. F. Engels, *The Origin of the Family, Private Property and the State*, Moscow, Progress Publishers, 1977, p. 73.
27. For instance, see Anne Phillips, *Engendering Democracy*, Cambridge, Polity Press, 1991, especially Chapter 4; Susan Moller Okin's critique of John Rawls, 'John Rawls, Justice as Fairness—For Whom?', in Carol Pateman and Mary L. Shanley, eds, *Feminist Interpretations of Political Thought*, Blackwell, Polity Press, 1991, and Okin's *Women in Western Political Thought*, Princeton, Princeton University Press, 1979.
28. Juliet Mitchell, *Woman's Estate*, Harmondsworth, Penguin, 1971, p. 100.
29. Michele Barrett, 'Rethinking Women's Oppression Today: A Reply to Brenner and Ramas', *New Left Review* 146, July–August 1984.
30. Nancy Hartsock, *Money, Sex and Power: Towards a Feminist Historical Materialism*, New York, Longman, 1983.
31. Linda Nicholson, 'Feminism and Marx: Integrating Kinship with the Economic', in Seyla Benhabib and Drucilla Cornell, eds, *Feminism as Critique*, Cambridge, Polity Press, 1987.
32. Gayatri Spivak, *In Other Worlds*, New York and London, Methuen, 1987, p. 103.
33. Anita L. Allen, *Uneasy Access: Privacy for Women in a Free Society*, Totowa, NJ, Rowman and Littlefield, 1988.
34. Discussed in Catharine MacKinnon: *Feminism Unmodified*, Cambridge and London, Harvard University Press, 1987, p. 96.
35. Susan Moller Okin, 'Gender, the Public and the Private', in David Held, ed., *Political Theory Today*, Cambridge, Polity Press, 1991, p. 86.36.
36. Susan Moller Okin, ibid.; Anita L. Allen, *Uneasy Access*.
37. Catharine MacKinnon, *Feminism Unmodified*, pp. 93–102.
38. Tove Stang Dahl, *Women's Law*, p. 75.
39. Mary Fainsod Katzenstein, 'Getting Women's Issues on the Public Agenda: Body Politics in India', *Samya Shakti*, vol. 6, 1991.

40. Seyla Benhabib, 'The Generalized and the Concrete Other: The Kohlberg-Gilligan Controversy and Feminist Theory', in Seyla Benhabib and Drucilla Cornell, eds, *Feminism as Critique*, Cambridge, Polity Press, 1987, p. 177.
41. Nandita Gandhi and Nandita Shah, *The Issues at Stake*, p. 271.
42. 1984 *All India Reporter* 66 Delhi. Discussed in Nandita Haksar, *Demystifying the Law for Women*, p. 58.
43. Frances E. Olsen, 'The Myth of State Intervention in the Family', in Frances E. Olsen, ed., *Feminist Legal Theory Volume II: Positioning Feminist Theory Within the Law*, Aldershot, Dartmouth Publishers, 1995, p. 185.
44. Jean Cohen, 'Democracy, Difference and the Right of Privacy', in Seyla Benhabib, ed., *Democracy and Difference: Contesting the Boundaries of the Political*, Princeton, NJ, Princeton University Press, 1996.
45. Michel Foucault, *The History of Sexuality, An Introduction*, Harmondsworth, Penguin (Peregrine Books), 1984, p. 101.
46. I. Snider, 'Legal Reform and Social Control: The Dangers of Abolishing Rape'.
47. Upendra Baxi, *Towards a Sociology of Indian Law*, New Delhi, Satvahan, 1986, p. 77.
48. Urvashi Butalia, 'Community, State and Gender: On Women's Agency During Partition', *Economic and Political Weekly*, 24 April 1993; Ritu Menon and Kamla Bhasin, 'Recovery, Rupture, Resistance: Indian State and the Abduction of Women During Partition', *Economic and Political Weekly*, 24 April 1993.
49 Veena Das, 'National Honour and Practical Kinship: Of Unwanted Women and Children', in *Critical Events: An Anthropological Perspective on Contemporary India*, Delhi, Oxford University Press, 1995, p. 80.
50. Joan W. Scott, *Only Paradoxes to Offer: French Feminists and the Rights of Man*, Cambridge MA, Harvard University Press, 1996, p. ix.
51. Letter on file with author.
52. Nelly Oudshoorn, *Beyond the Natural Body: An Archaeology of Sex Hormones*, London, Routledge, 1994.
53. Suzanne J. Kessler, 'The Medical Construction of Gender: Case Management of Inter-sexed Infants', in Anne C. Herrmann and Abigail J. Stewart, eds, *Theorising Feminism: Parallel Trends in the Humanities and Social Sciences*, Boulder, Westview Press, 1994.
54. Anonymous, 'Gender Hurdles', *Economic and Political Weekly*, 3 June 2000, p. 1877.

55. In this as in many other formulations (particularly on the notion of hegemony) my intellectual debt to the work of Ernesto Laclau and Chantal Mouffe will be evident. I have cited them at many places, and the bibliography lists that part of their work that I am familiar with. However, although I may not have cited them at every point, it will be clear that their pioneering efforts to build up a 'post-Marxist' mode of analysis has been formative for my thinking. Mouffe, of course, has moved in a somewhat different political direction since her joint work with Laclau, but I continue to find her questions and mode of engaging with them provocative and productive.

CHAPTER ONE

Rights: Putting History Back In

In the course of this chapter I will attempt to shift the assumption underlying understandings of rights, that these are universal and based on a generally accepted moral order. I argue that rights come into being within specific sets of shared norms of justice and equality. However, legal discourse, through which rights are sought to be institutionalised, is marked by the movement towards certainty and exactitude. What are the implications for the liberatory potential of rights once their meaning is fixed by law? If, as I seek to establish, rights are constituted by values derived from specific moral universes, there is a singularity to justice, a uniqueness, which, as Derrida puts it, must always concern 'individuals, irreplaceable groups and lives, the other or myself *as* the other in a unique situation'.[1] This uniqueness however, is at odds with law, which must take a general form, as norm and as rule.

In Derrida's understanding of justice, the very condition of justice is that one must address oneself to the other in the language of the other. There is violence involved in judging persons in an idiom they do not share, perhaps even understand. But this violence is obscured by the appeal to 'justice' as a universal value, as to a third party 'who suspends the unilaterality or singularity of the idioms'.[2] Derrida emphasises that to recognise this paradox is not to abdicate before the question of justice or to deny the opposition between just and unjust. Rather, it involves a responsibility to a 'historical and interpretative memory'— that is, to recall the history, the origin and subsequent direction, of concepts of justice and the law. In this way we would be desedimenting the values embedded in the idea of justice as a universal concept. These values have assumed the status of natural presuppositions and the violence of the moment of their imposition has been rendered invisible through a kind of historical amnesia. To interrogate points of origin constantly, to question the grounds of the norms which underline notions of justice at historically specific moments, is not to surrender an interest in justice. On the contrary, it 'hyperbolically raises the stakes of exacting justice'. [3]

In a critique of this essay Nancy Fraser argues that since, in Derrida's understanding, 'violence cannot fail to be implicated in any possible legal institution . . .' the implication is that 'it would be folly to try to eliminate it [violence]'.[4] She seems to suggest that Derrida forecloses the possibility of ending violence, thus giving up on democratic aspirations. However, Fraser reads the term 'violence' here too narrowly. In this essay Derrida uses the idea of 'violence' in the sense of closure, of bringing a halt to the play of meaning. It is this closure that is undemocratic, for it fixes one possible meaning finally as the only possible one. It is in this sense that violence is involved in any engagement with legal discourse. Thus, Derrida does not suggest the impossibility of 'eliminating violence' but rather, brings into question the relationship between law and justice, because law will always involve violence in his sense. Since Fraser cannot conceive of a society without *law* in its modern form, she reads Derrida as suggesting that a just society without *violence* is impossible.

To return to our argument here, what the discussion above suggests is that the achievement of justice in a universal sense is therefore, an impossibility. At particular historical moments and in different spatial contexts, 'justice' is constituted by specific moral visions, but the discourse of the law is predicated upon the assumption that justice can be attained once and for all by the fixing of identity and meaning. The meaning delivered by law as *the* only just one then gets articulated in complex ways with other discourses constituting identity, and tends to reinstate dominant and oppressive possibilities rather than release marginal and emancipatory ones.

The Emergence of Rights

As I have suggested in the title of this chapter, we need to rehistoricise the emergence of rights—we need to remind ourselves that the notion of 'rights' as we understand them today arose in a specific time/space configuration. The very assertion that rights are 'natural', 'inalienable' and so on, was possible only in the context of particular historical forces. The term 'history' in the title then, does not refer to History with a capital H as it were, or to some Truth. Rather, it alerts us to shifting contexts. It suggests that the meaning of notions such as 'rights' is not inherent in the terms themselves, but emerges out of the contexts in which they are placed.

Bhikhu Parekh traces the evolution of the understanding of rights from the first systematic development of the concept in ancient Rome, which was also, as he points out, the first western society to develop the concept of the private realm and to insist on its relative inviolability in relation to the public realm. For Roman jurists, rights, law and justice were inseparable, and the law was considered to be an expression of the community's conception of justice. Nevertheless rights did not imply absolute control, nor were they unlimited in scope. Rights operated in the realm of civil society, not in the realm of the state or the family, and governed relationships between individuals, not between individuals and the state. The law was not the only source of rights, which were also generated by customs, usages and traditions. Rights also did not imply absolute control, but were circumscribed in various ways. During the centuries of feudalism in Europe, rights continued to be conceived of in equally complex ways, with both individuals as well as communities and groups being the bearers of rights. Indeed, the 'individual' was not clearly separable from his community, work or land. The process of individuation that was to be both empowering as well as severely alienating, began later.

Moreover, rights continued to be derived from customs and traditions as well as from law, and all sources of rights had equal validity.[5]

From the seventeenth century, rights began to be seen as inhering in individuals, rather than in groups or communities. However, we need to remind ourselves, as Wendy Brown puts it, that:

> Historically, rights emerged in modernity both as a vehicle of emancipation from political disenfranchisement or institutionalised servitude and as a means of privileging an emerging bourgeois class within a discourse of formal egalitarianism and universal citizenship. Thus, they emerged both as a means of protection against arbitrary use and abuse by sovereign and social power and as a mode of securing and naturalising dominant social powers— class, gender and so forth.[6]

Take for example, the 'right to work' and the manner of its emergence. What paves the way for the capitalist system in Marx's view, is primitive accumulation— the process of violently expropriating from the labourer the means of production and transforming it into capital. While in the fifteenth and sixteenth centuries the process was carried out by individual acts of violence, the eighteenth century sees an advance in that the law itself becomes the instrument of theft of people's land. This process was accompanied by a disciplinary discourse on 'work' which criminalised and brutally punished the refusal to perform labour. Early colonising missions also used the policy of forced labour, particularly in Africa. The intervening centuries and developments in the global capitalist order have seen a radical reversal of this discourse. From the disciplinary discourse of the obligation to work, resisted by the target population, gradually there emerged the social and economic order in which 'work' is unavailable. And the resistance of the property-less to this order is manifested in struggles to embody the 'right *to* work'. But unlike in the early centuries of capitalist growth in Europe, the millions of people dislocated by capitalist development today, such as for example, by mega development projects, are not being absorbed, however violently and unwillingly, into capitalist production. They are being thrown into unemployment, or into the grossly exploitative conditions of work at the peripheries of capitalist production, where, far from being 'emancipated from serfdom', they experience crushingly coercive extra-economic forms of extracting surplus. Thus, in the era of globalised late capitalism, the relationship between 'work' and 'worker' has been fundamentally transformed, making the 'right to work' correspondingly more complicated.

The rights-bearing individual then, was a complex creation that emerged in very specific historical conditions. It should not surprise us therefore, that feminist critiques have pointed out that this individual, detached from social context and conceived of as constituted by the limits of the body, was clearly male. Male bodies, being clearly bounded and solid, were considered perfect. Female bodies, on the other hand, were seen as disorderly, penetrable and subject to cyclical changes. Their messy bodily processes challenged the idea of the closed and controlled body surface, and through reproduction, their bodies were divisible, suggesting the unlimitability of their boundaries. Thus they could never be the rational, indivisible, unambiguous individual. The bourgeois public sphere therefore, Joan Landes insists, was *essentially* and not just *contingently* masculinist. The central categories of bourgeois thought—universal reason, law and nature—were embedded in the ideologically sanctioned order of gender differences and the public–private dichotomy that underlay the new 'public' sphere.[7] The relationship of Enlightenment to feminism was therefore never a simple one of extending these new rights to women. Rather, the form of the family and the subordinated position of women in Western European commercial civilisation were seen as the highest form of development by European thinkers, and the justification of this inferior status of women was sought in science rather than in divine will.[8]

Joan Scott too, draws our attention to the 'universal definition and masculine embodiment' of the republican notion of the individual. Men's difference from women, she argues, was precisely what served to eradicate differences of class and race among men—the universality of the abstract individual was in this way established as a common maleness.[9]

It is from the seventeenth century that the source of rights shifted to the civil law, with customs, traditions and usages being gradually marginalised. Most significantly, Bhikhu Parekh points out, the scope of rights changed radically at this time. The natural world was no longer part of a whole in which human beings acquired their sense of self. Rather, it was external and alien to the individual who was to master it and tame it to his ends. This meant that men could have rights over everything in the external world. Not only the external world, but each of his capacities became quantifiable and alienable while at the same time, man had somehow to be considered separable from his capacities so that his 'self' could remain 'his' even as he sold or alienated aspects of himself. Man's 'self' then, was seen to reside in his capacity to choose, and as long as he chose freely, he was an autonomous individual, regardless of the ways in which his ability to choose was constrained.[10]

The idea then, of individuals as bearers of rights in their own capacities is barely four hundred years old. These centuries have seen the expansion of democratic rights to larger sections of people, and the discourse of rights has empowered different kinds of social movements. This process, when seen from the point of view of the transition from feudal communitarianism to capitalist individualism, has been significant in freeing the individual from the immutability of feudal hierarchies. As Habermas puts it

> By opening up the legal space for pursuing personal preferences, individual rights release the entitled person from moral precepts and other prescriptions . . . Whereas morality primarily tells us what our obligations are, law has a structure that gives primacy to entitlements. Whereas moral rights are derived from reciprocal duties, legal duties stem from the legal constraints on individual liberties.[11]

To this extent I would go along with a Habermasian account of the public sphere, where modernity produced the individual citizen empowered with rights, and freed from pre-modern tyrannies.

That is, while the 'fluid constructions of the self' that Ashis Nandy argues are characteristic of pre-colonial South Asian cultures may have provided protection from the alienation and objectification of atomistic individualism, this 'fluidity' did not extend to the possibility of renegotiating ascribed, even if multiple, positions within overlapping communities. This circumscription ensured the exclusion of lower castes, women and other stigmatised groups from socially valued cultural and economic resources. So it is not my claim that the modern public sphere transformed a hitherto democratic communitarian space, as Nandy himself might argue.[12]

I would differ too, from a totalising rendering of Foucault's idea of 'governmentality' such as for instance, by David Scott, that would deny that the modern public sphere ever had any emancipatory potential. Foucault termed as governmentality, a type of power 'first discovered in the eighteenth century', resulting 'on the one hand, in the formation of a whole series of governmental apparatuses, and on the other, in the development of a whole complex of '*savoirs*' (knowledges). This governmentality is at once internal and external to the state, 'since it is the tactics of government which make possible the continuous definition and redefinition of what is within the competence of the state and what is not, the public versus the private and so on . . .' This governmentalisation of the state is a 'singularly paradoxical phenomenon', says Foucault, because the techniques of government have become 'the only real space for political struggle and contestation' but on the other hand, it is precisely the governmentalisation of the state that has allowed it to survive.[13]

In David Scott's reading of this idea, the emergence of modern political rationality ensures that 'power works not in spite of but through the construction of a space of free social exchange, and through the construction of a subjectivity normatively experienced as the source of free will and rational autonomous agency'.[14] In other words, through the institutions of civil society, a 'new self-regulating field of the social' is created in which rights-bearing citizens 'do as they ought'.[15] What gets obscured in Scott's reading of 'governmentality' is the effect of local resistances to the construction of this subjectivity and the ways in which the intended objects also continuously elude the point of application of power. As Foucault himself has put it elsewhere, 'At the very heart of the power relationship, and constantly provoking it, are the recalcitrance of will and the intransigence of freedom.'[16] In other words, the emergence of the rights-bearing citizen was a historical process, the revolutionary and liberatory consequences of which should be engaged with in order to arrive at a fuller critique.

But the idea of the citizen empowered with rights in the public sphere derived its emancipatory potential precisely from its positioning against feudal absolutism. With the completion of the bourgeois revolution in the West, and the mediated and refracted manner in which this transformation takes place in colonial and postcolonial societies, it seems to me that the language of rights has lost much of its relevance. The extension of this language from rights of the individual against the state, to the rights of collectivities against one another and against individuals, as well as rights defined in such broad terms as 'the right to be fully human'[17]— these rights to be guaranteed *by* the state— raise contradictions which have not been adequately confronted. This chapter points out some of these contradictions and their implications for political practice.

Critiques of Rights

By the mid-twentieth century several influential critiques of liberal theories of rights had emerged. In this section we will pass carefully through this terrain in order to clear the space for my own argument to move forward. One of the classic liberal statements is that of Ronald Dworkin, who urges the understanding of individual rights as 'trumps'— that is, in any situation of conflict between individual rights and community welfare, the individual's rights should prevail over (or trump, as in a game of cards) what is perceived as the community's interest. He argues that rights arise from an appeal to equality as a value, for the theory of individual rights ensures that all people are treated equally, and nobody's interests are subordinated to some 'larger' good.[18]

The well-known Marxist critique comes from the position that 'rights' are juridical conceptions that mask substantive inequality. Although the doctrine of equal rights recognises the equal dignity of all human beings, embodying what Nicos Poulantzas calls the 'real rights of the dominated classes', these are 'material concessions imposed on the dominant classes by popular struggle'.[19] In his understanding, capitalist law does not just obscure real differences behind a screen of universal formalism but in fact, helps to 'establish and consecrate individual and class differences within its very structure'. Thus the role of modern law is not to intervene against state violence but rather to organise 'the exercise of violence, always taking into account the resistance of the popular masses'.[20] In this tradition too, is Nancy Fraser's political critique of 'the force of law' identifying, in the context of the USA, three levels at which 'masked, structural violence' enters institutionalised practices of legal judgement. The first is the level of basic constitutional principles, where the most problematic case is identified as the entrenched centrality of property right in the US constitution. This right to 'private property in the means of production' makes it possible in the legal system for small numbers of people 'to make decisions with impunity that imperil the health and livelihood of many others while degrading the quality of life of everyone'. The second is 'the deep grammar of our legal reasoning' by which the rights of social groups cannot be recognised. Fraser argues that a great deal of harm in the social system is not the result of individual action but of 'systemic processes' and 'structural relations among differentially advantaged social groups'. Since this cannot be recognised, there is embedded a masked, structural violence in the law. The third level of violence is that cultural assumptions underlie judgements by professional judges as well as by jury members. These cultural assumptions tend to work to the disadvantage of subordinated social groups. The task of critique is to expose this masked, structural violence.[21]

Like many other Marxist theorists Fraser tries to recover some of the emancipatory potential of rights, by transforming law through critique. Similarly, Christine Sypnowich, maintaining that rights themselves are not illusions, challenges the view that an ideal socialist society would have no need of law. She argues that the struggle is to metamorphose these empty juridical rights into real rights by transforming the structural conditions which disempower the labouring class. In this view, rights are considered to have a powerful liberatory charge, both at the level of rhetoric and symbol as well as substantively, with the revolutionary transformation of material conditions. For Sypnowich, any worthwhile socialist society would require legal institutions to adjudicate disputes between socialist citizens and between citizen and community. She holds that a socialist jurisprudence must draw from the liberal tradition, and using Ronald Dworkin's phrase, argues that it must retrieve the idea of the individual with rights which 'trump' society's policies.[22]

From another direction comes the critique offered by radical feminist Catharine MacKinnon who argues that liberalism supports state intervention on behalf of women as abstract persons with abstract rights, while in reality 'the state is male in the feminist sense'. Abstract rights only 'authorise the male experience of the world'. As a result, she holds, feminist understandings of the state have been 'schizoid'— on the one hand recognising the state as patriarchal and oppressive, and on the other, turning to the state to make the law less sexist. She sees the state as embodying and ensuring male control over female sexuality even while it juridically prohibits excesses. In fact the legal prohibition of and controls over pornography and prostitution are meant to enhance their eroticism— 'if part of the kick of pornography involves eroticising the putatively prohibited, pornography law will putatively prohibit pornography enough to maintain its desirability without making it unavailable or truly illegitimate.'[23] MacKinnon's critique of the law and her understanding of gender *as* dominance of women by men[24] has certainly served the purpose of radically questioning the myth of law's neutrality which continues to have a powerful hold over the feminist imagination.

Yet MacKinnon herself makes law the focus of her feminist politics in the USA. She has been the pioneer of legislation against sexual harassment and pornography, formulated in terms of employment rights and civil rights respectively.[25] I find it difficult to reconcile MacKinnon's attempts to transform sexist society through the law, with her critique of abstract rights, which is based on an understanding of 'the intractability of maleness as a form of dominance'.[26] Such an understanding leaves no space for women, let alone for feminist politics. Indeed, so dauntingly seamless does she make male dominance appear, that she dismally concludes, 'it may be easier to change biology than society.'[27] But if there were so perfect a fit between the 'intention' of male dominance and its effect, where is the space in which feminist critique, such as that of MacKinnon, is generated? Surely any radical politics has to proceed on the belief that the 'effect' of oppressive discourses always exceeds and escapes 'intention'. But even more interesting here for the argument that I make, is that despite this problematic and apparently insurmountable ubiquity attributed to male dominance, MacKinnon continues to expect to be able to force 'women's experience' into the law. All visions of political transformation seem to have become so focused on the state, that the most radical critiques of the state and its institutions, whether Marxist or radical feminist, end up merely realigning themselves once again on its territory.

This is particularly characteristic of analyses that suggest that the purposes of justice would be served better by stressing the relative importance of 'needs' as compared to 'rights'. Upendra Baxi, counterposing human rights to basic human needs, problematises the liberal conception of rights in a situation of mass poverty. He argues that the notion of human rights must be fused into a discussion of developmental processes, development in the sense of value for human dignity, both in an economic as well as in a political sense. He recognises that needs are 'sociogenic' and culture-specific, and that questions will therefore arise about the hierarchy of needs, about who determines this hierarchy, and the conflict between human rights and needs. Nevertheless he holds that the needs-approach is still the most proper way of understanding the possibilities of a just society. However, Baxi's analysis continues to focus on the state as the agent of change. For instance, he asks, 'Should not continued drought or famine in one state in India . . . justify a nation-wide ban on the conspicuous consumption of food on social events?'[28] But surely the state and the law are deeply implicated in the very processes which make famines, uneven development, and enclaves of wealth intrinsic parts of the Indian system? Baxi would share this analysis, so why would he expect this very state to enforce such a ban? In other words, the dilemma that Baxi poses can only be addressed in the realm of *political,* not merely *legal,* transformation. This distinction will become clearer as my argument proceeds.

Nancy Fraser believes that needs-claims can balance the competing claims of mutual responsibility and individual rights even though there exists the danger of playing into the hands of conservatives who prefer to distribute aid as a matter of need rather than right, precisely to avoid any assumption of entitlement. Since her analysis is geared towards retrieving aspects of the welfare state while critiquing its paternalism and androcentrism, she is quite unambiguously state-focused. Moreover she concludes by arguing that 'justified needs claims, must be translated into social rights'. This suggests a hierarchy, an understanding that 'needs' must graduate into 'rights' if they are to be taken seriously. It would seem then, that she sees needs-claims not as an improvement on rights-claims but merely as a preliminary stage to making rights-claims.[29]

Other feminist critiques of rights-claims have also come from the position that such claims place undue emphasis on the individual. They have therefore, attempted to redefine rights in a manner which would enable them to not be understood as purely individualist, but which does not dissolve possibilities of autonomy within 'the community'. For example, Martha Minow and Nancy Fraser have both tried to conceptualise rights so that they embody connectedness between autonomy and responsibility. Minow tries to redefine the substance of purportedly individualistic rights by developing the connection between rights and responsibilities, and by suggesting that rights claims can focus on the social and economic *preconditions* for rights.[30]

Similarly, Elizabeth Schneider argues that the experience of the women's movement has shown that a claim of right is not merely about the individual as bearer of rights but that such claims have a dialectical relationship with political struggle:

> The assertion or experience of rights can express political vision, affirm a group's humanity, contribute to an individual's development as a whole person, and assist in the collective development of a social or political movement . . .[31]

This brief overview of some significant attempts from within Marxist and feminist theory to reformulate orthodox liberal understandings of rights-claims by giving them an ethical and moral dimension, leads us to what I have suggested is a problematic relationship between rights and the law.

Morality as the Basis of Rights

I attempt to demonstrate in this section that critiques of rights that move towards asserting the moral and ethical underpinning of rights discourse, end up in irreconcilable contradiction with the requirements of legal discourse. It is important to remember at this point that both at a conceptual as well as at a political level, rights and law are quite distinctly connected. On the one hand, a social movement operating in the realm of law is constrained to use the language of rights because legal discourse is animated by the weighing of competing rights. In other words, to enter into the realm of law, rights-talk becomes obligatory. On the other hand, when a social movement makes claims based on rights, at some level these claims are predicated on the assumption that these rights should be protected by law. The language of rights thus tends to privilege the sphere of the state and its institutions.

One kind of argument draws on the idea that there are rights sanctioned by a moral order whether or not they have legal existence. Joel

Feinberg, for instance, emphasises a commonly accepted distinction between 'conventional' morality (which varies from group to group) and 'true' morality (which derives from some objective and universal principles of morality). Moral rights in this sense then, can be seen to be synonymous with natural rights.[32] Legality cannot encompass all of morality, and indeed, according to Feinberg, all moral rights should not be legal rights because of the potential for abuse. He cites as examples, the right to euthanasia and the right to rebel against a tyrannical government— the latter, if formulated as law, might 'encourage misguided violence and increase political instability'.[33] He does not address the contradiction generated by the fact that the right to rebel against government or other similar rights like the right of self-determination of nations would necessarily be beyond the ambit of existing laws.

From the above it is clear that the 'universal' morality Feinberg sees as a source of rights, would be bitterly contested. Another example he gives is even more stark in its incomprehension that what he considers to be 'universal' is in fact very particular. He suggests as an instance of a right arising from 'true' as opposed to 'conventional' morality, the right of 'an Indian widow not to be burnt with her dead husband'.[34] The problem of course, is that from the point of view of Indian society such an act could constitute 'true' morality in Feinberg's sense, while his objection to it would arise from the 'conventional' morality of his particular group. By simply asserting that certain rights (originating in the culture of western societies) are universal, the real dilemmas of rights-discourse are simply swept under the carpet.

I should clarify that my point here is not that favourite shooting-target of pro-rights arguments— I am not criticising rights-discourse as 'Eurocentric.' What is termed 'Eurocentrism', I suggest, is in fact a particular relationship to modernity. This relationship in post-colonial societies is fraught and complex, but I do not believe that this offers a legitimate excuse for denying democratic rights. I engage with this argument more thoroughly in the last chapter of this book. What I am arguing here is that while the moral basis of rights is assumed to be self-evident and universally shared, it is highly variegated, even within western culture itself. This has serious implications for the inevitable and unavoidable relationship of rights to law.

Agnes Heller, to take another instance, argues that rights are 'the institutionalised forms of the concretisation of universal values'. A value is universal she holds, if its opposite cannot be chosen as a value. In this sense freedom is a universal value because 'no one is publicly committed to unfreedom as a value'. She adds 'the value of life' as another value which 'comes close to attaining a universal status'. Rights are derived from these values and stem from the conception of justice. Therefore rights-language is and should be, she concludes, 'the lingua franca' of modern democracy.[35] Apart from the point I have already made, that what is presented as 'universal' arises from a particular context, the problem is that this kind of analysis allows no room to conceive of conflict among 'Universal Values' themselves. Heller, for instance, designates as universal values, both 'freedom' and 'the right to life', but it is precisely the contradiction between the two that operates in the abortion debate— the freedom of women to choose versus the right of the foetus to life.

Elizabeth Kingdom's critique of rights raises similar problems. She questions the desirability of generalising on a whole range of issues grouped together under the heading of 'women's rights' and urges instead that specific legislations be analysed from both 'feminist' and 'socialist' perspectives. She argues that this model allows for a more complex analysis of the issues covered by 'women's rights'. She takes up as an instance, the case of protective legislation (restrictions on the employment of women in hazardous work, night work, overtime, and so on), in which 'the protection of women's rights is inseparable from the struggle to improve working conditions for both men and women.'[36] Again, Kingdom assumes a shared morality when she assumes that it would always be possible to apply a 'feminist' or a 'socialist' understanding to specific legislations without the possibility of conflict between the two. However, the very example she suggests, that of protective legislation, has been the focus of other socialist-feminist studies as exemplifying the conflict within the working class between the rights of male and female workers.[37] Michele Barrett, discussing the support for protective legislation from British trade unions, argues that this was a deliberate strategy to reduce competition for male workers. She notes that such legislation was introduced in areas of competition rather than in all areas of work.[38] Once again, we see the possibility of contradiction between two sets of rights accepted by feminists as universal and desirable.

A more thorough feminist critique of rights is provided by Carol Smart. She holds that first wave feminists needed the concept of equal rights to fight against legally imposed impediments but that in the late twentieth century, while law remains oppressive for women, it no longer takes the form of denial of formal rights reserved for men. Continuing the demand for formal rights now is problematic. She suggests that 'the rhetoric of rights has become exhausted, and may even be detrimental'.[39] Rights can be appropriated by the more powerful; for example, the Sex Discrimination Act may be used as much by men as by women, to challenge affirmative action for women. She also points out that rights are often formulated to deal with a *social* wrong, but in practice become focused on the *individual* who must prove that her rights have been violated. Any redress too, will affect only that particular woman.[40]

Smart thus argues that posing a problem in terms of rights simply transposes that problem into one that is defined as having a legal solution. While accepting that rights do amount to 'legal and political power resources', Smart holds that the value of these resources seems to be ascertainable more in terms of the losses if such rights diminish, than in terms of gains if they are sustained.[41] This distinction that Smart makes is crucial to developing any critique of rights, for it forces a confrontation of the fact that while the existence of a given right does not guarantee its realisation, its denial may negatively affect the people who had held that right.

However, Smart's critique continues to be imprisoned in the terrain of the state, for she urges in place of rights, a reformulation of 'demands' grounded in 'women's experiences' rather than in 'abstract notions like rights'.[42] What form will these 'demands' take, and on whom will they be made? It is not clear how Smart's 'demands' will differ from 'rights' after all. Moreover the formulation of rights-as-abstract versus experience-as-concrete is misleading. We have seen how rights, despite their self-presentation, are derived precisely from within concrete universes of shared 'experiences'. The difference between abstract 'rights' and concrete 'experience' cannot be sustained.

A broad-based school of ethical critique of the law, called the Critical Legal Studies (CLS) movement, undertakes the most thorough deconstruction of rights-discourse and the law. Officially started in 1977 at the conference on Critical Legal Studies at the University of Wisconsin-Madison, its roots extend back to 1960 when many of its founding members participated in social activism surrounding the civil rights movement and the Vietnam war. CLS draws from several disciplines and philosophical trends, ranging from social and literary theory to economics and from Marxism to post-structuralism and postmodernism. As one scholar puts it, 'critical legal scholarship appears to be a strange blend of legal realism, the New Left, and literary criticism. It oscillates between wildly esoteric European philosophy and painstaking descriptions of the fine texture of mundane social interaction. It is left-wing, yet it is deeply critical of Marxism.'[43]

According to Cornel West, the basic issue dividing CLS and mainstream legal scholarship has to do with recognising the cultural context in which legal scholarship and education take place. CLS contests the existence of context-free, universal standards untainted by ideological prejudgements and outside of power struggles and political conflict. The point is not that there are no such standards but rather, that prevailing standards are 'part and parcel of a larger form of life— a cultural context of legal scholarship and education with great authority and power that invokes its standards, in part, in order to reproduce itself'. This reproduction, West holds, marginalises and devalues certain 'perspectives, orientations, questions, answers, styles, and persons'. If we view this complex process of reproduction as a thoroughly historical and political affair— from the kind of standards invoked to the type of members admitted— West insists, we are forced to become more relentlessly critical and self-critical of its results.[44]

Thus, as West argues, a basic purpose of CLS is to disclose the degree to which liberal perspectives are unable to be truthful about themselves owing to the blindnesses and silences reinforced by their assumptions and presuppositions. The 'standards' of judgement that 'shape liberal discourse make it difficult and even *illegitimate* to discuss certain issues— especially those that contest the very "impartiality" and "objectivity" that hide the operations of power in liberal discourses.'[45] By now, any critique that rejects the idea that law is objective or neutral, and locates law at the heart of power relations in society, comes under the rubric of CLS. Thus, a feminist theorist like Catharine MacKinnon is considered to be a CLS scholar, as is critical race theorist Patricia Williams. 'That life is complicated is a fact of great analytical importance,' says Williams, but 'Law too often seeks to avoid this truth by making up its own breed of narrower, simpler, but hypnotically powerful rhetorical truths. Acknowledging, challenging, playing with these *as* rhetorical gestures is, it seems to me, necessary for any conception of justice. Such acknowledgement complicates the supposed purity of gender, race, voice, boundary; it allows us to acknowledge the utility of such categorisations for certain purposes and the necessity of their breakdown on other occasions.'[46] Williams marks her distance from Critical Legal Theory however, by asserting the importance of rights: ' "Rights" feels new in the mouths of most black people. It is still too deliciously empowering to say . . . The concept of rights . . . is the marker of our citizenship . . .'[47]

The founding work of CLS though, is considered to be that of Roberto Mangabeira Unger, whose article, 'The Critical Legal Studies Movement', lays down the field that can broadly be defined as CLS. In that article, Unger claims that the critical legal studies movement, which he places in the tradition of 'leftist tendencies in modern legal thought and practice', has 'undermined the central ideas of modern legal thought'. These central categories that CLS criticises are *formalism*, which assumes that legal analysis is marked by rationality and can be clearly contrasted to 'open-ended disputes about the basic terms of social life, disputes that people call ideological, philosophical or visionary', and *objectivism,* which is the belief that authoritative legal materials embody and sustain an intelligible moral order. He develops the idea of 'deviationist doctrine' with a 'looser, more contestable morality', which 'begins all over again the fight over the terms of social life.'[48]

In more recent work, Unger criticises the obsession with judges and adjudication as the primary locus of legal analysis. Unger argues that this link may arrest democracy's development because the judiciary's non-democratic posture keeps it from engaging in the more revolutionary forms of legal analysis. Unger presents us with three alternatives: the 'extended social democracy', which radicalises the institutions of liberal individualism and the private sphere; the 'radical polyarchy', which places primary power in a loose-knit confederation of local communities; and the 'mobilisational democracy', which institutionalises consistent, broadened political activity by all citizens in the civic body. Unger thereby exemplifies his recommendation that legal analysis should be 'recast . . . as institutional imagination'.[49] Here his argument develops on his earlier work, in which he had been critical of liberal theories of rights for their individualistic thrust. He developed a notion of 'customary law', which is based on a consensus that pluralism is to be valued for itself: 'Openness towards the future means that one must value the conflictual process by which communities are created over time . . .'[50] This would require us to engage in a system of continuous institutional revision. Unger argues that his requirement rests on democratic grounds because democracy is nothing more than the attempt to wed institutions that allow for material progress with ones that allow for individual emancipation, a task that will require constant institutional change.[51]

Unger thus seems to suggest that justice must be sought outside the framework of the law. Justice becomes a complex, shifting goal to be continuously negotiated within overlapping local communities; it is no longer self-evidently identifiable with the state's legal systems and the judiciary. Other CLS theorists, as we have seen, do not take this final, radical step.

Communitarian critiques of liberal democracy bring into play the notion of morality and substantive conceptions of the good in a different way. Michael Sandel for example, is critical of liberal attempts to 'bracket' controversial moral conceptions for purposes of justice, and to base justice instead on a general theory of law that is neutral among competing visions of the good life. The appeal of this strategy, Sandel recognises, lies in the fact that in the face of deep disagreement about values, it offers a basis of political agreement based on toleration of one another's differing conceptions of morality. However, his contention is that such a 'bracketing' does not in fact succeed. Sandel examines the actual arguments used by judges and commentators in the USA, in cases dealing with abortion and homosexuality, to demonstrate that although these try to be neutral among questions of the good, they do in fact draw upon some shared notion of morality, but without explicitly acknowledging this. As a result, the moral arguments marshalled by opponents of abortion and homosexuality never get addressed directly. Further, Sandel holds that the bracketing of moral questions in constitutional discourse more or less forecloses the possibility of raising such questions elsewhere, since constitutional discourse has come to constitute the terms of political discourse in American public life generally. Assumptions of constitutional discourse—rights as trumps, the neutral state and the unencumbered self—increasingly set the terms for political debate in general. Sandel suggests that it is necessary to confront the fact that the justice or injustice of laws against abortion and homosexuality can only be addressed in terms of moral conceptions.[52]

The problem with this insight, whose basic premise I share, is that it still leaves us with the impossibility of addressing such moral complexity in the realm of the law. Sandel does not explicitly address this question, ending this essay with the suggestion that 'the justice or injustice of laws against abortion and homosexual sodomy may have something to do with the morality or immorality of these practices after all'.[53] If so, do we need to move to a point where we challenge the continued legitimacy of legal discourse itself, given its inability to reflect the multiple visions of justice that coexist in society?

Briefly to go over the picture outlined above—many critics of liberal theories of rights seeking to re-inscribe rights on to moral terrain do not have the notion of 'universal values' in mind. As we have seen, such critiques argue rather, that the notion of 'universality' only obscures the power dynamics by which some values are assigned greater status and others are marginalised and silenced. But at the same time, it seems that these attempts to refigure rights through morality invariably invoke what is assumed *should* be universal values, that is, feminist or other such values. These values are not at present dominant, but the belief is that they should (and can) be made universally applicable through law. For instance, as Nancy Fraser puts it, rights talk is not necessarily individualistic and androcentric. It becomes so 'only when societies establish the *wrong* rights, for example when the (putative) right to private property is allowed to trump other, social rights.'[54] Here Fraser is addressing an audience that would agree with her that the right to property is a 'wrong' right to endorse—she is making an argument within a *specific* moral universe but assuming *universal* agreement.

The discussion above underscores my point that what one 'ought' to do, or what constitutes a 'moral' action, makes sense only within shared sets of understandings on 'justice', 'equality' and so on. Thus, rights are justified on a terrain constituted by shared moral boundaries. What happens to rights in the realm of legal discourse? Appeals to the law are made on the assumption that rights are self-evident, universally comprehended and universally applicable, but some slippage in meaning takes place once they are in the legal arena where diverse discourses of rights converge. That is, what appears to be a right empowering women within feminist discourse can have an entirely contrary effect once it is materialised in the legal realm.

The next section will examine the manner in which legal discourse operates, seeking certainty and exactitude and bringing to a halt the play of meaning and contexts that give rise to rights.

Legal Discourse and the Fixing of Meaning

In India the understanding of 'law' fundamentally changed with the British conquest—legality replaced authority. Whereas in the classical system, judgement had no other object but to put an end to a particular dispute, it now began to constitute a precedent, a source of law. Even in the medieval period, there was great flexibility in the attachment of particular regions to one or the other school of interpretation. Sastric law was as likely to modify its principles to match local custom as custom might modify itself in deference to Sastric law. Both Islamic law and *Dharma* were based on revelation and in neither were decisions of the court the source of law. In both, interpretation and custom had the same importance.[55]

Under the British system however, the judge fixed interpretation once and for all, and further development of the law could take place only through cases. Even where custom was accepted as prevailing over Sastric law, it was fixed as legal rule. Once identified, 'custom' was understood to be fixed, and thereupon, rigidly codified. Thus, the dynamic interplay between custom and Sastric law was halted. A recent volume called *Changing Concepts of Rights and Justice in South Asia* brings together the work of several historians that points to the working of this dynamic.[56] Sumit Guha teases out conceptions of justice in seventeenth- and eighteenth-century Maharashtra through an examination of cases where rights were invoked or affirmed. There was a considerable range of authorities offering different types of justice, and a multiplicity of scriptural and customary sources of right. Rights were by no means universal or equal, and differing social categories had differing rights, deriving from customs, 'which aligned themselves silently along past lines of force', although they were continually subject to contest and redefinition.[57]

For a later period, Radhika Singha's study of Benares zamindari during 1781–95, traces the development of a sphere of civil authority through a criminal jurisprudence by which the colonial state claimed exclusive prerogatives of judicial and punitive authority. The state's efforts to consolidate a body of Hindu and Islamic law to vindicate its claim to be ruling on the basis of the laws and customs of the people in fact resulted in a body of jurisprudence that modified 'scriptures' in keeping with official objectives wherever necessary. Similarly, although colonial procedures of policing and prosecution were mediated by indigenous notions of rank and respectability, this was less due to a sensitivity to religious belief than to ensure that the standardised procedures of Indian courts would not be seen as threatening to Indian elites. Thus, all persons of 'high caste and rank' were exempted from taking a religious oath in court and could use an affirmation instead. Singha sees this concession as 'ironically introducing a certain ambivalence into the principle of equality before the law.'[58]

Upon her use of the word 'ironically' here, hangs a debate within contemporary Indian historiography which is puzzling for non-historians quite to get the hang of, and I would like to address it here. Singha is at pains to refute an argument, attributed primarily to Ranajit Guha, that colonial rule was 'an absolute externality'. She holds that 'new conceptions of sovereign right had to find expression through existing agencies of order and information', or as the editors put it in the Introduction, 'Denying . . . that the colonial judiciary began with a *tabula rasa,* she [Singha] shows nonetheless how both resistance from and co-option by indigenous ruling elites shaped the edifice of Anglo-Indian justice.'[59] Thus both the editors and Singha set up the contours of an argument that they are concerned to refute—this argument is apparently that colonial power acted upon a *tabula rasa* and reshaped Indian society out of thin air. Now who exactly makes such an argument? In Singha's paper, Ranajit Guha is quoted as making the argument mentioned above, that colonial rule 'had no mediating depths', and provided no space for 'transactions between the will of the rulers and the ruled'.[60] This perspective, argues Singha, would not take us very far 'in examining the realignments of agency, and the reorientation of cognitive structures involved in the construction of colonial law'.[61] But she concedes that Rule of Law under a colonial despotism was riven with contradictions, although it provided the legitimacy for British rule—a despotism based on law was said to be better than the arbitrary oriental variety of despotism. She also concedes that the colonial magistrates and judges while displaying a sympathy for patriarchal authority and values of masculine honour brought these norms (as they did other indigenous norms) in line with the legal claims to superiority of the state. That they engaged with indigenous norms at all (resulting in the 'realignments of agency' she refers to above), in her own argument is understood to be in order to ensure that the standardised procedures of British courts would not be threatening to Indian elites.[62]

What then is 'ironic' about the ambivalence in the Rule of Law as introduced by the British? It would seem this refracted operation of Rule of Law was the only possible form a colony could have. And how is this argument so different from Ranajit Guha's which, we discover on going back to the paper cited, refers to the 'fear which haunted so many of the more perceptive British observers during the second quarter of the nineteenth century . . . that the regime's isolation from the people under its rule would gravely undermine its security';[63] the British therefore adopted the political strategy of persuading the indigenous elite 'to attach themselves to the colonial regime'.[64] The colonial state, Guha says, was 'structured like a despotism' (as opposed to a bourgeois state; the term 'despotism' serves this specific purpose at this point in his paper) with 'no space provided for a transaction between the will of the rulers and the ruled'. Given such an argument, what Guha means is simply that the exchange between Indian elites and the state under these circumstances was moulded by reasons of the state's security, and was hardly an exchange between equals.[65] There is no suggestion that the colonial state operated upon a *tabula rasa.*

What emerges from Singha's rich and detailed research is that colonialism worked on contemporary indigenous modes of thinking, economy and social arrangements, shifting them in a new direction. The move was towards erasing the kind of ambiguity and multiplicity that marked existing forms of jurisprudence—the situation so clearly evoked by Sumit Guha in the earlier paper. Of course in this process it had to work with existing notions of justice, honour and so on, but as she demonstrates, as do Sandria Freitag, G. Arunima and Radha Kumar later in the book, the colonial intervention decisively transformed indigenous notions and brought them in line with the requirements of modern legal discourse.[66]

While it is true, as the editors say in their introduction, that some notions of justice and rights existed in Indian communities, the point is that 'rights' in the sense meant today did not exist in pre-colonial India. As all the five papers under discussion establish, rights in that sense were produced by colonial transformation of judicial discourse and administrative institutions. I believe of course, that the language of rights also empowered many subaltern sections against indigenous elites, but it is evident that its emergence was not unambiguously and universally emancipatory. As the work of these historians shows, the new language of rights had devastating consequences for many subaltern sections (*sansiahs,* Nayar women and female mill workers in Bombay) who were drastically marginalised and disciplined by the operation of modern codes of identity and governance.

In contemporary India too, as we shall see in the following chapters, the drive of law to fix identity has been problematic from the point of view of feminist politics. The work of Maitrayee Mukhopadhyay offers a striking illustration of this point. Her case studies of Hindu and Muslim women litigants who go to court for maintenance upon divorce or for a share in natal property, suggest that the force of the law tends to fix identity in such a manner that it is the dominant and oppressive possibilities that get reinforced. Mukhopadhyay points out that when women appeal to the state, they shift from the authority emanating in social relations to one that governs citizenship. Hypothetically, this shift has the potential to position both women and their male kin on the same plane as citizens, but this is rarely the case. The move to courts, she argues, rather than releasing women from 'the web of social relations that determine the meaning of wifehood', ends up not even simply reflecting that social identity, but reconstituting it and giving it renewed meaning.[67] As we have seen, this process of traditional identities acquiring new (and often more oppressive) meanings through the courts is a process that began with colonial jurisprudence.

Upendra Baxi argues that it was with 'ascendant capitalism and its Siamese twin colonialism' that the state appropriated to itself the legitimacy of being the sole source of law. All other forms of dispensing justice then began to be seen as inferior; these became designated as 'custom', 'community justice' or 'unofficial adjudication'. He holds that these should be called 'non-state legal systems" because to deny them the status of law is to accept the colonial devaluing of indigenous institutions.[68] However, simply to name them differently might be misleading. Modern legal systems are marked by 'a *quest* for . . . certainty, consistency and uniformity', as Baxi himself points out elsewhere.[69] This is not characteristic of pre-colonial indigenous justice-dispensing institutions, and the universal use of 'law' to refer to all forms of 'prescriptions, prohibitions, punishments'[70] would blur this crucial distinction.

Baxi himself does not consider the goals of 'certainty, consistency and uniformity' to be desirable and urges in fact, that there should be departures from them to ensure 'legal growth.' However, he does not address the question of how such departures are to be effected. The legitimacy of the law rests on the concept of Rule of Law, that is, the due observance of the procedures prescribed for making a valid decision. Departures from these procedures cannot be arbitrary. We find the same problem with Ronald Dworkin who, while questioning the rationalist and positivist certainties of law from a hermeneutical position, affirms law rather, as interpretation and meaning. However, he is clear that such interpretation has to follow 'the injunctions of a grammar of principles'. Ultimately, Dworkin assumes such principles to be drawn from the moral ideals of a subject assumed to be universal, for in his understanding, the job of the judge is to interpret the law in its best intellectual and ethical light so that it reflects the public standards of the community.[71] Clearly, any attempt to build into the law an openness to multivalence would have to be institutionalised if it is to be legitimate. The paradoxical nature of this formulation itself points to its impossibility. Without such institutionalisation, departures from consistency and uniformity can only be at the whim of individual judges, but once institutionalised, the desired 'openness' is at risk.

Such arbitrary departures from consistency are in fact, precisely the focus of critique of one feminist school of law. The perspective of 'legal realist rule scepticism' is that in actual practice, decisions are at the mercy of individual judges who make 'law' through their interpretation of ambiguous and open-ended practices. These interpretations reflect social and individual biases and practices, and the law is thus distorted from its purpose of neutral arbitration in the interests of social justice.[72] However, this understanding has been attacked from within feminism for reinstating the assumption that bias and prejudice are external to the law, that law proceeding from its parliamentary source is just and untainted by the values which influence individual judges.[73]

Marc Galanter's work is an acknowledgement of the need to confront the tendency of the law to fix meaning. He attempts to build into the law a conception of 'identity' not as a fixed, natural or inherent quality, but as something constituted by interaction and negotiation with other components of society. It is Galanter's view that this understanding of identity would require courts to adopt an 'empirical' as opposed to a 'formal' approach. The formal approach sees individuals as members of one group only, and therefore, as having only the rights to which that group is entitled. Thus, for example, one who attains caste status loses tribal affiliation as far as the law is concerned. The empirical approach on the other hand, does not attempt to resolve the blurring and overlap between categories and accepts multiple affiliations. It addresses itself to the particular legislation involved and tries to determine which affiliation is acceptable in the particular context. Galanter accepts that in this approach, some slippage is inevitable between judicial formulations and actual administration, for the courts must make subtle distinctions that must be translated into workable rules capable of being administered at lower levels.

It is clear that Galanter applies his understanding of identity as relative and shifting only to 'people', not to 'courts' or 'government'. The latter are assumed to be outside this grid of affiliations, to have a superior understanding of it, and to be capable of choosing the 'correct' perspective, whether empirical or formal. For example, he writes, 'it is beyond the courts to rescue these policies [reservation policies] from systematic cognitive distortion, for courts cannot control the way that various actors and audiences perceive judicial (and other) pronouncements.'[74] Moreover, government intention in framing and implementing reservations is assumed to be identical with the official stated intention, that is, promotion of social justice. Groups are then seen to relate to these policies in their own particularistic ways, while apparently, the government and courts have the overall and universal picture. Since Galanter retains the notion of the state and of law itself as the unified and self-transparent agency which will interpret the multiplicity of identities around it, his attempt to contest law's rigid codifying procedures remains unsuccessful.

An attempt to develop a 'postmodern jurisprudence' has been made by Douzinas, Warrington and McVeigh. They reject the orthodox jurisprudence of modernity that portrays the law as a coherent body of rules and principles. Dominant jurisprudence has always linked its claims to unity with the legitimation of power—that is, power is legitimate if it follows the law and law follows reason. Douzinas *et al.* argue that on the contrary, legal language games have proliferated endlessly and cannot be presented as 'the embodiment of the public good . . . or of some coherent system of principle . . .' In other words, their position is that the law is not the coherent system based on uniform principles it claims to be but rather, that its structures and institutions are multiple and work at different levels.[75]

Their analysis seems to suggest that the ensemble of modern law is already 'post-modern' in the sense of embodying multiple principles and functioning at a variety of levels in open-ended ways. The critique then, is aimed at the *pretensions* of the law to coherence and unity, not at its actual functioning in a way that tends to impose coherence and unity. If this is so, 'post-modern' jurisprudence merely involves uncovering the actually contingent and unstable nature of the law's functioning and bringing out 'the consequences of this for the legal subject'. In other words, 'the task of post-modern jurisprudence is to deconstruct the centrality of reason and law in the texts of the law.'[76] To the extent that Douzinas *et al.* are questioning the neutrality of the law in this process, and its claim to embody the General Will, their argument is well founded. But as the discussion in this chapter indicates, the drive of legality, of all judgements, judicial and quasi-judicial decisions and any form of adjudication in the formal legal sphere, is towards codifying conflicting meanings and identities, regulating them and rendering them uniform. If the law were indeed incoherent and multivalent, the kinds of dilemmas generated for a radical politics would have been very different. The drive towards erasure of ambiguity is not of course, always successful, but ambiguity is precisely what makes for *injustice* in the legal arena. Ambiguity in law does not benefit the powerless, but nor does certainty. The next section explores this contradictory situation in the feminist context.

The Sameness-*versus*-Difference Debate in Feminist Legal Theory

The fixity of meaning required by legal discourse has generated a dilemma for feminists which has come to be formulated as sameness-versus-difference. When 'equality before the law' is interpreted as men and women being the same as each other, courts do not uphold any legislation intended either to compensate for past discrimination or to take into account gender-specific differences like maternity. Thus the sameness approach cannot distinguish between 'differential treatment that disadvantages and differential treatment that advantages' as Ratna Kapur and Brenda Cossman put it.[77] Liberal feminists who subscribe to the sameness approach however, continue to insist that the way for women to achieve legal recognition of their equal status to men is to deny the legal relevance of their difference to the degree that it exists. Women should be recognised as gender-neutral legal persons.[78]

The opposing position from within feminism is that this accepts the masculine as the norm, and prevents the visibility of the unique experience of women. To consider ourselves as gender-neutral 'persons' can only marginalise us and devalidate our experience. However, the difference approach in law has at best been protectionist, thus denying women the claim to equality altogether. It has also been used by courts to justify discriminatory treatment on the grounds that women are different from men.[79] To put it in Frug's words, 'Sameness feminists have been thwarted by the repeated recognition of difference; difference feminists by the devaluing of *women's* difference.'[80]

Joan Scott's study of a sex-discrimination suit brought against Sears, the giant retailing company in the USA, by the Equal Employment Opportunities Commission (EEOC) in 1979, examines the notions of equality and difference that were brought into play in the courtroom. Two historians testified on opposite sides. Sears won the case and though this was in the overall climate of the Reaganist reversal of affirmative action policies in the 1970s, Scott points to the need to recognise that 'equality-versus-difference was the intellectual trap within which historians argued, not about tiny disparities in Sears' employment practices, but about the normative behaviours of men and women'.[81] Historian Elizabeth Kessler-Harris and the EEOC argued that Sears' hiring practices reflected inaccurate and inapplicable notions of sexual difference, while Sears argued that 'fundamental' differences between the sexes (and not its own actions) explained the gender imbalances in its labour force. Each of Kessler-Harris's carefully nuanced explanations of work history, says Scott, was forced into a reductive assertion by the Sears lawyers' insistence that she answer questions only with a yes or no. Further, the historian testifying for Sears, Rosalind Rosenberg, challenged Kessler-Harris with demands for absolute consistency. That is, she juxtaposed Kessler-Harris's testimony in court to her earlier research in which she had stressed differences between male and female workers in their approach to work, thereby suggesting that Kessler-Harris had misled the court. Scott points out that in the context of a critique of labour historiography, Kessler-Harris's different positions were legitimately different emphases for different contexts—'only in a courtroom could they be taken as proof of bad faith'.[82]

In other words, feminists seeking social justice through the law have come up against the limits set by the criterion that law be uniform and consistent. It can either recognise sameness (which disadvantages women) or difference (which justifies discrimination). An alternative approach suggested is that of 'substantive equality'.[83] The focus of this approach is not on equal treatment under the law, but on the impact that the law has. This is an attempt to make the law more sensitive to a more complex notion of equality that takes into account the comparative disadvantages of persons under existing unequal conditions. The proponents of this approach hold that in some contexts, the substantive model will require a sameness approach, and in others, a corrective approach to take into account difference as well as disadvantage.

This model quite clearly, is an understanding of how the law *ought* to function, and bears out the argument that is central to this paper, that rights are constituted within shared moral universes. The 'substantive equality' approach is an attempt to universalise one such moral universe through law. However, both conceptually as well as in terms of political practice, this approach is illustrative of the problematic nature of the discourse of legal rights. It assumes, to begin with, the independence and separateness of the judiciary and legal system from the institutions of the state and the economic and cultural practices that constitute present conditions of inequality. It seems to suggest that all that is required is for judges to be sensitised to the notion of substantive equality, and social conditions will be gradually transformed by law.

To put my objection to this simply, if the morality underlying the notion of substantive equality were so self-evident and unthreatening to the dominant social order, we would not need the law to bring about social justice. In the Sears case discussed above, for instance, Scott mentions the political climate only briefly, as an incidental factor. But the fact that the Reagan government's policies were transforming the economy and society at that time, during an overall global resurgence of neo-liberalism, is not a coincidence. The drive of law towards consistency and uniformity can only be expected to serve dominant interests. Indeed, one feminist teacher of law and legal activist has come to the conclusion that legal method may be 'impervious to a feminist perspective'.[84] She urges coming to terms with the fact that '. . . because there is so much resistance in legal method itself to ideas which challenge the status quo, there is no solution for feminists . . . except to confront the reality that gender and power are inextricably linked in the legal method we use.'[85]

Discussing the Canadian Charter of Rights and Freedoms of 1982, Judy Fudge makes a similar point. She concludes that once the demand for substantive equality for women is translated into legal rights, it becomes divorced from broader political demands:

> instead of directly addressing the question of how best to promote women's sexual autonomy under social relations which result in women's sexual subordination, feminists who invoke the Charter must couch their arguments in terms of the rhetoric of equality rights.

And courts interpret 'equality' as formal equality rather than contextualising it within a historical framework of current inequalities.[86]

One of the most passionate feminist declarations of difference is that of Robin West, who asserts 'the difference in women's hedonic lives'. 'The quality of our suffering is different from that of men's, as is the nature of our joy. Furthermore . . . the quantity of pain and pleasure enjoyed or suffered by the two genders is different: women suffer more than men.'[87] West is critical of both liberal and radical feminist models of legal theory, both of which adopt non-feminist normative models of legal criticism, which deny

> the normative significance of the subjective pleasure and suffering of our lives. Because of the normative models employed by modern legal feminists, the internal, phenomenological reality of women's lives—and its difference from men's—has become virtually irrelevant to feminist legal theory.[88]

West suggests a third strategy in order to make the larger legal culture sensitive to this difference:

> It is hard to empathise with the pain of another, when that pain is not understood . . . The strategic inference I draw is this: . . . the feel of our gender-specific pain must be described before we can ever hope to communicate its magnitude.[89]

She also rejects the Kantian assumption she sees as underlying both liberal and radical feminist theories, that to be human is to be autonomous. Women's lives, 'because of our biological reproductive role' are not autonomous, they are rather, 'profoundly relational'. This relationality is both empowering and burdening. Legal theory does not recognise this, nor do liberal and radical feminist theories of law. West insists that feminists need to force legal discourse to recognise women's humanity in this unique sense.[90]

This account is a perfect example of the impasse produced by the collision of richly textured, ethical accounts of experience with the requirements of legal discourse. West's account is impossible to accommodate within legal notions of truth and meaning, but neither is it uncontested within feminist legal theory itself. So hers is not even *the* feminist understanding of how women can be subjects in law, indeed, there can be no such single account. Difficult questions of politics and value cannot be simply turned into legal questions, as a commentator said in another context.[91] The terrain on which to deal with them might be entirely different.

If as I have attempted to demonstrate, rights are constituted by particular discourses, this resituates rights in a realm of complexity, ambiguity and undecidability. Law, on the other hand, sutures[92] open-endedness, and functions through the assertion of certainty and the creation of uniform categories. We come then, to a point where we must go further than saying simply this: the language of rights can be alienating and individualistic but since it refers to some desirable capacities and powers the oppressed should have, it can be empowering. We need to recognise rather, that the experience of feminist politics pushes us towards the understanding that social movements may have reached the limits of the discourse of rights and of 'justice' as a metanarrative.[93] It might even be that trying to bring about positive transformation through the law can run counter to the ethics which prompt entry into legal discourse in the first place.

Notes

1. Jacques Derrida, 'Force of Law: The Mystical Foundation of Authority' (tr. Mary Quaintance), in *Deconstruction and the Possibility of Justice*, a special issue of *Cardozo Law Review*, vol. II, nos 5–6, July–August 1990, p. 949.
2. Ibid., p. 955.
3. Ibid.
4. Nancy Fraser, 'The Force of Law: Metaphysical or Political?', in Manfred B. Steger and Nancy S. Lind, eds, *Violence and its Alternatives: An Interdisciplinary Reader*, London, Macmillan, 1999, p. 84.
5. Bhikhu Parekh, 'The Modern Conception of Right and its Marxist Critique', in Upendra Baxi, ed., *The Right to be Human*, New Delhi, Lancer, 1987, pp. 2–4.
6. Wendy Brown, *States of Injury: Power and Freedom in Late Modernity*, Princeton, Princeton University Press, 1995, p. 99.
7. Joan Landes, *Women and the Public Sphere in the Age of the French Revolution*, Ithaca, Cornell University Press, 1988.
8. Jane Rendall, *The Origins of Modern Feminism*, New York, Schocken, 1984.

9. Joan Scott, *Only Paradoxes to Offer*, pp. 9–11.
10. Bhikhu Parekh, 'The Modern Conception of Right . . .', pp. 5–9.
11. Jurgen Habermas, 'Remarks on Legitimation Through Human Rights' (tr. Max Pensky), in *The Postnational Constellation, Political Essays*, Cambridge, Polity Press, 2001, p. 114.
12. Ashis Nandy, 'The Politics of Secularism and the Recovery of Religious Tolerance', in Veena Das, ed., *Mirrors of Violence: Communities, Riots and Survivors in South Asia*, Delhi, Oxford University Press, 1990.
13. Michel Foucault, 'Governmentality', in Graham Burchell, Colin Gordon, and Peter Miller, eds, *The Foucault Effect: Studies in Governmentality*, London, Harvester Wheatsheaf, 1991, pp. 102–3.
14. David Scott, 'Colonial Governmentality', *Social Text*, no. 43, 1995, p. 201.
15. Ibid., p. 203.
16. Michel Foucault, 'The Subject of Power', in Dreyfus and Rabinow, eds, *Michel Foucault: Beyond Structuralism and Hermeneutics*, Chicago, University of Chicago Press, 1982, p. 221.
17. Charles Taylor, 'Human Rights: The Legal Culture', in *Philosophical Foundations of Human Rights*, UNESCO and International Institute of Philosophy, 1986, p. 57.
18. Ronald Dworkin, *Taking Rights Seriously*, London, Duckworth, 1977; 'Rights as Trumps', in Jeremy Waldron, ed., *Theories of Rights*, Oxford, Oxford University Press, 1984.
19. Nicos Poulantzas, *State, Power, Socialism* (tr. Patrick Camiller), London, New Left Books, 1978, p. 84.
20. Ibid., pp. 87, 92.
21. Nancy Fraser, 'The Force of Law: Metaphysical or Political?', pp. 86–7.
22. Christine Sypnowich, 'The Future of Socialist Legality: A Reply to Hunt', *New Left Review* 193, 1992, pp. 86–7.
23. Catharine MacKinnon, 'Feminism, Marxism, Method and the State', pp. 643–4.
24. Catharine MacKinnon, *Feminism Unmodified*, pp. 32–45.
25. Ibid., pp. 103–16, 163–97.
26. Catherine MacKinnon, 'Feminism, Marxism, Method and the State', p. 636.
27. Ibid.
28. Upendra Baxi, 'From Human Rights to the Right to be Human', in Upendra Baxi, ed., *The Right to be Human*, New Delhi, Lancer International, 1987, pp. 190–5.

29. Nancy Fraser, *Unruly Practices, Power, Discourse and Gender in Contemporary Social Theory*, Minneapolis, University of Minnesota Press, 1989, pp. 182–3.
30. See discussion of Martha Minow's work in Elizabeth Schneider, 'The Dialectics of Rights and Politics: Perspectives from the Women's Movement', in Martha Albertson Fineman and Nancy Sweet Thomadsen, eds, *At the Boundaries of Law*, New York and London, Routledge, 1991, p. 311; Nancy Fraser, *Unruly Practices*, pp. 312–16.
31. Elizabeth Schneider, 'The Dialectics of Rights . . .', p. 312.
32. Joel Feinberg, 'In Defence of Moral Rights', *Oxford Journal of Legal Studies*, vol. 12, no. 2, Summer 1992, pp. 151–3.
33. Ibid., pp. 160–2.
34. Ibid., p. 152.
35. Agnes Heller, 'Rights, Modernity, Democracy', in *Deconstruction and the Possibility of Justice*, a special issue of *Cardozo Law Review*, 1990, p. 1384.
36. Elizabeth Kingdom, *What's Wrong With Rights? Problems of Feminist Politics of Law*, Edinburgh, Edinburgh University Press, 1991, pp. 26–45.
37. Sally Alexander, 'Women's Work in Nineteenth-Century London; A Study of the Years 1820–50', in Juliet Mitchell and Anne Oakley, eds, *The Rights and Wrongs of Women*, Harmondsworth, Penguin, 1976; Michele Barrett, 'Rethinking Women's Oppression Today: A Reply to Brenner and Ramas', *New Left Review* 146, July–August 1984.
38. Michele Barrett, 'Rethinking Women's Oppression', p. 171.
39. Carol Smart, *Feminism and the Power of Law*, London and New York, Routledge, 1989, p. 139.
40. Ibid., p. 145.
41. Ibid., p. 143.
42. Ibid., p. 159.
43. James Boyle, 'The Politics of Reason: Critical Legal Theory and Local Social Thought', *University of Pennsylvania Law Review*, April 1985.
44. Cornel West, 'CLS and a Liberal Critic', *Yale Law Journal* 97, Yale L.J. 757, April 1988.
45. Ibid.
46. Patricia J. Williams, *The Alchemy of Race and Rights: Diary of a Law Professor*, Cambridge, MA, Harvard University Press, 1991, pp. 10–11.
47. Ibid., p. 164.
48. Roberto Mangabeira Unger, 'The Critical Legal Studies Movement',

Harvard Law Review, 96 Harv. L. Rev. 561, January 1983, pp. 561–5, 581–3.

49. See Robin Bradley Karr, 'Review of Roberto Unger's *What Should Legal Analysis Become?*', *Yale Law Journal*, vol. 106, no. 8, June 1997, pp. 2685–90.
50. Roberto Mangabeira Unger, *Law in Modern Society*, New York, Free Press, 1976, p. 241.
51. Robin Bradley Karr, 'Review of Robert Unger's . . .
52. Michael J. Sandel, 'Moral Argument and Liberal Toleration. Abortion and Homosexuality', in Amitai Etzione, ed., *New Communitarian Thinking*, Charlottesville, University Press of Virginia, 1995.
53. Ibid., p. 87.
54. Nancy Fraser, *Unruly Practices*, p. 183.
55. A.S. Altekar, *Sources of Hindu Dharma*, Sholapur, Institute of Public Administration, 1952; Robert Lingat, *The Classical Law of India* (tr. J. Duncan M. Derrett), Berkeley, University of California Press, 1973; Upendra Baxi, *Towards a Sociology of Indian Law*, New Delhi, Satvahan, 1986.

    Tahir Mahmood argues that custom is not an independent source of law in the legal theory of Islam, and that British administrators misunderstood custom to have the same significance in Islamic as within Hindu law. The reference to 'usages' may have been inspired, according to him, by the practices of Hindu converts to Islam, who continued to follow certain aspects of Hindu law and custom. But if this was prevalent, then to what extent did a pure Quranic law operate for Muslims any more than Sastric law did for Hindus? It was only at the beginning of the twentieth century that the *ulema* began to compulsorily enforce Shari'a law. See Tahir Mahmood, 'Custom as a Source of Law in Islam', *Journal of the Indian Law Institute*, vol. 7, 1965.
56. Edited by Michael Anderson and Sumit Guha, Delhi, Oxford University Press, 1998.
57. Sumit Guha, 'Wrongs and Rights in the Maratha Country: Antiquity, Custom and Power in Eighteenth Century India', in *Changing Concepts of Rights and Justice in South Asia.*
58. Radhika Singha, 'Civil Authority and Due Process: Colonial Criminal Justice in the Banaras Zamindari, 1781–1795', in *Changing Concepts of Rights*, p. 38.
59. Introduction, *Changing Concepts of Rights*, p. 7.
60. Ranajit Guha, 'Dominance Without Hegemony and its Historiography';

Ranjit Guha, ed., *Subaltern Studies VI*, Delhi, Oxford University Press, 1989, p. 274.

61. Radhika Singha, 'Civil Authority and Due Process', p. 59.
61. Ibid., pp. 38–9.
63. Ranajit Guha, 'Dominance Without Hegemony and its Historiography', p. 243.
64. Ibid., p. 242.
65. Ibid., pp. 273–4.
66. Sandria Freitag, '*Sansiahs* and the State: The Changing Nature of "Crime" and "Justice" in Nineteenth-Century India', pp. 82–113; G. Arunima, 'A Vindication of the Rights of Woman? Families and Legal Change in Nineteenth Century Malabar', pp. 114–39; Radha Kumar, 'Sex and Punishment Among Mill-Workers in Early-twentieth Century Bombay', pp. 179–97; in *Changing Concepts of Rights.*
67. Maitrayee Mukhopadhyay, *Legally Dispossessed: Gender, Identity and the Process of Law*, Calcutta, Stree, 1998, pp. 182–3.
68. Upendra Baxi, 'The State's Emissary: The Place of Law in Subaltern Studies', in Partha Chatterjee and Gyanendra Pandey, eds, *Subaltern Studies VII*, Delhi, Oxford University Press, 1992, pp. 251–2.
69. Upendra Baxi, *Towards a Sociology of Indian Law.*
70. Upendra Baxi, 'The State's Emissary: The Place of Law in Subaltern Studies', p. 251.
71. Ronald Dworkin, *Law's Empire*, Cambridge, MA, Harvard University Press, 1986, Chapter 11. See also the discussion of Dworkin's work in Costas Douzinas, Ronnie Warrington, and Shaun McVeigh, *Postmodern Jurisprudence, The Law of Texts in the Texts of Law*, London, Routledge, 1991, pp. 24–30.
72. A. Sachs and J.H. Wilson, *Sexism and the Law: A Study of Male Beliefs and Judicial Bias*, Oxford, Martin Robertson, 1978; S. Atkins and B. Hoggett, *Women and the Law*, Oxford and New York, Basil Blackwell, 1984.
73. Beverley Brown, 'Litigating Feminisms', *Economy and Society*, vol. 20, no. 4, November 1986; Elizabeth Kingdom, *What's Wrong With Rights?*
74. Marc Galanter, *Competing Equalities: Law and the Backward Classes in India*, Delhi, Oxford University Press, 1984, p. 357.
75. Costas Douzinas, Ronnie Warrington, and Shaun McVeigh, *Postmodern Jurisprudence: The Law of Texts in the Texts of Law*, p. 27.
76. Ibid.

77. Ratna Kapur and Brenda Cossman, 'On Women, Equality and the Constitution: Through the Looking Glass of Feminism', *National Law School Journal*, vol. 1, 1993. Republished in Nivedita Menon, ed., *Gender and Politics in India*, p. 261.
78. Ibid., pp. 216–17.
79. Ratna Kapur and Brenda Cossman, 'On Women'; Mary Joe Frug, *Postmodern Legal Feminism*, New York, Routledge, 1992.
80. Mary Joe Frug, p. xv.
81. Joan W. Scott, 'Deconstructing Equality-Versus-Difference: Or, the Uses of Poststructuralist Theory for Feminism', in Frances E. Olsen, *Feminist Legal Theory I: Foundations and Outlooks*, Aldershot, Dartmouth Publishing Company, 1995, p. 271.
82. Ibid., p. 269.
83. Ratna Kapur and Brenda Cossman, 'On Women', pp. 20–1.
84. Mary Jane Mossman, 'Feminism and Legal Method. The Difference It Makes', in Martha Albertson Fineman and Nancy Sweet Thomadsen, eds, *At the Boundaries of Law*, p. 297.
85. Ibid., p. 298.
86. Judy Fudge, 'The Public/Private Distinction: The Possibilities and Limits to the Use of *Charter* Litigation to Further Feminist Struggles', *Osgoode Law Journal*, vol. 25, no. 3, 1987, pp. 49–50.
87. Robin West, 'The Difference in Women's Hedonic Lives: A Phenomenological Critique of Feminist Legal Theory', in Frances E. Olsen, ed., *Feminist Legal Theory Volume I*, p. 423.
88. Ibid., p. 426.
89. Ibid., p. 425.
90. Ibid., pp. 439–40.
91. T.M. Scanlon, 'Partisan for Life', in *The New York Review*, 15 July 1993, p. 45.
92. I use the term 'suture' in the sense in which Ernesto Laclau and Chantal Mouffe do, implying a 'filling in'—'Hegemonic practices are suturing insofar as their field of operation is determined by the openness of social, by the ultimately unfixed character of every signifier. This original lack is precisely what the hegemonic practices try to fill in.' *Hegemony and Socialist Strategy: Towards a Radical Democratic Politics*, London, Verso, 1985, p. 88.
93. This recognition is emerging from within other contexts as well. Mahmood Mamdani points out in the case of Africa that the liberal notion of rights

as an attribute of citizenship has increasingly anti-democratic consequences for large numbers of Africans who are migrant labour and do not live in the countries of their birth. Mamdani points to the 'statist' character of the liberal theory of rights and urges a re-examination of the claim that the right to self-determination is not possible without the establishment of a state and that the bearer of 'human rights' should be a member of 'the political (state) community.' While Mamdani does not reject altogether the emancipatory potential of rights, and would work towards reinstituting them in a non-state context, the implications of this project are clear. To suggest that rights be abstracted from the arena of the state and its institutions is to radically question the current understanding of rights that social movements operate with, and the possibility of having reached the limits of rights-discourse is once again foregrounded. See 'Africa: Democratic Theory and Democratic Struggles', *Economic and Political Weekly*, vol. 27, no. 41, 10 October 1992, pp. 2228–32.

CHAPTER TWO

Abortion: When Pro-Choice is Anti-Women

In this chapter we explore the dilemmas that arise for feminist discourse on abortion as a result of the phenomenon of selective abortion of female foetuses in India. Abortion has been legal in India since the Medical Termination of Pregnancy Act of 1971, but that legislation originated from the population control imperatives of the Indian state, not from feminist politics. There has been no consistent and organised anti-abortion opinion in the country but since the 1980s, Indian feminists have found themselves in the paradoxical position of demanding curbs on access to abortion in the face of rising instances of selective abortion of female foetuses.

The Abortion Question in Feminist Politics

Western feminism has traditionally taken the position that the right to abortion is a fundamental and non-negotiable demand, a right to self-determination to which all women are entitled. By the 1960s, the right to abortion came to be seen as essential to women's right to equality as 'individuals'.[1] The slogan that was adopted was that of 'choice', thus emphasising autonomous decision-making rather than abortion itself. The movement generally focused on legal barriers to the realisation of individual liberty and thus implicitly denied the validity of any social regulation of reproduction.[2] On the other hand, campaigns against abortion also shifted their emphasis from the selfishness of women who would avoid their maternal calling to the rights and personhood of the foetus. Thus an anti-abortion discourse was created which was compatible enough with women's rights to be supported by many who are not anti-feminist.[3] Feminist critiques of foetal rights arguments see these as merely another attempt to regulate the bodies of women, for they are not concerned with poverty, large-scale pollution by powerful industries and such other factors which can equally affect the birth and quality of life of foetuses.[4]

Nevertheless, there is considerable rethinking among feminists in the West about conducting the discussion on abortion in the language of liberal rights discourse. First, this has to do with the changing image in the popular imagination, of the woman who wants an abortion. From the victim of the 1960s, she is now seen as the irresponsible 'Women's Libber'. Linda Gordon feels that this shift has come about precisely because of the success of the feminist attempt to pose abortion in terms of self-determination rather than as a form of medical treatment, and this change in image makes the formulation of feminist claims in terms of rights increasingly unpopular.[5]

Second, with advances in medical technology, it now seems possible that the foetus can be identified as separate from the mother far earlier than ever imagined before. It can thus be made to appear, as Carol Smart points out, that one branch of medicine has the capacity to 'save' foetal lives while another, at the instigation of feminists, is terminating them.[6] Further, rights talk can produce counter claims in terms of foetal rights and fathers' rights which may well prove to have greater political purchase than women's rights.

A third, more fundamental critique of setting abortion in the realm of rights is that the right to 'choose' makes little sense in the context of economic and cultural constraints that limit women's possibilities of choice. Abstract ideals of individual self-determination unaccompanied by any obligation on the part of the state to secure these can leave women without the institutional support necessary to realise their rights.[7] At the same time, as Carol Smart puts it, 'Neither laissez-faire nor state regulation are automatically good or bad. State regulation may force women to have only one child, while laissez-faire may offer her expensive medical abortions or cheap and dangerous backstreet ones. In the former she appears to have no choice, in the latter she has Hobson's choice.'[8] This is the basis on which Catharine MacKinnon attacks *Roe v. Wade* (1973) which is seen as the landmark judgement which legalised abortion in the USA. This judgement guaranteed abortion as a right to privacy, included in the constitutional right to privacy. The logic of *Roe* was, she argues, consummated in *Harris v. McRae* (1981) which decided that the right to privacy guaranteed only the individual woman's decision to terminate her pregnancy; it did not mean that federal funding must be available for abortions. MacKinnon argues against abortion as a right of privacy for another reason—insisting that sex is a private matter implies that the violence that women face in what is designated as 'private' is not a matter of public concern.[9]

Another influential feminist critique of abortion as a right to privacy is that of Robin West, who like most feminists, does not hold that a foetus is a person with moral rights of its own, but does insist that it is a creature of moral consequence. West argues that if the Supreme Court ever overturns *Roe*, and the issue of abortion is to be decided in the legislatures, women will not succeed in defending abortion rights if they emphasise privacy, which suggests selfishness and freedom from accountability. Rather, they should emphasise responsibility. 'Whatever the reason, the decision to abort is almost invariably made within a web of interlocking, competing, and often irreconcilable responsibilities and commitments.'[10]

Drucilla Cornell argues for the right to abortion in terms of the necessity of establishing the minimum conditions of individuation, which she sees, not as a natural process but as precariously achieved through relations with others. Cornell uses Lacan's theory of the mirror-stage to say that the ability to internalise the projection of bodily integrity so that one experiences oneself as whole, is central to a conception of selfhood. Therefore, denial of the right to abortion is a serious symbolic assault on women's sense of self because it thwarts the projection of bodily integrity and places her body in the control of the imaginings of others who deny her coherence by separating her womb from her self. Further, since the conditions of individuation are social and symbolic, the right to bodily integrity cannot be understood as the right to privacy. It is not enough for the state not to block access to abortion. It must establish the conditions whereby safe abortions are available to all women.[11] Although Cornell's conclusions are in tune with feminist positions generally, this emphasis on individuation may not be one that many feminists agree with.

For instance, the classic and often-cited study of Carol Gilligan (1982) had argued that in American society, women think about moral issues in distinctively different ways from men. Her work was based largely on interviews with twenty-nine women contemplating abortion, which led her to believe that, faced with difficult moral decisions, women are less guided by abstract moral principles than men are, and place greater emphasis on the responsibility to care for others and to prevent or minimise pain. Decisions about abortion therefore grew out of a perceived conflict between two sets of responsibilities, towards themselves and to the future child. Gilligan concluded that women define self-worth in terms of the ability to care for and protect others.[12]

Thus, feminist discussion on abortion in the West attempts to conceptualise abortion in moral terms, compatible both with generally held notions of the value of life as well as with feminist visions of sexual and reproductive autonomy. Discussing feminist debates on abortion, Ronald Dworkin concludes,

> Deciding about abortion is not a unique problem, disconnected from all other decisions, but rather, a dramatic and intensely lit example of choices people must make throughout their lives, all of which express convictions about the value of life and the meaning of death.[13]

This discussion is set in the context of the growing strength of campaigns to criminalise abortion once again. The political thrust therefore, is on retaining women's access to safe and legal abortions, and ensuring that the state intervenes positively through laws and administrative measures.

Abortion and the Indian Women's Movement

In India, the issue of abortion has entered the lexicon of feminist struggle through a very different trajectory from that followed in the West. Here, the 'right' to abortion has never been at the centre of much debate since it is seen as a measure to control population growth. The dominant ideology in, and about, countries such as India presents poverty as a function of rising population. One consequence of this ideology is that population control has been a central focus of governmental programmes for economic development.

If the issue of abortion is not framed within the political economy, its legalisation could appear to be the 'revolutionary' achievement of a progressive Indian state 'while women the world over are still striving to get abortion legalised.'[14] A brief discussion is therefore in order here, contextualising the issue of abortion in terms of the political economy of development in India. At independence, it was recognised by the Indian bourgeoisie that in order to promote industrialisation, it was essential to create a market by reducing poverty in the countryside. As originally conceived, this objective was to be achieved by substantial land reforms. However, the presence of powerful landed interests meant that effective land reforms were never carried out. Subsequently, economic policies in post-independence India have attempted to balance the interests of the different sections of the ruling classes—bourgeoisie, landed interests, the urban professional middle classes and the upper castes.

Successive governments have therefore pursued simultaneously, two conflicting sets of policies: growth strategies based on incentives to private investment, and distributive strategies requiring government investment on loans, technical training for the unemployed and other short-term measures. The tensions between the two types of policy are obvious. Governmental financing of distributional programmes entails diversion of resources from the creation of incentives for private capital. At the same time, if distributive policies are not implemented, mass poverty would make it impossible to achieve and sustain high growth rates. Since fundamental agrarian change in India has been ruled out, all attempts to tackle economic crises are situated within this contradictory matrix. Since the 1980s, under the tutelage of the World Bank, the Indian economy has undergone liberalisation and restructuring. More than ever, overpopulation is cast as the cause of poverty.[15]

Population control policies tend to be coercive towards the poor. During the Emergency of 1975–7 the government carried out compulsory mass sterilisation of men in slums. The strong reactions to this policy led the government gradually to target women as the object of family planning policies. District collectors have been offered incentives to meet their 'sterilisation targets' and there are instances in which employment on famine relief works has been refused to women workers who have not undergone sterilisation.[16] Far from having to struggle for the right to abortion, feminists find that government-sponsored programmes as well as private clinics like Marie Stopes, explicitly advocate the use of abortion as a method of controlling population.[17]

Further, governments have used incentives and disincentives to influence the decisions of government employees with respect to family size, and it can determine the availability of different kinds of contraceptives through pricing and subsidy policies. The small family norm is sought to be imposed even where factors like high infant mortality rates and insecurity of incomes make it rational to have large families. In the wake of the National Population Policy, 2000, several states have announced population policies that have a strongly punitive and anti-democratic thrust.[18] It is within such imperatives of population control that the Indian state moved towards the legalisation of abortion. Clearly then, the legal sanction for abortion does not arise from feminist principles at all, but it exists, nevertheless.

It is therefore, for quite a different reason that abortion has become an issue for Indian feminists. Since the 1980s, amniocentesis has been used to determine the sex of foetuses in order to abort female foetuses.

The vocal public debate on this practice including feminist responses, highlights issues located precisely at the points of tension in the feminist discourse on abortion.

First, the assumptions underlying the feminist demand for curbs on sex determination tests overlap assumptions behind justifying restrictions on abortion itself. In other words, arguments deployed to support a ban on sex determination tests can also be used to support a ban on abortion. This can give rise to very serious political contradictions. The dilemmas for the movement arising from this form of engagement with law, are explored later in this chapter.

Second, there is a profound philosophical incoherence involved in arguing for abortion in terms of the right of women to control their bodies and at the same time, demanding that women be restricted by law from choosing specifically to abort female foetuses. It is essential that feminists avoid being forced to counterpose the rights of (future) women to be born against the rights of (present) women to control over their bodies. This chapter will also therefore, examine in conclusion some of the problems that arise at the level of philosophy from setting abortion in the matrix of rights-talk.

The Medical Termination of Pregnancy Act

In 1965 a UN mission evaluating India's population policy recommended legalising abortion.[19] In 1966, the Shantilal Shah Committee submitted its report, recommending that access to abortion be liberalised in order to put an end to the large number of illegal and unsafe abortions. The Committee specifically denied that its recommendation was intended to serve the aim of population control. It stated that since the medical facilities to support an intensive abortion programme were not available, liberalising abortion with a view to family planning could in fact be counterproductive for the programme.[20]

The Act was passed in 1971 quite independently of the women's movement. The declared objectives of the Bill when it was introduced in Parliament were (a) humanitarian: to help the 'unfortunate women' who are the 'victims of forcible sexual acts'; (b) health: 'we should be sympathetic' to those who become pregnant because of failure of contraception; and (c) eugenic: to reduce the risk of 'crippled' children.[21]

In the debate in the Lok Sabha, the overwhelming majority supported the Bill, and insisted on making the point that the real objective was clearly population control, although the Bill did not mention this. Savitri Shyam, for example, stated that failure of contraception as a ground for abortion can be justified only in the context of population control. The government should accept, she said, that the family planning programme had not been successful and that this measure was simply an additional tool.[22] J.M. Gowder applauded the Bill as 'we have been spending crores of rupees on family planning programmes because of our unwarranted hesitancy in legalising abortion'.[23] Some felt that the conditions hedging access to abortion were unnecessary and hypocritical and opened the doors to corruption. Nawal Kishore Singh[24] and Vikram Chand Mahajan[25] for instance, argued that the Bill should simply allow abortion for women who wish to terminate their pregnancies.

Some MPs stated the 'social' reasons for their support of the Bill—that is, the 'social stigma' that unmarried women face if they get pregnant. Dr Melkote made a distinction between an 'unnecessary' child (which according to him, had to do with family planning), and an 'unwanted' child (which had to do with unmarried women and rape). The Bill would take care of both contingencies, he noted approvingly.[26] Lakshmikantamma held that we need the MTP Act since Indian society is not as 'advanced' as in the West, where women can openly bear illegitimate children.[27]

Only two MPs, M.M. Joseph and Muhammed Sheriff, opposed the Bill, on the ground that abortion is murder.[28]

What the Parliamentary debate on the Bill establishes is that there is no serious anti-abortion stream of opinion in India despite the fact that the major religions—Hinduism, Islam and Christianity—have textual traditions that denounce abortion as sin.[29] However, it is also clear, both from the debate as well as from the discussion in the previous section, that the reasons for widespread support for liberalising abortion arises from impulses quite at variance with feminist concerns about reproductive freedom. Access to abortion is upheld (a) through a sanctifying of social norms which are in fact antithetical to feminism, and (b) on the grounds that overpopulation is the reason for mass poverty, an argument used by the ruling elites to justify the development strategy they have adopted.

Despite the MTP Act the number of unsafe abortions continues to be high. Only 10 per cent of total induced abortions are performed through licensed safe medical services.[30] According to the Parivar Seva Samstha which runs the Marie Stopes clinics, about 6.6 lakhs of women die every year due to illegal abortions, that is, abortions performed by unqualified personnel. India's maternal mortality rate is the second highest in the world and 22 per cent of this is due to abortions. The problems with abortion services are lack of information, limited publicity and the widely held belief that abortion is illegal. Added to this is the fact that facilities and trained personnel are inadequate, especially in rural areas. Legalisation has not, in short, been buttressed by safe and humane abortion services.[31]

However, the focus of feminist activity on abortion has not been on these issues. Rather, it has been on a serious subversion, from the feminist point of view, of the liberatory potential of access to abortion.

The Campaign Against Sex Determination Tests: Political Contradictions

In 1975 the All India Institute of Medical Sciences initiated experiments in using amniocentesis for detecting foetal abnormalities. A by-product of the test was knowledge about the sex of the foetus, and most of the couples who learnt that the foetus was female went in for abortion. Subsequently, through an order of the Indian Council for

Medical Research, the use of the amniocentesis test was restricted to cases of suspected genetic diseases.[32] Between 1977 and 1985 three circulars to government departments at the centre and in the states made the use of pre-natal sex determination for the purpose of abortion a penal offence.[33]

The ban on the use of this technology in government institutions led to its privatisation and commercialisation. Sex determination clinics mushroomed all over the country. Districts which lack such basic amenities as potable water and electricity have pre-natal sex determination clinics. Rural health centres with no facilities for the testing of sputum for tuberculosis or to maintain the cold chain for oral polio vaccines send samples of amniotic fluid in ice-packs to the nearest towns for sex determination tests. A study showed that even landless labourers and marginal farmers were willing to take loans at high rates of interest to avail of these tests.[34]

A campaign against the practice of pre-natal sex determination was launched by women's groups as well as civil liberties and health movements. In 1984 a broad coalition was formed, the Forum Against Sex Determination and Sex Preselection (FASDSP). The FASDSP operated on many levels. It conducted research studies, held seminars and workshops, produced information sheets and so on. However, the primary focus of its activity was the mounting of a sustained campaign for legislation to ban sex determination tests.

In 1988 there was a legislative breakthrough at the state level when the government of the state of Maharashtra brought into force the Maharashtra Regulation of the Use of Prenatal Diagnostic Techniques Act. After this, the FASDSP began a campaign for central legislation.

The FASDSP clearly saw restrictive legislation as an important strategy of progressive social change. After the passing of the Maharashtra Act, it asserted in its newsletter that the Act proved 'it is possible to pressurise the government to take a progressive step provided all progressive forces join hands.'[35] Many activists however, were disappointed with the Act, as reflected in Flavia Agnes's comment that '[t]his moment which should have been one of jubilation turned out to have been one of doubt and misgiving.'[36] Of greater concern though, is the FASDSP's unqualified acceptance of the progressive potential of the government, even though it does recognise that the government responds only when confronted by overwhelming democratic pressure. As we have seen, the 'progressive' attitude of the Indian state towards abortion is dictated by compulsions other than a commitment to women. If the logic of these very compulsions were extended, the government could well support selective abortion of female foetuses.

In fact, there already exists a vocal and influential school of thought which justifies the selective abortion of female foetuses as a form of population control. The argument is in essence, that to permit abortion of female foetuses would stop couples from continuing to have children until the desired son was produced.[37] At a seminar in 1984 a government official stated that sex determination tests must be allowed because our population problem calls for desperate measures.[38] Similarly, the Head of Obstetrics and Gynaecology at the government general hospital in Bokaro has said, 'Our priority is population control by any means. Amniocentesis should be used as a method of family planning and should be made available to everyone at a minimum cost or even free.'[39]

Moreover, although the government does not openly advocate sex determination tests, the selective abortion of female foetuses seems to have been built into the population control policies of the Sixth and Seventh Plans. These Plans set a target of a Net Reproduction Rate (NRR) of one (that is, one woman should replace her mother) and it is expected that this goal, together with the objective of limiting births to two to three per woman, will be achieved by 2006–11. It would appear that one implication of these polices is that 'excess' girls will have to be killed at the foetal stage to maintain the NRR of one.[40]

As long as poverty is tackled as a function of overpopulation, the availability of abortion facilities is unlikely to be questioned. The corollary of this policy however, is that it is not at present in the interest of the dominant elites to curtail abortions in any way. Therefore, while the compulsions of democracy are such that a vocal, visible and organised women's movement may achieve legislative reform, such reforms are bound to be unsatisfactory. Legislation cannot but be embedded in the dominant values of systems and very often distorts the purpose intended by marginal groups.

Thus it is not surprising that the legislation in Maharashtra which purports to curtail pre-natal sex determination is full of loopholes. First, the legislation does not ban private genetic laboratories and clinics which carry out sex determination (SD) tests but only provides for their registration. Second, the Act enables the state government to overrule the decisions of the highest monitoring body set up by the Act with respect to cancellation or suspension of the licence of a clinic or laboratory. Third, the government can exempt any public lab or clinic from the provisions of the Act. Fourth, the ordinary citizen cannot directly move the courts if s/he comes acrosss a case of sex-selective abortion but must approach the monitoring bodies. Finally, the monitoring bodies can refuse to make records or information available to the complainant 'in the public interest'.[41]

Even if it were possible to pressurise the government into enacting a foolproof law against the abortion of female foetuses, there remains an important dilemma for feminists. We have to examine the political implications of pushing for legislation that could entail restricting a woman's right to abortion. In fact, two of the legal initiatives against SD tests were based on premises which questioned the unrestricted right to abortion. A women's group in Bombay filed a petition in the High Court in 1986 arguing against SD tests on the grounds that such tests violated Article 21 of the Constitution, that is, the right to life. This argument could well be extended to the right to abortion itself. The second instance is a Private Members's Bill introduced in Parliament to amend the MTP Act. The amendment sought to empower the medical practitioner to refuse termination of pregnancy 'if he or they have reason to believe that such termination is sought with the intention to commit female foeticide.'[42] Both initiatives were opposed by the FASDSP as potentially restricting the right to abortion. Nevertheless, it must be recognised that in many ways, arguments against selective abortion of female foetuses occupy the same terrain as those against abortion. Reflecting on the campaign against SD tests, an activist writes, 'Today . . . some of us feel that the poster and other visuals used in the campaign might have been misinterpreted as being anti-abortion.'[43]

This is why, although the FASDSP holds that it seeks only to restrict SD tests, not the access to abortion itself, it remains unable to separate the two issues. One example of the problems that can arise is to be found in the reaction the FASDSP had to one of the critical provisions in the draft of the Central legislation which has since been passed. While it awaited presidential assent, it was circulated for discussion. The definition clause of the draft legislation defined 'selective abortion of female foetus' as that which is performed on the pregnant woman 'on grounds other than those listed in the MTP Act of 1971.' Under this Act, an abortion is legal up to twelve weeks without restriction, up to twenty weeks if the physical or mental health of the woman or child is at risk and after twenty weeks only if it is certified as immediately necessary to save the life of the pregnant woman. Thus, by the terms of the proposed Bill, monitoring agencies would consider the possibility that an abortion was selectively directed at a female foetus only if it clearly falls outside these conditions. That is to say, the regulatory regime would be breached only if (a) termination after twenty weeks of pregnancy cannot be supported by evidence of a sufficiently grave threat to the life of the pregnant woman, or (b) in terminations between twelve and twenty weeks, sufficient evidence cannot be shown that the pregnancy threatened the physical or mental health of the mother or child.

The FASDSP opposed the definition clause of the draft legislation that excluded from its purview abortions which were permissible under the MTP Act. It pointed out that on occasion doctors have interpreted the 'mental health' clause to include the trauma that the woman would be subjected to if she had a female child, and on this basis have conducted abortions up to twenty weeks. Thus, the existing provisions of the MTP Act can legally permit selective abortion of female foetuses. The FASDSP argued, therefore, that the definition clause of the Bill discussed above ('grounds other than those listed in the MTP Act of 1971') should be deleted.[44] However, the dropping of the clause has grave implications because it opens up the possibility of any abortion coming under the scrutiny of the proposed legislation against SD tests. In effect, while the FASDSP is very clear that on no account should the MTP Act be amended to curb SD tests, its opposition to the clause discussed above could open up entirely new ways of reviewing many routine abortions carried out under the MTP Act.

Furthermore, increasingly simpler techniques of sex determination are being developed, and abortion of female foetuses being rendered unnecessary by sex pre-selection techniques, which decide the sex of the foetus at the time of conception. The FASDSP therefore, calls for a ban on such pre-selection techniques and for their regulation in future. The extent to which state intervention is being actively solicited should give rise to considerable unease.

While sharing the concern of the FASDSP over technologies that would have the same effect on the sex ratio as the selective abortion of female foetuses, one must recognise the dangers inherent in seeking the intervention of law to restrict the development of any technology that could be judged capable of being used for sex pre-selection. It is true that technology is not neutral in relation to power structures and that it tends to reinforce existing patterns of power. Nevertheless, the solution cannot be to hand over entire areas of science and knowledge to bureaucratic control. Such a strategy is in fundamental contradiction to any feminist ideal of democracy.

It has been almost two decades since the campaign was launched, and there is evidence of growing introspection and reflection within the movement. Thus there is increasing discomfort with the term that gained currency during the first phase of the campaign, 'female foeticide'. Responding to an article against the practice recently published in a journal of medical ethics, a feminist wrote, 'Female "foeticide", undoubtedly a catchy phrase, implies the murder of the female foetus, and imbues the foetus with a life, a soul and rights, including the right to life.'[45] The term, used unproblematically for many years by many feminists, including myself, partly for its convenience and 'catchiness', is increasingly being replaced by the more cumbersome but less problematic phrases 'femicide of foetuses' or 'selective abortion of female foetuses'.

The extent to which 'abortion' and 'female foeticide' can run together in the common perception is evident in the invitation card to an event organised by the Delhi NGO Network to launch a campaign against femicide of foetuses. The logo on the card is of a foetus in a womb, and the slogan around it says: '*bhrunhatya roko abhiyan*', that is, 'Campaign to stop *foeticide*.' The word *kanya* for 'female' is missing, apparently through oversight or proofreading error, for there were feminists and feminist NGOs among the organisers whose support for legal access to safe abortion is well known.[46] My point is that the conflation is widely prevalent.[47]

On another front, an activist reviewing the years of struggle relocates SD tests as a wider issue that raises questions about democracy and decision making.

> We would assert that a few bureaucrats and/or scientists/technocrats should not have the right to decide on matters which affect society as a whole. We should try to initiate a process whereby a technology would be allowed to operate within a society only after ascertaining its benefits and risks to all concerned.[48]

However, this kind of perspective cannot merely be added on to a legalistic and state-centred campaign. It suggests a radical rethinking of the issues and strategies involved, and a definite move away from demands for more legislation. So overpowering however, is the hegemonic perception of law as a transformative instrument, that this writer concludes, 'we should ask for banning the misuse and at the same time for regulating the proper use of these techniques.'[49]

After this long and troubled campaign, a piece of legislation finally emerged. In the next section, we will look at this Act more closely.

The Pre-Natal Diagnostic Techniques (Regulation and Prevention of Misuse) Act (1994)

The Pre-Natal Diagnostic Techniques (PNDT) Act, first introduced in 1991 as Bill No. 155, was sent to a Joint Select Committee of Parliament, and after subsequent discussion, was unanimously passed in July 1994. Its only focus of regulation and control is techniques of pre-natal sex determination, not the access to abortion in any form. That is, the Act does not concern itself with selective abortion of female foetuses as such, but rather, with medical procedures to detect the sex of the foetus, which can lead to femicide. Thus, unlike the draft earlier discussed, there is no definition of what constitutes femicide of foetuses. As the Act stands, therefore, it seems that the access to abortion in general has been kept entirely clear of its scope. This certainly resolves one of the political contradictions for feminism discussed earlier, although the inconsistency at the level of philosophy remains, which we will go into later in this chapter. However, it is precisely the narrow focus of this Act that protects the Medical Termination of Pregnancy Act from coming within its scope—but this has left the legislation incapable of tackling effectively the problem of even SD tests. Both these contentions will be explored later in this section.

The Act specifies that pre-natal diagnostic tests can be conducted for the detection of five types of abnormalities—chromosomal abnormalities, genetic metabolic diseases, haemoglobinopathies, sex-linked genetic diseases and congenital anomalies. It also lays down certain conditions under which these tests can be conducted—if the pregnant woman is over thirty-five, if she has a history of two or more spontaneous abortions, if there is a family history of mental retardation or physical deformities, or if she has been exposed to potentially teratogenic agents such as drugs, radiation, infection or chemicals.

The Act lays down that no person conducting pre-natal diagnostic procedures shall communicate to the woman or her relatives the sex of the foetus. All genetic counselling centres, labs and clinics are to be compulsorily registered, and their licences are liable to be suspended or cancelled in case of complaints. There is a ban on the advertising of SD tests, with the publishers sharing equal culpability with the advertisers. The punishment can be up to three years of imprisonment and a fine of Rs 1000. There are similar rules for medical practitioners, who can be deregistered by the Medical Council for two years for a first offence and permanently for a subsequent one. The woman undergoing the test will be presumed to have been compelled to do so unless the contrary is proved, in which case she too, is liable for punishment.

Women's groups were dissatisfied with the Bill in the form it was passed, and in August 1994 urged the President to send it back for reconsideration to Parliament. The points that their memorandum raised were as follows:

(a) The registration of private clinics will only regularise them, and they can continue to determine the sex of foetuses by misusing tests meant for the purposes permitted by the Bill. Only government clinics therefore, should be permitted to conduct pre-natal tests.

(b) All ultrasound machines and other equipment which can be used for SD tests should be registered. The Joint Committee had earlier considered this suggestion and rejected it as unfeasible because such equipment is used for various purposes other than pre-natal testing. A Note of Dissent to the report of the Joint Committee, by MPs Geeta Mukherjee, Sarla Maheshwari and Malini Bhattacharya, had endorsed these two recommendations made at that time by women's groups.[50]

(c) Future techniques for sex determination as well as for sex preselection should be brought within the ambit of the Bill.

(d) Punishing the woman is misguided even on the presumption that she was coerced unless proved otherwise. The husband and relatives can escape punishment if they hold the woman responsible. This is unjust in a context where women rarely take autonomous decisions. The Bill in this respect is anti-woman, and would create conditions that would limit its effectiveness.

(e) Knowledge of the sex of the foetus is to be kept only from the woman and her family and relatives. There is nothing in the Bill which prohibits the communication of such information to non-relatives.

(f) No minimum punishment has been specified, which means that actual punishment can remain only nominal.

(g) There is no provision in the Bill for setting up of local vigilance committees which could contribute to the effective implementation of the Act. [51]

These objections were not taken note of, and the Bill became law in the form it was passed by Parliament, in 1994. The years since the Act have passed without effect. The Census of 2001 has aroused considerable concern about the continuing decline in the sex ratio, particularly in the age group 0–6 years—a clear indicator of large-scale femicide of foetuses and infants. In February 2000, a Public Interest Litigation was filed in the Supreme Court by a group of NGOs and individuals, seeking directives to state and central governments to implement the PNDT Act, and second, to interpret/amend the legislation to include sex pre-selection techniques. The PIL argued that the PNDT Act had not been taken seriously, the machinery to enforce the Act had not been put into place, nor had the required resources been provided. In May 2001 the Supreme Court passed an order which aims to ensure the implementation of the Act, to plug loopholes and to launch a media campaign highlighting the issue. However, there is no reference to the second aim of the PIL, to ban/regulate sex pre-selection techniques, although the order does ask the central supervisory board to examine the necessity of amending the Act.[52]

So ineffective has the Act been, that in 2001 the State Consumer Disputes Redressal Commission (a government body) of the state of Gujarat (one of the states in which the decline in sex ratio has been most marked) awarded a large cash compensation to a couple who filed a complaint that they had been erroneously told that a foetus was female, when after abortion, it turned out to be male. The doctors in question have been asked to pay cash damages with interest to the couple. Said Justice Mahendrabhai Parikh, chief of the Commission, when questioned by reporters, 'We have only seen the case from the scientific point of view and the doctor should have conducted the test carefully.' He added that since the complaint was filed in 1992, the test might have been done before it was banned. However, the Family Welfare Secretary at the Union Ministry of Health and Family Welfare is of the opinion that the case comes under the existing law, and that both the parents and the doctors can be imprisoned and fined[53] (although till the date of going to press, nothing of the sort has happened).

It is clear that most of the loopholes of the Maharashtra Act of 1988, as perceived by women's groups, persist. However, simply tightening these would involve stringent state control, about which misgivings have been expressed earlier in this chapter. Further, if SD tests are sought to be entirely delinked from selective abortion of female foetuses, which is necessary in order to protect the MTP Act, they cannot be effectively curbed, because most of the equipment is used for other purposes as well. This is the double bind into which, I argue, legal discourse pushes social movements like feminism—the more narrow the focus of a piece of legislation, the less it serves its purpose, but the broader it is, the more it subverts the ethics underlying the very demand for legislation. We will find similar dynamics at work when the issue of sexual violence is explored in the next chapter.

Another important question arises from the memorandum of women's groups to the President in 1994. It is true that women may be implicated by families and end up being punished when they rarely are in a position to make choices. Nevertheless, what are the implications of denying agency altogether to women on the grounds that they are never responsible for their decisions and therefore, should not be considered culpable at all? Within the realm of legal discourse, it is dangerous for feminists to construct women as incapable of taking autonomous decisions—the consequences for women's struggles against legally sanctioned discrimination in other spheres could be fatal.

Finally, the new legislation and feminist responses to it establish that we remain unable to confront the ethics of condoning abortions on the grounds of 'abnormalities' in foetuses. This question will be addressed more fully in the last section of this chapter.

The Right to Abortion in India's Legal Discourse

It is now necessary to examine just how strongly entrenched the right to abortion is in India. Is it of little more than academic interest to speculate on the danger to the access to abortion if curbs are demanded on selective abortion of female foetuses? A close examination of the MTP Act and of judicial pronouncements on abortion however, reveal that this 'right' is circumscribed by the *absolute* discretion of medical opinion.

Jesani and Iyer in their study of the MTP Act point out that the pregnant woman cannot avoid giving an explanation in order to avail of abortion. She cannot simply state that it is an unwanted pregnancy. 'She is required to furnish explanations that fit into the broad liberal—and yet restrictive—conditions listed in the Act.'[54] These conditions confer a monopoly on medical opinion, which has the power to decide whether the woman meets the requirements of the Act. Thus, during the first twelve weeks of pregnancy, termination is available on the certification of one registered gynaecologist or obstetrician. From twelve to twenty weeks, termination requires two registered gynaecologists or obstetricians to certify either that the pregnancy involves a risk to the life of the woman or would cause grave injury to her physical or mental health, or alternatively, that there is a substantial risk that a seriously handicapped child would be born. After twenty weeks a pregnancy can be terminated only if two registered gynaecologists or obstetricians testify that it is immediately necessary to save the life of the pregnant woman. The Act does not define 'health', 'substantial risk', 'seriously handicapped' and so on. It is left to the medical practitioner to decide how these terms are to be interpreted, although two explanatory notes indicate that pregnancy in the case of rape (excluding marital rape) and contraceptive failure (in the case of a married woman) may be treated as causing injury to mental health. In fact, even the words 'abortion', 'miscarriage' and 'termination of pregnancy' have not been defined, either in the Act or in the relevant sections of the Penal Code, which leaves individual medical opinion on these matters sacrosanct.

Thus, the 'liberal' provisions of the MTP Act could become restrictive without, as Jesani and Iyer put it, 'a single word of the text being altered.'[55] It has been pointed out that in one sense, Section 312 of the IPC is broader than the MTP Act, because it allows the termination of pregnancy in order to save the life of the pregnant woman, while the MTP Act only allows this if it is 'immediately' necessary to save her life.[56] Similarly, Alice Jacob points out that the MTP Act, by permitting only registered medical practitioners to terminate pregnancies, renders illegal any emergency operation by the woman herself or any layperson. Thus the MTP Act is more restrictive, she feels, than Section 312 of the IPC, which permitted any person to terminate pregnancy in order to save the life of the woman.[57]

Clearly then, what appears to be a well-established right in the Indian context is constituted in a very complex way. A shift in the configuration of political and cultural elements could radically affect the economic compulsions that at present give legal sanction to abortion. One scenario that is not entirely beyond the realms of possibility is a government interested in selective population growth within specific communities. In the climate of increasing communalism in India, there is considerable discussion on the supposed decrease in the numbers of Hindus in comparison to other religious communities, especially Muslims. An illustration of the potential danger for women's control over their reproductive capacity can be seen in the ceremony organised in 1986 by a group called the Hindu Munnani to honour, with the title 'Brave Mother', four Hindu women, each of whom had borne ten children. The awards were distributed by the Shankaracharya of Kanchi who said that while he did believe that Hindus should practise family planning, other communities were not being controlled.[58] In Mumbai, which has been controlled by the Hindu right-wing Shiv Sena for many years now, billboards condemning abortion have become a common sight.[59]

Most recently, after the 2001 census showed a significant drop in female-to-male sex ratio, the government has increased its efforts to publicise the illegality of selective abortion of female foetuses. Part of its propaganda has been through mobilising religious bodies to declare femicide of foetuses to be a sin. However, the statements made by Hindu religious leaders at a convention against femicide of foetuses organised by a governmental body, the National Commission for Women, in association with the Indian Medical Association and UNICEF, give us no reason to believe that their concern is for women's right to life and dignity. Most of them declared abortion itself to be a sin, and femicide of foetuses was only a part of that understanding. Moreover, in accordance with the Shastras, they endorsed the practice of sati and denounced vasectomy and widow remarriage.[60] Thus, not only is the legal sanction for abortion precarious in itself, social sanction for it cannot be taken for granted either.

I would emphasise here that the lack of clarity in definitions that marks the MTP Act and the relevant sections of the IPC does not indicate the ability of legal discourse to be flexible. Rather, it underscores the move towards fixing meaning that, I argue, is characteristic of the Law. In the case of abortion, this fixing is sought through the supposed 'neutrality' and 'scientificity' of medical discourse which will determine exactly the period of gestation, the precise degree of risk of a disabled foetus, the possibility of mental injury and so on. Such a move towards rigidly codifying and normalising the ambiguities and ambivalences inherent in decisions to abort can only be antithetical to the morality underlying the feminist defence of abortion rights.

The second problem with the MTP Act is that it is precariously balanced on patriarchal assumptions. What animates the legal discourse on abortion is not concern for women's health or their autonomy, but a punitive spirit which treats abortion as a crime unless performed under specified conditions. An abortion which does not meet the conditions set by the MTP Act is an offence under the IPC, Sections 312 to 316, which used to govern abortion before 1971 and which still exist on the statutes. Under Section 312, causing miscarriage, even with the consent of the woman, is punishable by law unless it is to save the life of the woman.

The 'liberality' of the MTP Act has rarely been put to test because of the acceptance of abortion as a mode of family planning. However, in the few cases regarding abortion which have come to court it becomes evident that a concern for the autonomy or physical health of women is not what motivates judicial discourse. Four cases are discussed below, which illustrate the preoccupation of the courts with the reproductive role of women and its centrality to maintaining the social order.

Under the Act, termination of pregnancy requires the consent only of the woman if she is above eighteen and sane. However, while such a woman cannot be punished for the act of abortion itself, a Delhi High Court judgement in 1983 held that abortion without the consent of the husband constitutes 'cruelty' within the meaning of the Hindu Marriage Act. The husband was therefore granted divorce as, in the words of the judgement, the wife had refused to 'satisfy a husband's natural and legitimate craving to have a child'. The judgement goes on, 'This is more so . . . where the parties to the litigation are Hindus. In this sort of case the court has to attach due weight to the general principle underlying the Hindu law of marriage and sonship and the principle of spiritual benefit of having a son.'[61] What are the implications of such a judgement for the selective abortion of female foetuses?

In a case before the Madras High Court in 1993, the father of a sixteen-year-old girl petitioned that the pregnancy of his daughter be terminated on the grounds that she was legally and mentally too young to take the decision to bear a child. The Additional Public Prosecutor who presented the case of the girl, defended her right to bear the child on the grounds of the right to privacy. He argued that this right was a fundamental right included in the right to life and liberty and that the Constitution made no distinction between majors and minors when it came to fundamental rights.

The Bench accepted the public prosecutor's arguments and said that this issue could be taken as one which involved the basic right of an individual. However, it made two additional pronouncements which are deeply disturbing from the feminist point of view. One, it rejected the petitioner's argument that delivery in the case of minors was medically dangerous. On the contrary, said the judges, 'The younger the mother, the better the birth.' Termination of the first pregnancy could lead to sterility, they added. Two, they quoted from Hindu, Muslim and Christian scriptures that destruction of life even in the mother's womb had no moral sanction.[62]

Given these explicit values underlying the judgement, it does not seem possible that the right to individual liberty would have been upheld had the situation been the reverse, that is, had the girl been a minor wanting to terminate her pregnancy in the face of opposition from her guardian.[63]

In 1966, in a case that came up before the Allahabad High Court, the judgement held that the child in the womb is a person. This judgement is interesting because such a conclusion does not appear to have been indispensable to holding the appellant guilty of assault resulting in miscarriage. The circumstances were that the appellant pushed down a woman and kicked her. Since she was seven months pregnant, this resulted in her prematurely delivering a baby which died. The trial court convicted the appellant under Section 316 which applies if the death of a quick unborn child (the term 'quick' refers to an advanced stage of pregnancy) is caused by an action that can be classified as culpable homicide (that is, an action with the knowledge and/or intention that it would cause death).

The judge held on appeal that Section 316 does not apply as the appellant could not have intended to kill the woman by merely pushing her down and kicking her. Since his act did not amount to culpable homicide, it did not come under the purview of Section 316. Nor did it come within Section 313, which covers causing miscarriage without the consent of the mother. In the opinion of the judge, the assault came within the meaning of Section 304A which deals with death caused to a person by a rash and negligent act not amounting to culpable homicide. The foetus in the womb was adjudged to be a 'person' within the meaning of this section whose death had been caused by the appellant's rash act. The maximum punishment under Section 304A is two years of imprisonment while Section 316 has a maximum punishment of ten years. Thus the appellant received a much lighter punishment than had been awarded by the trial court. More significantly from our perspective, the principle was established that the term person as used in Section 304A includes an unborn child in the mother's womb if it is an advanced stage of pregnancy. The rationale the judge used was that at seven months the child is capable of independent existence.[64] What implications this judgement can have for the access to abortion has not been put to test yet, but it reinforces the idea of the mother as a mere environment which bears the foetus.

The greater importance assigned to the unborn child over the mother is illustrated also in a case before the Madhya Pradesh High Court in 1992. A doctor administered an injection to a woman to determine pregnancy. She was twenty-four weeks pregnant and died the next day. The doctor's conviction under Section 312 was upheld, that is, voluntarily causing miscarriage. It is significant that though the woman died as a result of the injection, the doctor was not convicted for her death but, in essence, for the death of the foetus.[65]

In short, while the 'morality' of abortion remains undebated in India, this is because of a particular hegemonic perception of the reason for widespread poverty. Within a changed cultural and ideological matrix, we may well find ourselves battling to retain even the restrictive provisions of the MTP Act.

Reproductive Autonomy Versus Population Control

Maria Mies, analysing 'global capitalist patriarchy', holds that reproductive technology is yet another manifestation of 'technopatriarchal' control over women. Mies suggests that the international battle over women's bodies has entailed a dual strategy of discouraging poor women from the South from breeding poor people, while middle-class women of the North are encouraged to breed because they add to consumption demand, which drives capital accumulation.[66]

Clearly then, the issue of abortion appears to feminists of the South in quite a different way than it does to feminists of the North. The latter see it as endangered by the moral offensive of the Right, and their concern accordingly, is with developing a philosophical justification which would delicately balance autonomy with responsibility. Politically, they are concerned with protecting access to safe and legal abortions as well as ensuring the possibility of choice in matters of contraception.

Feminists of the South, while recognising that access to abortion must be retained, do not see it as being under threat in their societies. To them, abortion appears as one more tool with which the reproductive autonomy of women is sought to be controlled. As Nalini Karkal points out, in India the 'right' to abortion is often little more than a measure forced on women by husbands who refuse to use contraceptives.[67] One attempt to bridge these two positions has been to recast abortion in the context of 'reproductive rights' as many feminist groups now do.

For example, the Roundtable on Women's Perspectives on Family Planning, Reproductive Rights and Reproductive Health which met in Ottawa in 1993 stated,

> All persons have inherent reproductive rights including the right to have or not to have, children. Reproductive rights also imply reproductive responsibilities, including the responsibilities men have to their children, their communities and future generations. At the same time, communities and governments have a responsibility to organise themselves in ways that help people achieve good sexual and reproductive health and overcome barriers to successful child-bearing and child-rearing.[68]

The key to women's empowerment, the statement adds, 'lies in women acting individually and collectively to exercise their rights, in particular, their reproductive rights.'[69]

Similarly, a Women's Global Network for Reproductive Rights leaflet describes reproductive rights as 'women's right to decide whether, when and how to have children—regardless of nationality, class, ethnicity, race, religion, disability, sexuality or marital status—in the social, economic and political conditions that make this possible.'[70] Again, the International Conference on Population and Development at Cairo in 1994 was influenced by feminist initiatives into transforming the agenda from the achievement of demographic targets to the enhancement of women's sexual and reproductive health, choice and rights.[71]

However, the notion of 'reproductive rights' too, is criticised as retaining the focus of 'white middle-class feminist'. A group in Chennai sees present campaigns as rooted in the liberal individualistic tradition related to birth control advocacy, when their own concern as feminists from the South, is the opposite, that is, population control policies that coerce women by control of their fertility. They also point out that the slogan of reproductive rights has been co-opted by governments for their anti-natalist population control strategies. This, they claim, is true even in the developed countries of the North where poor and non-white women are forced, by government funding and policies, into sterilisations, harmful hormonal contraceptives and so on.[72] In order to reclaim the radical nature of reproductive rights, therefore, this group urges a critique of the development model and the need to create alternatives. It should always be more than a legal struggle or a struggle at governmental level. 'Reproductive Rights should always be about women achieving things for themselves, about getting political power necessary to change things, about changing relations in society.'[73]

Similarly, Pravin Visaria argues that studies and field experience show that poor peasant women's protective, conservationist and nurturing attitudes to natural resources cannot be the real threat to the global environment as the official international view seeks to project. This threat comes from the ideal of unlimited consumption as presented by developed countries. Visaria urges, therefore, looking at population policies as inseparable from sustainable livelihood, shelter, effective access to minimum needs, childcare, and child development. 'Population has been defined so narrowly that important factors like the declining sex ratio, morbidity and malnutrition are not considered significant variables in demographic studies.' The only demographic sector which has received an overdose of policy attention is fertility, and even this focus has been 'an absolute obsession with sterilisation, contraception and abortion' while access to health care has been ignored.[74]

The differences among feminists in the perception of reproductive rights underscores once again the central argument of this study, that rights are constituted by particular discourses. Rights cannot be seen as 'inherent', as for example the statement on reproductive rights quoted above asserts. On the contrary, they come into being only within shared assumptions and shared political circumstances. As such, the assertion of rights can serve to make a statement about what the vision of a movement is, but it does not seem possible that rights can actually be 'achieved' in any concrete sense by embodying them in law.

As we have seen, the law embodies the dominant values of a society and tends to freeze identities and to regulate and normalise behaviour. The feminist understanding—or rather, feminist understandings—of reproduction and sexuality is characterised by ambiguity and ambivalence. As a matter of practical strategy, it may be useful to work around existing laws that can be positive for women, such as the MTP Act, for example, but this must be accompanied by a constant sense that its potential to subvert the feminist vision is as great as its potential to realise it. Certainly it would appear to be counterproductive to seek *new* laws or state regulation to meet our goals. Such laws would further categorise, concretise and regulate behaviour, and this can only be inimical to the interests of marginal groups.

Abortion, Femicide of Foetuses and Feminist Ethics

In conclusion, let us address some of the deeper philosophical dilemmas that arise from the issue as outlined in this chapter. If abortion is a right over one's body, how are feminists to deny this right to women when it comes to selective abortion of female foetuses? For Rosalind Pollack Petchesky the answer is clear, but the reasoning still needs to be worked out:

> Should women get an abortion on the grounds that they prefer a different gender? . . . Such a decision would be blatantly sexist . . . That is, a women's 'right to control her body' is not absolute, but we have not developed a socialist feminist morality that would tell us what the exceptions would be.[75]

Conversely, from another kind of feminist position it is possible to argue that a legal ban on the selective abortion of female foetuses is violently contrary to every feminist principle. Writes Manjula Padmanabhan:

> Could there be anything more grotesque than to be forced to carry an unwanted living presence within the sanctum of one's own body? . . . In a twisted sort of way, women who abort their female foetuses are voting against their own misogynist culture and in that sense, are subverting it . . . Abortion is never a happy solution to the problem of how we humans restrict our number . . . But given the world we have now, it is far better to enable women to take this life-denying decision of their own accord, under medically and legally safe conditions than to saddle them with babies whom they will revile and devalue as they were reviled and devalued . . .[76]

If indeed abortion is a self-evident right, then it would seem that exceptions can be justified only by reference to a morality assumed to be shared by the very group to whom that right is being denied. The

FASDSP takes this a step further by seeking to translate this notion of morality into specific legal provisions. As we have seen, one of its demands on the proposed central legislation was that the woman who aborts a female foetus should not be punished at all. This stand is justified on the grounds that women who 'choose' this option are not really exercising their free will but have been indirectly influenced by the prevailing social ethos or compelled to act by husbands and families.[77]

The assumption seems to be that decisions to abort taken in other circumstances, based on any other consideration than the sex of the foetus, reflects the woman's 'free will', unmediated by social or cultural pressures. However, decisions to abort are almost always shaped by factors like the stigma of illegitimacy, lack of social facilities for childcare, economic constraints and so on. Under such circumstances decisions to abort are no more reflective of a woman's autonomy than her decision to abort a foetus because it is female. Nor are such decisions any less determined by the constraints of a patriarchal society. Feminist understandings of women's autonomy always tread that uncertain ground where we must recognise that oppressive conditions produce a 'free' will constrained by harshly limited choices, but where we must also ensure that women are seen to act as agents nevertheless. Or, to put it another way—'a feminist view of autonomy must acknowledge that oppression impedes autonomy, without stripping women of the autonomy that they have managed to wrest from a patriarchal, racist, heterosexist, class-stratified world.'[78] How is this nuanced and complex understanding of autonomy to be translated into terms that make sense within legal discourse? I suggest that this is an impossible endeavour.

This discussion brings us to an understanding of the manner in which notions of rights come into being. It is clear that within a feminist worldview, it does make perfect sense to say that access to abortion is consistent with the feminist vision, and that femicide of foetuses is not. If we unravel the subterranean thread of reasoning behind this belief, we arrive at something resembling the following position:

The constraints of a patriarchal society (including the low priority given to research on safe contraceptive methods) are largely responsible for the necessity of abortions in most cases. Such constraints would be much greater if fewer and fewer women were born, for societies with a low female-to-male ratio are demonstrably more sexist. The logic of the market—that is, low supply leads to greater demand—does not operate here. So abortion must be available to women who want it, while selective abortion of female foetuses must be stopped.

If this is the argument being made, and I suggest it is, then the implication is that 'rights' over 'one's' body are not natural, timeless and ahistorical. They do not exist except within specific sets of agreements as to what constitutes one's 'own' body, the meaning of consent or responsibility, the degree to which present social and economic arrangements are equitable, and the nature of the desired society of the future.

Quite a different level of moral complexity is opened up when we examine the validity of using amniocentesis to determine foetal abnormality. The FASDSP is clear that it does not want a blanket ban on pre-natal testing, and thus implicitly endorses such testing for the detection of 'abnormal' foetuses and their subsequent abortion.[79] However, once we accept that there can be a hierarchy of human beings based on physical characteristics, and that it is legitimate to withhold the right to be born from those at lower levels of this hierarchy, then this reasoning can be extended to other categories, whether female, 'inferior' races or any other. One feminist response to this dilemma is to argue that since women would have to look after handicapped children, they should be able to decide whether to bear them or not. It hardly bears repeating that the identical argument can be made about female children—that because the social pressure to bear male children falls entirely on the woman, she should have the right to abort a female foetus.

The work of Rayna Rapp on genetic counselling in New York City radically problematises the language of individualism and pro-choice feminism that validates the abortion of 'abnormal' foetuses.[80] She urges moving the focus from the individual woman and her family to the larger community. The perception of disability and the mechanisms of coping vary dramatically with class and community. For a low-income Afro-Puerto Rican woman in New York, the risks of running out of food, of having a son or brother die in street violence, or of being evicted from her home, are all greater than the chances of having a child with chromosomal abnormality at age thirty-five.[81] It is only when all these social, political and economic 'risks' are screened out, Rapp argues, that amniocentesis seems to 'cut risks' and 'offer control'.[82]

Immigrant communities in the USA seem to expect to rely on a kinship network for sustained support, and thus are more prepared to bring up children with disabilities. Rapp's extensive interviews remind us that the quality of life is not determined by absolute biological incapacities, but by prejudice and stigma, by the cultural meanings assigned to these incapacities. Not everyone sees Down's Syndrome as so debilitating that it would have been better not to be born. As one Afro-American mother said, 'My kid's got a heart problem. Let me deal with that first, then I'll figure out what this Down's business means.'[83] Contrast this with the white professional couple who said, 'If he can't grow up to have a shot at becoming President, we don't want him.'[84]

While feminist discourse on abortion, including the choice to abort 'abnormal' foetuses, is cast in terms of freeing women from images of selfless and endlessly nurturant maternity, Rapp points out that the imagery which is to replace it is no less oppressive, 'for the "New Woman" of prenatal diagnosis may feel like an agent of quality control on the reproductive production line.'[85] Both images, she argues, are deeply embedded in patriarchal cultural discourses, 'the one traditional and religious, the other modern and medically technocratic.'[86]

Similarly, Veena Das points out that it is not inscribed in the nature of things that a physically or mentally retarded individual should have a poor quality of life. It is the great value placed on individual autonomy and on competition that makes this seem like a self-evident fact.[87]

Neither Das nor Rapp offers facile solutions to the dilemmas involved, but their argument foregrounds the moral and ethical vision of feminism, with all its rich ambivalence and self-doubt, a vision impossible to straitjacket into the certainties of legal discourse.

Thus feminist understandings need to confront the fact that the pro-abortion position is not necessarily a feminist decision to take. I found interesting a recent Hindi film, *Kya Kehna*,[88] that complicated the simple feminist pro-choice/anti-feminist pro-life polarisation. This film was hugely successful despite not having a star cast, and was billed as a 'family film'. According to film magazines, the audience was largely middle-class women. The heroine, Priya, is a brave and gutsy young college-going woman. (The opening scene of the film is her school-leaving function, at which she publicly denounces a male teacher who has been sexually harassing female students.) While in college, she has sex with a fellow student and becomes pregnant. Her loving and close-knit family (particularly the father) is at first appalled and disowns her, but comes round to supporting her, especially her decision not to have an abortion. This decision mobilises all possible pro-life tropes including her fantasy that the divine baby Krishna appeals to her, calling her Ma (Mother). Many feminist friends found the film to be reactionary and dangerous, particularly since 'pro-life' arguments are not common sense in India. Indeed, one of them pointed out that the colloquial term used in Hindi for abortion is *safai karna,* simply, 'to clean up'.[89] In other words, decisions to abort are largely unsentimental, and tend to be seen in practical terms. This is largely true, but I think *Kya Kehna* radically shifted the terms of discourse about 'illegitimacy', 'autonomy' and 'patriliny' in directions that can be called feminist.

Under the circumstances in which Priya became pregnant, with the man who made her pregnant refusing to marry her, a decision to abort can also be seen as capitulating to the pressures of patriarchal society in which 'illegitimacy' is a fate worse than death. Priya speaks out on several occasions, defending her decision to have her baby, denouncing the hypocrisy of valorising motherhood only within marriage, and ultimately she shames her college and the entire town. In a scene that is surprising for its overturning of conventional tropes of Hindi cinema as well as of Indian middle-class values generally, a vastly pregnant Priya (in dungarees, not a modest sari) at the library, is warmly encouraged by student after student to go up to the top of a long queue, while the man now identified as the father of her baby, is isolated, at a table by himself, watching in disbelief. Her own family too, is publicly supportive of her, and there are scenes of joyful nurturing of the pregnant Priya that are remarkable in the context of North Indian patriarchy in which such adoration of a pregnant woman is legitimate only when she is the daughter-in-law carrying forward the name of her husband's family. Priya writes her exams, gives birth to a daughter, turns down an offer of marriage from the penitent lover, and decides to marry instead, her faithful suitor who has stood by her through all of this. When the rejected ex-lover claims the baby as his, she declares proudly, 'It is mine.'[90]

What is significant here is that this was not 'offbeat' cinema, but a mainstream Hindi commercial film, which did very well at the box-office. Moreover, while being understood as a 'family' film, it celebrates the love and solidarities of the natal family of the woman, not of the family into which she marries. Again, this runs counter to Indian (particularly North Indian) 'family values' in which a daughter is *paraya dhan*—wealth belonging to another—to be kept in safe-keeping by her natal family till she can be given away to her 'real' family in marriage. In this particular cultural context, Priya's 'pro-life' decision can be understood as a feminist one. It seems to me worth reiterating that the ideal feminist world would not be one in which abortions are free and common, but rather one in which most of the social constraints and technological inadequacies that make for unwanted pregnancies, would have been dealt with. Ultimately as feminists we must affirm 'life'—not in some absolute sense, but as it appears within our specific moral and ethical universe—while at the same time, in a hugely imperfect and unjust world, accepting the need for abortion and struggling for safe and universal access to it.

Notes

1. Kristin Luker, *Abortion and the Politics of Motherhood*, Berkeley, University of California Press, 1984, p. 92.
2. Linda Gordon, *Woman's Body, Woman's Right*, New York, Penguin Books, 1990, p. 406.
3. Ibid., pp. 409–10.
4. Carol Smart, *Feminism and the Power of Law*, pp. 101–2.
5. Linda Gordon, *Woman's Body, Woman's Right*, pp. 403–4.
6. Carol Smart, *Feminism and the Power of Law*, p. 148.
7. This argument has been made by Catharine MacKinnon, *Feminism Unmodified*; Rosalind Pollack Petchesky, *Abortion and Women's Choice: The State, Sexuality and Reproductive Freedom*, New York, Longman, 1984; Linda Gordon, *Woman's Body, Woman's Right*; Elizabeth Kingdom, *What's Wrong with Rights?*
8. Carol Smart, *Feminism and the Power of Law*, pp. 152–3.
9. Catharine MacKinnon, *Feminism Unmodified*, pp. 93–7.
10. Robin West, 'Taking Freedom Seriously', pp. 84–5.
11. Drucilla Cornell, *The Imaginary Domain*, New York and London, Routledge, 1995, Chapter Two.
12. Carol Gilligan, *In a Different Voice*, Harvard, Harvard University Press, 1982.
13. Ronald Dworkin, 'Feminism and Abortion', *The New York Review*, 10 June 1993, pp. 27–9.
14. Sunita Bandewar, 'Unsafe Abortion', *Seminar* 489, May 2000, p. 39. Madhu Kishwar too seems to believe that it is because of India's pro-women tradition that the right to abortion was won in India 'without a fight' while it took 'decades of struggle in the West'. 'Women and Politics: Beyond Quotas', *Economic and Political Weekly*, 26 October 1996, p. 2867. See discussion in Chapter Four.
15. See Sukhamoy Chakravarty, *Development Planning: The Indian Experience*, New Delhi, Oxford University Press, 1987; Sudipta Kaviraj, 'A Critique of the Passive Revolution', *Economic and Political Weekly*, Annual Number, 1988; C.T. Kurien, *Global Capitalism and the Indian Economy*, New Delhi, Orient Longman, 1994.

16. *Development for Whom? A Critique of Women's Development Programmes*, Report prepared by women's groups—Saheli, Sabala Sangh, Action India and Disha (Delhi); Women's Centre, Forum Against Oppression of Women and Awaz-e-Nizwan (Bombay), 1991, pp. 9–10.
17. Amrita Chhachhi and C. Satyamala, 'Sex Determination Tests: A Technology Which Will Eliminate Women', *Medico Friends Circle Bulletin*, New Delhi, November 1983, p. 4.
18. See Mohan Rao, 'Population Policies: States Approve Coercive Measures', *Economic and Political Weekly*, vol. 36, no. 29, 21 July 2001, pp. 2739–41.
19. B.P. Singh Sehgal, *Women, Birth Control and the Law*, New Delhi, Deep and Deep Publishers, 1991, p. 12.
20. Malini Karkal, 'Indian Family Planning Programme. A Historical Perspective', undated, unpublished. On file with Jagori Women's Resource Centre, Delhi.
21. Lok Sabha Debates, Fifth Series, vol. 7, pp. 160–2.
22. Ibid., pp. 312–16.
23. Ibid., p. 176.
24. Ibid., p. 177.
25. Ibid., p. 194.
26. Ibid., pp. 186–7.
27. Ibid., pp. 185–6.
28. Ibid., pp. 196–200.
29. Sehgal, *Women, Birth Control and the Law*, pp. 38–41. At the same time, there is sufficient evidence that can be marshalled to show that abortion was acceptable both in Hindu and Islamic traditions. The physician Susruta permitted abortions if the woman's health required it and Acharya Lohimba Raj in the seventeenth century suggested a herb for abortion to be used by 'pregnant women in poor health, widows and women of liberal morals'. Similarly in Islam, it is possible to argue that contraception and abortion in specific circumstances were in practice in the Prophet's lifetime and that it was not explicitly disallowed. And in Christianity, only the Catholic Church holds out uncompromisingly against abortion.

    It is significant that this evidence has been adduced by Sripati Chandrasekhar, a former Minister for Health and Family Planning, in a book tellingly entitled *Abortion in a Crowded World*, London, George Allen and Unwin Ltd, 1974.

30. Rani Bang and Abhay Bang, 'Contraceptive Technologies. Experience of Rural Indian Women', *Manushi*, no. 70, 1992, p. 29.
31. See Sunita Bandewar, 'Unsafe Abortion'; Vimal Balasubramaniam, 'Who's Not Afraid of Family Planning', *Seminar* 331, March 1987; Amar Jesani and Aditi Iyer, 'Women and Abortion', *Economic and Political Weekly*, vol. 28, no. 48, 27 November 1993.
32. Sanjeev Kulkarni, *Sex Determination Tests and Female Foeticide in the City of Bombay*, Report commissioned by the Secretary to the Government, Department of Health and Family Welfare, Government of Maharashtra, 1986, p. 19.
33. Ibid., p. 2.
34. Forum Against Sex Determination and Sex Pre-selection and Saheli, 'Information Sheet on Sex Determination and Sex Pre-selection Techniques', undated, unpublished. On file with Jagori Women's Resource Centre, Delhi.
35. FASDSP Newsletter, 1988.
36. Flavia Agnes, 'A Critical Review of Enactments on Violence Against Women', in Maithreyi Krishna Raj, ed., *Women and Violence: A Country Report*, Bombay, SNDT University, 1991, p. 146.
37. Arvind Kala, 'Banning Sex Tests. Unfair, Unworkable', *Times of India*, 25 January 1991, p. 8.
38. Bharati Sadashivam, 'The Silent Scream', *The Illustrated Weekly of India*, 14 September 1986, p. 40. Note that the title of this piece, which is a feminist attack on femicide of foetuses, replicates the title of the well-known anti-abortion film used in right-wing campaigns in the USA.
39. Sanjeev Kulkarni, *Sex Determination Tests*, p. 23.
40. Bharati Sadashivam, 'The Silent Scream', p. 40.
41. FASDSP, 'Note About Proposed Central Legislation to Ban Sex Determination Tests', 1988. On file with Jagori Women's Resource Centre, Delhi.
42. Flavia Agnes, 'A Critical Review', p. 147.
43. R.P. Ravindra, 'Campaign Against Sex Determination Tests', *Lokayan Bulletin*, no. 8, 1990, p. 31.
44. FASDSP, 'Note Sent to Women's Organisations', undated. On file with Jagori Women's Resource Centre, Delhi.
45. Laxmi Murthy, 'Female "Foeticide": Should We Use this Terminology?', Letter to the Editor in response to Mohan Rao, 'Female Foeticide: Where Do We Go?', in *Issues in Medical Ethics*, no. IX (4), October–December 2001.

46. This campaign is called 'Karvan' (Caravan), and the programme was held on 20 November 2001 in Delhi.
47. Another such example is a news report on steps taken by the Government of Haryana to 'curb prenatal tests leading to foeticide', meaning the selective abortion of female foetuses. The heading of the report is 'Steps to Curb Foeticide', *The Hindu*, 26 November 2001, p. 5.
48. R.P. Ravindra, 'Campaign', pp. 29–30.
49. Ibid.
50. Report of Joint Committee of Parliament on the Pre-Natal Diagnostic Techniques (Regulation and Prevention of Misuse) Bill, 1992. Lok Sabha Secretariat, Delhi, pp. 20–1.
51. Saheli Newsletter, January 1995, pp. 11–13.
52. Ravi Duggal, 'PNDT Act and People's Action', *Economic and Political Weekly*, 2 June 2001, p. 1930.
53. Ayesha Khan and Sanchita Sharma, 'When Foeticide Gets You Money From the Court', *The Indian Express*, 4 August 2001, p. 1.
54. Amar Jesani and Aditi Iyer, 'Women and Abortion', p. 2592.
55. Ibid.
56. B.P. Singh Sehgal, *Women, Birth Control and the Law.*
57. Alice Jacob, 'Abortion Law Reform: A Study of the Medical Termination of Pregnancy Act, 1971', *Journal of the Indian Law Institute*, vol. 16, 1974, pp. 572–3.
58. Vimal Balasubramaniam, 'Who's not Afraid of Family Planning?'.
59. Sunita Bandewar, 'Unsafe Abortion', p. 43.
60. At the convention, these views were contested only by Swami Agnivesh, who is a social activist as well as being a Hindu religious leader. See Swati Bhattacharya, *'Kanya bhrun hatya bishayak sabha paryabashit nari abamananaye'* (translation from Bengali—'Meeting on Female Foeticide Turns into Insult of Women'), *Ananda Bazar Patrika*, 25 June 2001, pp. 1, 6. I am grateful to Monobina Gupta for bringing this report to my attention.
61. *Satya v. Siri Ram*, AIR 1983 P&H 252 at 253.
62. News report, *The Hindustan Times*, 3 December 1993.
63. In this context, it is appropriate to point to an anomaly in the notion of consent involved in the MTP Act. Pregnancy resulting from rape is covered by the Act. Since by Section 375 of the Penal Code, sexual intercourse by a man with his wife if she is below fifteen is rape, the husband is also the guardian, and the woman cannot have an abortion if he withholds consent.

64. 1966 Cri. L.J. 1363. vol. 72, CN 410.
65. 1992 Cri. L.J. 1680.
66. Maria Mies, *Patriarchy and Accumulation on a World Scale: Women in the International Division of Labour*, London, Zed Books. Cited in Naila Kabeer, *Reversed Realities: Gender Hierarchies in Development Thought*, London, Verso, p. 199.
67. Malini Karkal, 'Indian Family Planning Programme', p. 13.
68. 'Roundtable on Women's Perspectives on Family Planning, Reproductive Rights and Reproductive Health' (based on workshop in Ottawa, Canada), 1993. On file with Jagori Women's Resource Centre, Delhi, p. 1.
69. Ibid., p. 3.
70. Undated, unpublished. On file with Jagori, Delhi.
71. Discussed in Susan Greenhalgh, 'Fresh Winds in Beijing: Chinese Feminists Speak Out on the One-child Policy and Women's Lives', *Signs*, vol. 26, no. 3, Spring 2001.
72. Discussion paper, *Teaching Politics*, vol. XIX, nos 1, 2, 1993, pp. 4–7.
73. Ibid, pp. 11–12.
74. Pravin Visaria, 'A Population Policy for the Twenty-first Century: Perspectives from the Women's Movement', undated, unpublished. On file with Jagori, Delhi, pp. 6–7. For other critiques of governments' neglect of women's reproductive health, see also Yamini Mishra, 'Unsafe Abortions and Women's Health', *Economic and Political Weekly*, 6 October 2001, pp. 3814–17 and for India specifically, Kalpana Vishwanathan, 'Whose Body Whose Health?', *Seminar* 505, September 2001, pp. 36–9. Another interesting study is based on a review of the official journal on family planning, *The Journal of Family Welfare*, over twenty years. Sangeeta Chattoo suggests that both the medical community and the state conceptualise men as essentially 'sexual beings' and women as 'reproductive beings'. In an overwhelming number of the follow-up studies on vasectomy there is an obsessive involvement with questions on 'impact on sexual function' and 'sexual satisfaction'. These questions are never raised in studies on female sterilisation. Rather, to women who had IUDs inserted, questions were asked about husbands' sexual satisfaction. See Sangeeta Chattoo, 'A Sociological Study of Certain Aspects of Disease and Death: A Case Study of Muslims in Kashmir', unpublished PhD thesis, Department of Sociology, Delhi University, 1990.
75. Rosalind Pollack Petchesky, *Abortion and Women's Choice*, p. 7

76. Manjula Padmanabhan, 'Outlawing Sex Determination No Solution', *The Pioneer*, 22 September 1993.
77. FASDSP, 1988, 'Note', p. 7.
78. Diana Tietjens Meyers, 'The Rush to Motherhood: Pronatalist Discourse and Women's Autonomy', *Signs*, vol. 26, no. 3, Spring 2001.
79. Ravindra R.P., 'Campaign', p. 30.
80. Rayna Rapp, 'The Power of "Positive": Diagnosis: Medical and Maternal Discourses on Amniocentesis', in Karen Michaelson, ed., *Childbirth in America: Anthropological Perspectives*, South Hadley, Massachusetts, Bergin and Harvey, 1987, p. 30. 'Accounting for Amniocentesis', in Shirley Linderban and Margaret Locke, eds, *Knowledge, Power and Practice: Medical Anthropology*, Berkeley, University of California Press, 1993; 'Risky Business: Genetic Counseling in a Shifting World', in Jane Schneider and Rayna Rapp, eds, *Articulating Hidden Histories: History, Anthropology and the Influence of Eric. B. Wolf*, Berkeley, University of California Press, 1994.
81. Rayna Rapp, 'Risky Business: Genetic Counseling in a Shifting World', p. 25.
82. Ibid., p. 26.
83. Ibid., p. 18.
84. Rayna Rapp, 'Accounting for Amniocentesis', p. 16.
85. Rayna Rapp, 'The Power of "Positive", p. 30. Diagnosis: Medical and Maternal Discourses on Amniocentesis', p. 115.
86. Ibid.
87. Veena Das, 'Deciding on Moral Issues: The Case of Abortion', in Diana L. Eck and Devaki Jain, eds, *Speaking of Faith*, New Delhi, Kali for Women, 1986.
88. An expression of admiration suggesting that words fail one.
89. Thanks for the invigorating argument, Ranjani Mazumdar and Shikha Jhingan!
90. The film ending with her decision to marry can be seen as her recuperation into traditional society, but again, her remaining unmarried would be what traditional society would expect of her: by remaining a single woman devoted to motherhood, she would 'pay her dues'. On the other hand, a woman marrying a man who is not the father of her child, does destabilise traditional notions of the patrilineal family.

CHAPTER THREE

Sexual Violence: Escaping the Body

The universality of women's experience of sexual violence has always provided an immediate entry-point for feminist intervention. Whatever the analysis of patriarchy and its relationship to class, caste, community or race, feminist politics of all hues is able to relate directly to sexual violation, experienced in different ways and to differing degrees, but an intrinsic part of all women's lives. What are the codes that enable such immediate recognition of 'sexuality' and 'sexual' violence? Are they indeed so universally recognised by all cultures, by all women? And is this recognition something that *enables* feminist politics, or does it paradoxically, *limit* the possibilities of feminist transformation? These questions become even more critical when sexual violence is sought to be made meaningful in legal terms, as the logical culmination of feminist intervention in this area. In line with the general argument that I advance, my concern is not with the sexism of the legal system, the intransigence of authorities and other such factors that make feminist engagement with the law so frustrating. Rather, we will focus on what goes wrong even when the law is 'on our side'. In this chapter we will consider two areas of concern for feminists—the first section will look at rape/sexual assault and the second, at sexual harassment in the workplace.

Rape/Sexual Assault

As we focus on the discourse about rape produced by feminist and legal practices, we come up against two assumptions:

(a) The belief that it is possible for the law to establish, where it is the case, the culpability of the accused and the violation of the victim. If this happens very rarely, it is because (from the feminist perspective) the law needs to be made more reflective of the reality of women's experience. Once this is achieved, the demonstration of the guilt of the accused and his punishment would deliver justice to the woman and strike at the dominant misogynist values of our culture.

(b) The understanding that 'the body' is a natural and physical object and that 'sex' is a phenomenon that exists prior to all discourse, simply distinguishable from other kinds of human interaction.

We need to question both assumptions:

(a) The binary logic of the law cannot comprehend the complexity of the way sexual experience is constituted. Even when justice appears to be done, the very demonstration through legal discourse of the violation of the woman re-enacts and resediments dominant patriarchal and misogynist values.

(b) More fundamentally, 'the body' and 'sex' are not 'natural' but produced by discourses. This is not to deny their 'reality' but to question the assumption that this 'reality' can be accessible outside of particular contexts. It would then become necessary to rethink the attempt to universalise one particular 'reality' through law.

Is there a strength we can lay claim to precisely in accepting 'sex' as constituted by different discourses rather than as a natural prediscursive reality? As I have been arguing, legal discourse functions by fixing meaning, by creating uniform categories out of a multiplicity of possibilities, by suturing open-endedness. The experience validated by feminism as 'real' on the other hand, acquires meaning precisely through an interplay of contexts, and may be rendered sterile within the rigid codification required within legal discourse.

Defining Rape: The Legal Discourse

Section 375 of the Indian Penal Code explains rape in the following way, 'Penetration is sufficient to constitute the sexual intercourse necessary to the offence of rape.' A man is said to have committed rape, according to this section, if he has sexual intercourse with a woman in circumstances falling under any of the six following descriptions:

- against her will.
- without her consent.
- with her consent when the consent has been obtained by putting her or any person in whom she is interested, in fear of death or hurt.
- with her consent if her consent is given because she believes the man to be her lawfully married husband, when the man knows he is not.
- with her consent if she is unable to recognise 'the nature and consequences' of that to which she gives consent because of intoxication or unsoundness of mind.
- with or without her consent if she is under sixteen years of age.

The exception to these circumstances is that sexual intercourse by a man with his wife, the wife not being below fifteen, is not rape.

Apart from Sections 375 and 376 (which deals with punishment for rape), other related sections of the IPC are 354 (assault or use of criminal force with an intent to outrage a woman's modesty), 377 (sexual intercourse 'against the order of nature', which is understood to refer to sodomy), 509 (violating a woman's modesty with word or gesture), 511 (attempt to commit rape), 109 (aiding and abetting rape), and 34 (common intention or gang rape).

In India the issue of rape was placed on the public agenda in the late 1970s, when women's groups mobilised around a Supreme Court judgement acquitting the police rapists of a young tribal girl, Mathura. Since then, rape and sexual violence against women has been one of the most visible and strongly articulated issues in the women's movement. Sections 375 and 376 of the IPC had remained unchanged in the statute books since 1860. A sustained campaign was mounted against these antiquated laws after the Mathura case. Redefining 'consent' was one of the major thrusts of the campaign, since the case had shown that it is extremely difficult for a woman to prove that she did not consent 'beyond all reasonable doubt', as was required under criminal law. In response to the campaign, the government set up a Law Commission whose recommendations included the main demand of the campaign, that in rape cases the onus of proving consent should shift to the accused. That is, once sexual intercourse was proved, if the woman states that it was without her consent, the court should presume she did not consent. However the Criminal Law Amendment Act which was passed in 1983 accepted this demand only partially, in the case of custodial rape alone—that is, rape by police, public servants, managers of public hospitals and remand homes, and wardens of jails. Also the mandatory minimum punishment was made more rigorous.[1]

One of the leading activists in the campaign against rape, Flavia Agnes, who has been writing extensively about her misgivings on the use of the law by feminists, urges the necessity to evolve a new definition of rape. She regrets that the campaign did not succeed in this:

> In fact the same old notions of chastity, virginity, premium on marriage and fear of female sexuality are reflected in the judgements of the post-amendment period. Penis penetration continues to be the governing ingredient in the offence of rape. The concept of 'penis penetration' is based on the control men exercise over 'their' women. Rape violates these property rights and may lead to pregnancies by other men and threaten the patriarchal power structure. We have not gone beyond this definition.

It is in keeping with this understanding of rape, she points out, that while in all criminal offences, injury and hurt caused by weapons is considered more grievous and deserving of greater punishment than that caused by limbs, in the case of sexual assault, injury caused by iron rods, bottles or sticks does not even amount to rape. She urges therefore, the use of the term 'sexual assault' to replace the categories of rape, attempt to rape and violation of a woman's modesty, the latter two categories at present earning lighter punishment regardless of the harm done to the woman. As some countries have already done, the use of 'sexual assault' to cover all such attacks would ensure that the punishment would be determined by the injury caused to the woman.[2]

Defining Rape: Feminist Discourse

Feminist understanding of rape seems to simultaneously (a) set up sexual violence as having an existence and reality prior to the law and (b) look to the law to recognise this reality and grant it legitimacy. This section takes up three instances of feminist interventions in the legal process. From a study of these I suggest that we can discern broadly three feminist positions on what rape is:

(a) Rape is violence, not sex.
(b) Rape is violence, but a unique form of violence because of its sexual character.
(c) Rape is violence and violence precisely *is* sex.

The first position is exemplified by two pieces of legislation which have served as models for feminists around the world, Michigan State's Criminal Sexual Conduct Act of 1974 and the Canadian legislation on rape, 1982. These had considerable input from feminist lawyers, academicians and women's groups both at the level of research as well as public awareness raising. The Michigan Act created 'a ladder of offences' each of which is described as criminal sexual conduct. Each degree covers a range of sexual assaults, differentiated according to the amount of coercion used, whether or not penetration has taken place, the extent of physical injury inflicted and the age and incapacitation of the victim. In this way it was hoped that defendants who are guilty would plead guilty. Under the present system in other parts of the world, the penalty is so high and the prospects of conviction so low that most defendants feel it wiser to plead not guilty. Also, the word 'rape' has connotations and conjures up images that very often do not match actual incidents of sexual assault. It was hoped that juries might be more willing to convict of a crime called 'criminal sexual conduct in the third degree' than to convict for 'rape'. The law has had no appreciable effect on cases of rape reported but there has been a clear increase in the number of arrests and convictions for conduct of this kind.[3]

In the Canadian legislation the central proposition is that rape is a form of assault. As the Working Paper on which the legislation is based put it, 'the concept of sexual assault more appropriately characterises the actual nature of the offence of rape because the primary focus is on the assault or the violation of the integrity of the person rather than sexual intercourse.'[4] By this legislation, the crime of rape no longer exists in Canada. Instead there is a gradation scheme which creates three offences of sexual assault, distinguished in terms of the violence used, with no distinction made between penetration and other sexual acts.

The second position can be illustrated by a document suggesting amendments to the rape law in India. This was prepared in 1993 on behalf of the National Commission for Women by a group of eleven lawyers and feminist activists in Delhi and was widely circulated for debate among women's groups all over the country.[5] Nothing has come of the document, and now a fresh set of recommendations to the Law Commission, drawing extensively on the earlier document, has been prepared by three of the people involved in the earlier exercise, and is currently in circulation.[6] However, at this point we will take up only the 1993 document (hereafter, the 1993 Draft) because it is more than a draft legislation—it is a feminist statement on sexual violence. It remains significant for its reflection of the careful negotiation of meaning that feminist understandings of sexuality must undertake at the interface with legal discourse. The current draft will be discussed later in the chapter in another context.

The 1993 Draft recognises 'the unique character of the nature of sexual assault' and aims to 'provide a comprehensive definition of sexual assault to cover the full range of such crimes against women and children.'[7] It points out that the legal definition of rape at present, recognising as it does, only vaginal penetration by the penis as rape, does not take into account a wide range of assaults which are sexual in nature. Particularly in the case of very young children, especially those below twelve, 'rape' can be committed without penetration and a number of serious injuries caused. The definition of rape has therefore to be expanded to 'take in a wide range of violations in addition to actual penetration'.[8] The expanded definition suggested by the 1993 Draft would be covered by Sections 375(1) and (2), while the existing Sections 375, 376, 377, 354 and 509 would be deleted. These sections deal with, respectively, rape, punishment for rape, sexual acts 'against the order of nature', outraging a woman's modesty by use of criminal force and outraging a woman's modesty by word or gesture.

The amended Sections 375(1) and (2) set out the content of sexual assault which includes penetration into any orifice by a penis or any other object, as well as, 'for a sexual purpose', touching, gesturing or exhibiting any part of the body, if any of these activities are carried out against the will or without the consent of the other person. If the other person is a minor then the question of consent is irrelevant. A further explanation clarifies, 'Any consensual sexual activity between two adults does not fall within the purview of this section.'[9]

A category of aggravated sexual assault has been introduced in Section 375A, the offences under this section being considered 'grievous' and deserving of more severe punishment. These are: sexual assault on a minor, a mentally or physically handicapped person, or a pregnant woman; on a woman or minor by a person abusing a position of power or authority; sexual assault which results in grievous bodily harm, is protracted over a period of time, or is by more than one person. The family is recognised as the 'greatest threat' where sexual assault is concerned, specially for minors.

The two radical points of departure that the 1993 Draft makes from common conceptions of rape as well as from prevalent legal wisdom in India are that:

(i) it reformulates entirely the harm perceived to be caused by rape. The harm of sexual assault, it is argued, lies not in the causing of physical damage but in the 'violation of a person's bodily integrity'[10] and

(ii) it introduces the possibility of recognising rape within marriage by dropping the exception to the present Section 375, which reads, 'sexual intercourse by a man with his own wife, the wife not being under fifteen years of age, is not rape'. The Draft document explicitly states, 'the continuous rape of adult females within marriage or by other adult members of the family has also been covered.'[11]

We might formulate the main principle animating each of these two positions in the following way. The Michigan and Canadian legislations try to establish rape as a crime of violence, not sex. Such an understanding had been theorised most notably by Susan Brownmiller who holds that the human anatomy is such that men can rape women while women cannot rape men. This according to her, is the root of women's subordination.[12] Rape then, is not an act of sex at all but one of power and domination. By taking the 'sex' out of rape as it were, feminist strategies tried to combat the sexism of the legal system. It was seen as a way of improving the treatment of raped women by the criminal justice system so that they could be seen as the victims of violent assault rather than accomplices in a consensual act.[13]

The Indian document on the other hand, seems to stress the 'unique character of *sexual* attack'.[14] Although the position taken in the 1993 Draft, that rape is a violation of bodily integrity, seems to parallel the notion of 'violation of the person' in the Canadian legislation, there is nevertheless, an emphasis on the 'sexual purpose' of touch, gestures or sounds /words which would make these actionable under the law.[15] The understanding here is that rape is a form of violence but a unique form of violence because of its sexual character.

A third position on this continuum is one that collapses the distinction between sex and violence in the opposite direction to that taken by the Canadian and Michigan legislations. That is, not 'Rape is a crime of violence, not sex', but 'Rape is a crime of violence and violence *is* sex'. This position is exemplified by Catharine MacKinnon, whose work has arguably been one of the most influential analyses of rape in the last ten years. She sees the social relation between the sexes as organised so that 'men may dominate and women must submit and this relation is sexual—in fact, is sex'.[16]

Gender in MacKinnon's understanding then, is not a difference, which suggests equality, but a hierarchy. To construe gender merely as a difference is to obscure the power relations which impose this difference by force. Violence against women has been eroticised, and men violating women therefore, has a sexual content:

> What this critique does that is different from the 'violence, not sex' critique is to ask a series of questions about normal heterosexual intercourse and attempt to move the line between heterosexuality on the one hand—intercourse—and rape on the other, rather than allow it to stay where it is.[17]

MacKinnon is arguing that the sharp distinction that men make between 'normal' sex and rape does not exist for women: 'What we are saying is that sexuality in these normal forms often *does* violate us.'[18]

For MacKinnon then, rape is inextricably bound up with heterosexuality. In other words, 'instead of asking, what is the violation of rape, what if we ask, what is the non-violation of intercourse?'[19] The difficulty that courts have in distinguishing between rape and seduction is precisely because there is not much difference between the two—all heterosexual sex is coercive. And exactly what 'heterosexuality as a social institution is fixated around' is what legally defines rape—that is, penetration. This is a very male point of view, says MacKinnon, on what it means to be violated, for penetration is not all there is in rape that is 'intrusive or expropriative of a woman's sexual wholeness'.[20]

What is the understanding of 'sex' that emerges from the three positions discussed above? The first two—the Canadian and Michigan legislations and the Indian Draft Bill—assume a universal understanding of what 'sex' is. Neither statement, 'Rape is violence, not sex', nor 'Rape is a unique form of violence because of its sexual character' undertakes an explanation of what makes an act sexual.

The third position, that of MacKinnon, does clearly define what it understands to be 'sex'—the hierarchical and violent relationship between men and women is sex. However, such an understanding, that all (hetero)sex is violence, reduces one to paralysis. It denies one the possibility that women can redefine and affirm themselves outside the rigid codes of a male-defined sexuality. If violence is sexuality and sexuality is male, there is a daunting seamlessness to male dominance. Where does MacKinnon see the space for feminists to refigure received notions of pleasure, pain or fulfilment?[21]

Even from a merely legal point of view, if rape cannot be distinguished from intercourse, then it would seem to be impossible to prosecute for rape at all. And yet, MacKinnon does see the law as a crucial weapon to fight sexual violence against women. The ordinance on pornography that she drafted with Andrea Dworkin is a landmark in feminist politics in the USA.[22] The focus of her legal campaign is the recasting of all forms of sexual assault as civil, not criminal offences, which she believes is a more effective way of ensuring convictions. Civil wrongs are wrongs against individuals, criminal wrongs, offences against the state. MacKinnon argues that civil suits would leave the legal procedure in the control of the victims, rather than handing over control to the state. However, there remains the inconsistency involved in characterising all (hetero)sex as rape on the one hand and on the other, seeking the recognition and punishment of sexual assault as a crime.

Finally, feminist critics also have a problem with MacKinnon's essentialising of 'women' into a natural category whose relations with men are fixed into static patterns of domination and power. Although she accepts that gender is socially constructed, the reduction of women to their sex becomes inevitable given that the only perspective available to us in her understanding is the 'male gaze'. As Drucilla Cornell points out, with such a rigid understanding of the way gender is constructed, the 'social' category of gender becomes as irrevocable as if it were biological.[23]

An exercise that is central to each of the three positions discussed above is the attempt to enable women to recognise that they have a right to feel violated even if what they have experienced is not 'rape' as it is generally understood. In other words, the explicit purpose is to criminalise a whole range of behaviour which women accept as 'normal', but by which they feel humiliated and oppressed, or at the very least, uncomfortable. As a survey in the USA revealed, many women do not know the legal definition of rape, but felt victimised even if they believed that the legal standards for 'rape' had not been met.[24]

Thus, a handbook issued by two activists working in the area of sexual violence spells out—

> You have been sexually assaulted if . . . Against your will you have been:
>
> 1. Kissed
> 2. Fondled
> 3. Handled
> 4. Forced to have sexual intercourse
> 5. Sexually violated through oral or anal intercourse
> 6. Penetrated with a foreign object.
>
> The law recognies only No. 4 as the very serious crime of rape and all others as lesser crimes. But for women, all six constitute equally serious violations of their freedom and their being.[25]

Further, the booklet notes, these sexual violations 'constitute a crime. The State defines them as crimes and they are not simply social misdemeanours even if men and society would like us to believe so.'[26]

There are then, two simultaneous impulses at work in feminist analyses of rape. The one revealing the limitations of the law and its inability to encompass the lived experience of women; the other seeking to legitimate this experience precisely through having it recognised by the law as authentic, 'to write the experiences of women and minor children into the law'.[27] In other words:

(a) Certain experiences assumed to be clearly recognisable as 'sexual', are posited as having a reality and an existence prior to legal discourse; legal discourse is seen as limited and incomplete to the extent it is incapable of recognising these experiences, but at the same time

(b) these experiences need to be authenticated by law to have social value and be recognised as 'real'. To this extent then, they are to be constituted as real and legitimated by legal discourse.

Law as the Primary Legitimating Discourse

Recourse to the law is seen as necessary and inevitable because it is believed that designing a law around an experience proves 'it matters'; law is 'the concrete delivery of rights through the legal system'.[28] For example, activists in Britain fighting to get male rape classified as 'rape' and not merely 'sexual assault' argue that recognising male rape as a crime 'would give men a signal that this is . . . very serious . . .'[29] Or as another writer puts it, publicising private injuries, that is, making them legally cognisable, politicises them. 'The specific legal strategy advocated here is that we publicise and thus politicise those injuries—those intimate intrusions into our lives—which we want to make legally cognisable.'[30] Law is seen as the primary legitimating discourse and it is believed therefore that legal criminalisation would socially delegitimise a practice.

However, as other feminists have pointed out, dominant modes of constituting the self—as woman, as criminal, as victim—are maintained and reinforced through the conventions of legal language. Kristin Bumiller for instance, argues that the courtroom trial is 'a forum that projects authoritative messages through language and legal form about identity and social relationships in a struggle between the antagonistic world views of the defence and the prosecution.' She suggests therefore, that some symbolic trials can be moments at which 'the rejection of these categories may come about through resistance to legal discourse.'[31] As Foucault puts it, judgement is passed not only on the 'crimes' defined by the code, but on 'the shadows lurking behind the case', 'on passions, instincts, anomalies . . .'[32] In short, judgements are never only about the 'crime' being discussed in the trial, but constantly imply and refer to deviations from dominant norms. Thus, the law legitimates dominant norms, which ultimately, is what feminist practice contests.

Moreover, in postcolonial societies, as I argued in the earlier chapter, the establishing of law as the only legitimating discourse has meant marginalising and devalidating other legitimating discourses—this process was not necessarily unambiguously emancipatory, contrary to the claims of the language of universal rights.

In this context let us examine a judgement which awarded a conviction in a rape case on the grounds that the Hindu Marriage Act supersedes all other forms of custom.[33] Three men had forcibly abducted a girl, said to be fourteen or fifteen years of age, and one of them had raped her. Though medical examination had shown her to be above the age of consent, the district court accepted her word that she had submitted passively on fear of death, and the men were awarded two years of prison. Considering the circumstances, this was a very short term in prison. On appeal, the accused men deposed that being Bhils of Jhabua District, they had only been following the tribal custom of Bhagoriya marriage by which the woman is abducted, the couple have sexual intercourse, and then the boy pays an agreed upon amount to the father of the girl. They alleged that the girl's father lodged a complaint with the police only because the bargaining was unsatisfactory and a quarrel took place. In the meanwhile, during the pendency of the appeal the prosecutrix and her father entered into an agreement with the appellants and wished to discontinue prosecution. However the judgement held that

(a) Offences under Sections 366 and 376 (abduction and rape) are non-compoundable, i.e. cannot be settled out of court, and

(b) '. . . it is difficult to take legal notice of custom opposed to law be it in the tribals or non-tribals'[34]

Nevertheless, the sentence was reduced to six months from two years in view of the appeal for compounding. In other words, the crime was treated as a light one even before the plea for compounding was made, when it had been clearly established that the woman had been forcibly abducted and raped. On appeal the already light sentence was further reduced. At the same time, the principle that has been embodied by the law as precedent is that 'law' supersedes 'tribal custom'. Serious negative implications may arise from the judgement for tribal communities and particularly women. Since many tribes have customs which give women more autonomy in marriage than the Hindu Marriage Act does, it can be detrimental to the interests of women in some tribes to have the law supersede tribal custom.[35]

This argument is not intended to valorise pre-colonial communitarian values as egalitarian and just. On the contrary, 'the community' is marked by exclusion along the axes of caste, gender, class and so on; inegalitarian power relations are the fulcrum on which 'the community' turns. But at the same time it would be simplistic to assume the neutrality of the modern legal system. Social movements tend to work on the belief that even if law is as enmeshed in the power structures of society as 'the community' is, it can be forced into the service of progress and change by the pressure of democratic movements. However, as Upendra Baxi points out, underlying the concept of 'Rule of Law' (the due observance of the procedures prescribed for making a valid decision) is the idea that power should become impersonal and be constrained through rules applied by an independent judiciary and autonomous legal profession. But this formal legal rationality does not always constrain the arbitrary exercise of power; Baxi argues that on the contrary, it often helps to camouflage the latter.[36]

What does it mean for feminists to insist that this 'formal legal rationality' should delimit the contours of a particular experience, and that it should legitimate this experience? Do we not, by implication, accept that without such validation, the experience itself has no reality? We need to recognise that legal rationality cannot comprehend the complex ways in which sexual violence is constituted.

Sexual Violence and the Binary Logic of Law

It is a well-documented fact that all over the world, only a fraction of instances of rape/sexual violence are reported, and only in a fraction of these are convictions obtained. In Bombay in the period 1985–9 for example, of 504 cases registered, only 469 were charge-sheeted, of which there were thirteen convictions and ten acquittals, and 441 were pending trial in 1990. Also, a large number of convictions in the Sessions Courts are overturned on appeal, or the sentences reduced.[37]

This is partly because, as Flavia Agnes points out, the criminal justice system envisages an all-powerful state prosecuting the vulnerable accused, and so the maxim on which it functions is that the benefit of doubt should go to the accused. In cases of rape however, she holds, the woman 'stands outside the power equations between the state and the accused.'[38] In crimes against women, 'which are private and personal in nature', it is virtually impossible to prove the case beyond reasonable doubt as required by the criminal justice system. She urges the evolution of 'totally different criteria' for convicting the accused and a 'totally different concept of justice'.[39]

Another factor that hampers the conduct of rape cases according to Agnes, is that rape is a criminal offence. Since offences under the Criminal Code are crimes against the state, only the state can prosecute in a rape case. The woman raped is represented, not by her own lawyer, but by the Public Prosecutor. The positive aspect of this is that it is the responsibility of the state to make preliminary investigations and collect evidence. On the other hand this also means that apathy on the part of the police and the Public Prosecutor can seriously hamper the progress of a case. Defence lawyers engaged by the accused are paid high fees and are in general more motivated. Thus, treating rape as a criminal offence, which is meant to establish the greater magnitude of the crime, in effect seems to hamper prosecution.[40]

Nevertheless, in the case of custodial rape by police or rapes by army personnel there is agreement among feminists that the state should accept responsibility. A significant case which focused on the responsibility of the state in a different context was the rape of a village-level worker (*sathin*) of the government's Women's Development Programme in Bhateri village, Rajasthan. In 1992, the sathin was punitively raped by two men of a family that had been prevented from conducting a child-marriage by the district authorities on the basis of her reports. After the rape the authorities colluded with the family, which belongs to the dominant caste in the village, to hamper registration and investigation of the case, and women's groups in the country rallied around. The case was transferred to the CBI, and later the District Court acquitted the rapists on the grounds that upper-caste men would not even touch, let alone rape, a lower-caste woman. The appeal is pending in the High Court.

The point that the women's groups have been stressing is that the sathin is a government employee carrying out responsibilities given to her by the government. The state therefore is responsible for what amounts to injury in the course of work. Nevertheless, the fact that this particular injury is sexual situates it firmly in the vise of the law's binary logic, and the CBI inquiry too, has followed predictable paths, casting doubts on the victim's testimony, humiliating her and so on.

No wonder then that exhausted feminists have come to feel that 'even though the law exists to protect your rights . . . It is often put into effect by men who have no understanding of what a sexual assault means to a woman.'[41] Or even more strongly, that 'liberal legalism' is itself misogynist.[42] At the very least there is the recognition of 'the limited ability of the law to provide a complete remedy to the problem of rape.'[43] However, this is usually understood to be a result of the sexist interpretation of the law by insensitive judges and lawyers. In other words, the limitation is seen to lie in the interpretability of the law, not its rigidity. It should follow that if a foolproof law were to be enacted according to feminist norms, and administered strictly, 'the problem of rape' can be solved more satisfactorily. It is the contention of this study that the more foolproof the law in feminist terms, the more it refracts the ethical and emancipatory impulse of feminism itself.

Let us begin by examining whether the 1983 Amendment to the Criminal Law was necessary, from a feminist perspective. Flavia Agnes points out that the legal position regarding consent before the Mathura trial was not as adverse as might be assumed. In fact the judgement in the Mathura case was contradictory to the generally accepted legal position set by the Rao Harnarain Singh case of 1958 in which the court had held that there is a distinction between submission and consent and that submission under terror is not consent.[44] An even earlier case than the one Agnes mentions is *Rameshwar v. State of Rajasthan 1952*, in which the Supreme Court had taken the view that in the case of rape, the necessity of corroboration was to be treated only as 'a rule of prudence . . . There is no rule of practice that there must be in every case, corroboration before a case can be allowed to stand.'[45]

Later judgements which Agnes lists, include *Rafiq v. State of UP, 1980*, in which the Supreme Court held that the testimony of the rape victim should not be rejected 'unless there are very strong circumstances mitigating its veracity . . .' In 1981 in *Harpal Singh and Another v. State of Himachal Pradesh*, the opinion of the court was that 'the fact that . . . the girl is used to sexual intercourse is immaterial in a rape trial.' In 1983, in *Bharwada Bhogibhai Hirjibhai v. State of Gujarat*, the court held that corroborative evidence of the woman's testimony is not necessary. This last judgement however, came in the course of the public campaign to amend the rape laws and was probably influenced by feminist propaganda.[46]

While there have been progressive judgements on the issue of corroborative evidence even before the amendment, equally there have been retrogressive judgements after the amendment. These have stressed the necessity of injury both to the accused as well as to the victim, or the imputed promiscuity of the raped woman.[47] In the

USA too, a survey of rape law in six states showed that pre-reform rulings had accomplished much of what reform laws were designed to do.[48]

From her analyses of judgements in rape cases, Agnes's conclusion is that the law can be interpreted progressively if the judiciary wishes. The 1983 Amendment was supposed to close off the possibility of retrogressive interpretations by providing certain guidelines, but, as she establishes, in the post-amendment period, provision for more stringent punishment has in fact resulted in fewer convictions.[49] The new law, it would seem, has served no purpose, and if anything, has reduced the prospect of securing convictions. Could better-framed guidelines have made the law tighter, less prone to interpretation, more able to secure convictions? Or is sexual violence incapable of being comprehended by law?

Carol Smart outlines the contours of this complexity in the following way. Law's claim to truth is based on a binary logic which sets up oppositions like truth/untruth, guilt/innocence, consent/non-consent. This binary logic, she argues, is completely inappropriate to what she calls 'the 'ambiguity' of rape.'[50] In criminal law the object is to establish guilt or innocence, and in rape cases, the establishing of either, turns on another pair of opposites: that of consent/non-consent. The dualism of consent/non-consent is

> completely irrelevant to women's experience of sex. Neither begins to approach the complexity of a woman's position when she is being sexually propositioned or abused . . . (T)he 'telling' of a story of rape or abuse inevitably reveals ambiguities. Hence a woman may agree to a certain amount of intimacy but not to sexual intercourse. In the legal model however, consent to the former is consent to full intercourse . . . (I)n legal terms submission fits on the consent side of the dichotomy. The only alternative when non-consent is not established is to presume consent.[51]

Let us consider a judgement by the Calcutta High Court in a case of a woman seduced with the promise of marriage and abandoned when she became pregnant. She sued the man for rape, contending that her consent to sexual intercourse was given on the basis of a false promise and hence was not valid consent. The court rejected her plea, holding that 'Failure to keep the promise at a future uncertain date does not amount to misconception of fact. If a fully grown girl consents to sexual intercourse on the promise of marriage and continues to indulge in such activity until she becomes pregnant, it is an act of promiscuity.'[52]

Flavia Agnes cites this judgement as displaying 'an extremely negative view of women's sexuality'.[53] Her criticism arises from the notion of 'promiscuity' underlying the judgement, which immediately contextualises it in terms of the moral norms sanctioning only marriage as a legitimate forum for sex. At the same time, as feminists, we are sharply critical of these moral norms; Agnes would not use 'promiscuity', with all its derogatory connotations, to refer to sex outside marriage. That is, if an adult woman consents to sex outside marriage, we would object to this being termed 'promiscuity', rightly holding that this is a sexist term redolent of sexual double standards. We would, like Agnes, see such a description of the case as a 'negative view of women's sexuality'; but then it seems to me that we cannot at the same time, support the woman's claim that her consent was not valid since she had given it on the promise of marriage. Her contention is valid only within a discourse that constitutes 'non-promiscuous/good' women as those who would not agree to sex outside marriage. In other words, if the woman consented to sex, it is not rape merely because the man later refused to marry her—if as feminists we were to see it as rape, we would be participating in a discourse that sets up sex as legitimate only within the framework of marriage.

It is not my contention that the girl was not cheated and exploited. Rather, this case is clearly illustrative of what Smart calls 'the ambiguity' of women's experience of sex, to which the law is unable to respond. Seen purely in the context of consent/non-consent, there is no doubt that the woman did consent, and not out of fear. Unless we accept MacKinnon's position that all heterosex is violent and male-directed (and we have discussed earlier how taking this position would make it impossible to engage with the law at all, as well as entail the rejection of the possibility of female subjectivity altogether), we have to retain the space to comprehend 'women's experience of sex' as other than simply 'consenting' to male pressure. A judgement convicting the man of rape in this case could only have been on the basis of a reaffirmation of patriarchal norms of marriage and female sexuality. At the same time, the judgement as it stands has not given the woman 'justice' in any sense. Thus, while recognising the relative powerlessness and lack of autonomy that characterise women's relations with men, the point here is to radically question the possibility of addressing this experience in the realm of legal discourse.

One way of inserting this particular case into the clear-cut dualism of the law might be to empty it of its 'sexual' content and see it as a case of cheating, for there is no disagreement on the fact that the man had promised marriage. Section 90 of the IPC, which lists General Exceptions, lays down the conditions under which 'consent' is not consent as intended by the Code. One of these conditions is if the consent is given under misconception of the fact and the other person knows that consent was given under these circumstances. Using this provision, would it have been possible to convict the man for cheating and fraud rather than rape? It seems unlikely that this would have worked, because the trial would have been inevitably 'sexualised', given the nature of the issues involved. This is what happened in a case in 1955.[54] Two constables lied to a woman that they had a warrant for her arrest and induced her to have sex with them in order to avoid being arrested. She did so, but later went to court claiming that her consent was vitiated by the fact that the policemen had lied to her. The court aquitted the accused since the woman had given her consent, even though under a misapprehension of fact. The precedent relied upon was an English judgement of 1888[55] in which it was held that consent to sexual intercourse obtained by fraud still must be considered consent: 'If a man . . . gives (a woman) bad money in order to procure her consent to intercourse with him he obtains her consent by fraud, but it would be childish to say that she did not consent.'

Would the judgement have been the same if a man had given bad money to buy property? Clearly the 'sexualisation' of consent transforms its meaning.

Consent and the Age Factor

The question of consent becomes crucial in a case of sexual assault in a way in which it does not in an act of non-sexual violence. The victim of a violent assault is never assumed to be an accomplice, but if such an assault can be described as sexual, the victim must establish her lack of consent, which is otherwise assumed. If consent is established, the act is considered legitimate. At the same time, sexual acts not sanctioned by prevailing codes of conduct are illegitimate regardless of whether consent was given, as with people who do not have 'adult' status (in terms of age or mental capacity) or between parents and children, or in India, sexual acts 'against the order of nature', which refers to sodomy, with men or women. Conversely, consent of both parties is assumed in sexual acts sanctioned by the social order which are therefore perpetually legitimate, as for example, sex within marriage. 'Marital Rape' does not exist except within the feminist lexicon, unless it is sodomy, in which case both husband and wife are guilty of a criminal act if the wife consented, and the husband alone, if she did not. 'Consent' therefore, is not always legitimate, nor lack of consent always illegitimate.

A crucial factor that decides the legitimacy of consent is age. In India, the legal age of majority, also the minimum age for marriage, is eighteen. However, under Section 375 of the IPC, the age of consent for marriage has been accepted as fifteen: 'Sexual intercourse by a man with his wife, the wife not being under fifteen years of age, is not rape.' Feminists have pointed out often enough that the marriage of a woman below eighteen is not legal and to recognise such marriages as legal through Section 375 is a great anomaly.[56]

The 1993 Draft therefore, seeks to correct this anomaly by fixing the minimum age of consent to sex as eighteen for the purposes of the Bill. However, from the note accompanying the Bill it is clear that this decision was arrived at after considerable debate: 'Some members were concerned that if the age was as high as eighteen then even consensual sex between adolescents in the sixteen-eighteen age group would be an offence. This position could be constructed (*sic*) as highly puritanical and moralistic.'[57] The decision was finally taken on the consideration that the age of majority for voting is eighteen. At the same time, in order to deal with the sexual assault of minors while not unduly penalising the possibility of consensual sex between adolescents, greater punishment has been laid down for the assault of children below twelve than in the age group twelve to eighteen. Thus the state of mind labelled 'consent', which is constituted in a complex way, as feminists would be the first to acknowledge, must be pegged rigidly to a linear notion of physical growth if it is to make sense within legal discourse.[58]

With the development of forensic medicine it is possible to codify 'the body' more and more rigorously, and ossification tests to determine age are routinely ordered when there are no documents to attest to the age of the raped woman, which is very often the case. Courts tend to give credence to ossification tests even when documents are available. In one case for example, the judge held that the school-leaving certificate of the woman, which showed her to be a minor, appeared to be suspect. The ossification test, which established her to be over the age of consent, was accepted, and since she had gone with the accused of her own will, the case was dismissed.[59] This judgement overruled an earlier one, which had held that the best evidence of age is the date of birth according to the school register if available, since the ossification test is not infallible.[60] No permanent precedent has been set in this regard, and individual judges continue to decide whether they will give greater weight to medical evidence or to birth and school certificates.

Once again, these multiple interpretations, far from demonstrating the elasticity of the law, point to precisely the opposite—the inevitable movement within legal discourse to codify, fix and regulate meaning. Different judgements may validate different kinds of evidence as more reliable, but 'more reliable' in the sense of better able to establish conclusively whether the woman was above or below the

Age of Consent. Below this age a woman cannot be deemed to have acted on her own volition in matters of sex; that is, she can be understood only as Victim or Dupe. Above this age, even if it is by a few months, she is radically transformed from Victim to Accomplice.

The 1993 Draft is marked by a deep discomfort with the fixing of one specific physical landmark as the point at which Consent changes its meaning. As a result much ambiguity remains. The definition of Minor, for example, is given as 'a person who is eighteen years of age or under.'[61] The age was arrived at on the consideration that the voting age is eighteen, but in this formulation a person who is eighteen is a minor. Similarly, in the section explaining the conditions vitiating consent, one condition is, 'If the person is or *appears to be* a minor.'[62] The concern underlying this deliberate ambiguity is clear. The attempt to fix 'minority' at a higher level in terms of age and simultaneously to leave the boundaries of 'minor' status permeable, results in opening up the possibility of more people being classified as minor, so that more cases of rape can be classified as Aggravated Sexual Assault, deserving of greater punishment. This must be seen in the context of the increasing number of sexual attacks on children, and the growing awareness of sexual abuse of women and children within families. The Committee makes it clear that it feels that the danger of sexual abuse of minors going unpunished is greater than the possibility of adolescents being punished for consensual sex.[63] However, the final form of the law cannot possibly retain the sort of ambiguity the Draft embodies.

More importantly, we cannot be blind to the implications of constructing 'sexuality' for young women entirely in terms of victimhood. And yet, perhaps the very logic of legal discourse leaves us with little room to deal in complexity. We are forced into the language of patriarchy despite ourselves. For instance, the Committee, while discussing the possibility that defining 'minority' so broadly could criminalise consensual sex between adolescents, came to the conclusion that there would be very few cases in which a family would make a false charge of sexual assault because such a charge would 'implicate their "family honour and dignity" '.[64] The quotation marks around the phrase 'family honour and dignity' do indicate that it is self-consciously used. Also, this argument has in fact been used in many judgements to dismiss the need for corroborative evidence in cases of rape. However, as the next section will demonstrate, accepting the notion of 'honour' as the basis for believing women's testimony in rape cases has serious consequences antithetical to the feminist project.

The Reinstatement of Dominant Norms through Discourse on Rape

The very idea of rape as 'violation' is located within a patriarchal and patrilineal discourse. To the extent that feminists share this understanding of rape, the implications can be disturbing. For instance, Croatian feminists termed the rapes and forced pregnancies of Croatian and Bosnian women in the violent aftermath of the break-up of Yugoslavia, as 'a method of ethnocide' or 'genocidal rape'. What is the understanding of lineage and community identity at work here? How can enforced pregnancy be understood as 'ethnocide' unless one subscribes to the aggressor's understanding that a woman is only the bearer of a man's seed, and that the child 'belongs' to the father's race? Under the circumstances of unimaginable violence and terror such as the former Yugoslavia witnessed, it seems that many feminists too were caught up in masculinist discourse about Nation and Community in such a way that even they could comprehend rape only in terms of the harm to the community.[65]

Another problematic area feminists are increasingly becoming aware of is the fact that even where convictions have been secured, the process of the trials as well as the judgements powerfully reinstate patriarchal and sexist norms of female sexuality and of legitimate codes of female behaviour. Kristin Bumiller's analysis of the 1984 rape trial of six Portuguese immigrant men in New Bedford, Massachusetts, raises many of these issues.[66] The woman who had been raped received general public support and sympathetic media coverage, and four of the defendants were convicted, so it would seem to have been a 'successful' rape trial from the feminist point of view. And yet, the demand of the law for objective evidence to prove the abuse of the victim makes it necessary to establish the victim's 'innocence'—that is, her non-complicity and non-consent according to commonly held notions. The demand for 'objectivity' also makes it difficult to establish the woman's 'innocence' in more ambiguous situations where rape differs from the kind of act recognised as 'real' rape which has to involve strangers, the use of weapons and a public scene. (Or what Flavia Agnes calls an 'ideal' situation for the police—a gang rape of an infant girl resulting in multiple injuries and with eyewitnesses ready to give evidence).[67]

In the New Bedford case the fact that the victim and the defendants were Portuguese was used to reinforce stereotypes of immigrant communities as violent and uncivilised. At the same time, the behaviour of the woman in going to a tavern at night, alone, came under scrutiny in terms of being compared to 'reasonable' standards of women's propriety. The trial in effect, turned on the victim's freedom from guilt, reinforcing the presumption that punishing violent men is justified to the extent that women are worthy of trust and protection.

In India particularly, judgements which have taken a progressive position on the issue of corroborative evidence in rape trials have been based on the most patriarchal notions of a woman's 'virtue' and 'chastity'. For example, in the 1983 judgement cited earlier, the explanation for the non-necessity of corroborative evidence was that 'a girl or woman in the tradition bound, non permissive society of India would be extremely reluctant even to admit that any incident which is likely to reflect on her chastity had ever occurred'.[68]

However, Justice Thakkar added, 'Corroboration may be insisted upon when a woman having attained majority is found in a compromising position and there is a likelihood of her having levelled such an accusation on account of the instinct of self-preservation.' That is, the very values which Justice Thakkar cites as the reason why false accusations of rape would be unlikely in India—the values informing a woman's overwhelming desire to preserve public belief in her 'chastity' and 'virtue'—could equally motivate, in his understanding, a consenting woman found in a 'compromising situation', to preserve her reputation—by denying that she had consented.

The implication is more serious therefore, than feminist critique recognises. In such decisions it is not simply that, as one author holds, the Court passively accepts rather than challenges, the belief in the need to protect women's chastity.[69] The seriousness lies in recognising the assumption that if the 'tradition bound society' of India would make 'innocent' women reluctant to level false accusations of rape, it would at the same time motivate 'promiscuous' women to hide their promiscuity precisely through such accusations. The rape trial thus turns once more on the 'guilt' or 'innocence' of the raped woman. Hence, the trend of decisions since the 1980s to reduce the importance of corroborative evidence in rape cases is not really an indication that there is growing recognition of the fact that women rarely make baseless allegations of rape. On the contrary, it merely reinstates the duality of the innocent woman who should be protected from rape and the promiscuous woman who cannot be raped.

The *National Law School Journal* (*NLSJ*) points out that the problematic assumptions about women's sexuality are most clearly seen when judgements make comparisons of the Indian context with 'the West'. Such comparisons suggest that 'more stringent rules of corroboration may be justified in 'the West' because Western women attribute no value to chastity and are thus more likely to make false allegations of rape. Implicit in these arguments is the assumption that the more aware women are of their sexuality, and the more obvious they are in the expression of their sexuality, the less they can be trusted to speak honestly and in turn the more likely they will become to lie about rape.'[70]

Another problematic assumption that was validated by a judgement convicting a rapist, was the belief that rape and sexual violence are impossible within marriage. Overturning the defence argument that the woman's injuries were caused by her husband and not by the defendant, the Supreme Court stated, '. . . [I]t is not possible to believe that when a married woman has sex with her husband in the privacy of their bedroom she would suffer abrasions.'[71] Thus the judgement reinforces 'traditional and sexist assumptions about women's sexuality and the nature of violence in their lives.'[72]

An analysis of the debate in the Lok Sabha on the Criminal Law Amendment Bill of 1983 (at which most of the benches were empty, as MP Geeta Mukherjee pointed out), reveals that the discussion was far removed from the feminist concerns of dignity, selfhood and bodily integrity of women. The Bill was passed, but it is significant that the instances of MPs' views given below were the rule rather than the exception.[73]

Fears about the trapping of innocent men by women willing to claim falsely that they were raped—'In such a situation the woman would not have been raped, but the poor man will certainly be raped in court.' (Moolchand Daga)[74]

A statement approvingly quoted from the Eighth Report of the National Police Commission—'Women, largely because they have come out of their homes to study and to work, are now more exposed to dangers in society . . .' (Ram Singh Yadav)[75]

The recommendation that any sexual relationship between a man and a woman who are not married should be treated as rape. This would be more in keeping with 'our own sexual morality'. Conversely, the concept of rape by a husband should not be entertained. (A.T. Patil)[76]

Opposition to the suggested amendment to debar publicity for rape cases. Apart from arguing that publicity ensures a fair trial, the MP held that social attitudes must change; merely protecting the identity of the woman could perpetrate 'the greater horror' of the girl later getting married without her husband or his family knowing about her rape. (N.J. Shejwalkar)[77]

Objection to the clause vitiating consent if given when intoxicated. What if the woman intoxicates herself and then disclaims responsibility; '. . . after all, we're not dealing all the time with virtuous women. We may also deal with some women who unfortunately, do not conform to normal standards of womanhood.' (Ram Jethmalani)[78]

These then, are the values and assumptions that animate the 1983 amendment that was passed by Parliament. The fear of the autonomous sexuality of women is the spectre that haunts the entire discussion. If rape is to be punished, it is because the enforced chastity of women is the cornerstone of patriarchal society. It is clear the law's comprehension of sexual violence can only be through misogynist and paternalist categories even as it condemns and attempts to punish sexual violence.

Activists working in the area of sexual violence are increasingly coming to feel that there is a need to adopt strategies other than law reform. Having conducted a workshop on sexual assault, a lawyer and feminist activist reports that the participants felt that they should shift focus from 'mainstream remedies to a sense of justice within'. This meant focusing on the victim's sense of self, denied to her by both the rapist and the enforcement agencies. More importantly, they felt they should work towards reinstating her within her community through gender education and awareness.[79] This growing awareness that 'rape' needs to be reconstituted in ideological terms is also evident in the campaign on the rape of the sathin in Bhateri, discussed earlier. One of the central slogans was, '*Izzat gayi kiski? Bhateri ki, Bhateri ki*' (Whose honour is it that is lost? The village Bhateri's)—thus turning around the colloquial Hindi phrase for rape, *izzat lutna,* or 'loss of honour' for the woman. Most importantly, unlike other rape cases where the rape survivor remains only a name to call the case by, in this instance, Bhanwari Devi has become an icon for the women's movement, speaking widely in public forums, and a well-known face associated with the struggle for women's dignity and identity.

What are the implications of reconstituting 'a sense of self' after sexual assault? We are pushed inevitably, into questioning 'sexuality' itself, a term assumed to be clearly comprehensible to everyone. And in one sense it is. We need to radically deconstruct this apparently universal, shared understanding of 'sexuality' to reveal the tenuousness of its foundations. The NLSJ concludes a feminist critique of judgements in rape cases with a statement which lays down the agenda for feminist practice:

> While we welcome the reduction of the corroboration requirements in rape cases, we must vigilantly reveal and challenge the problematic assumptions about women's sexuality that continue to inform these decisions. Feminist understandings of female sexuality and of women's rights to control our bodies, stand in stark opposition to the patriarchal pedestals of 'chastity and virginity'—pedestals that are securing the conviction of rapists at the cost of reinforcing the very assumptions that subordinate and oppress women.[80]

This statement fails to comes to terms with the fact that the reduction of corroboration requirements in rape cases is not just incidentally linked to problematic assumptions about female sexuality, as we have seen. More fundamentally, the statement fails to question the assumptions that underlie feminist understandings of 'women's rights to control our bodies' and 'female sexuality'.

Rape and Rights-Talk

Let us examine some of the implications of setting rape within the discourse of rights so that it can 'make sense' within law.

The 1993 Draft contains a Note from one of the members of the Committee, urging further debate on Section 375(2) (a) as it has been drafted. This section classifies the sexual assault of pregnant women as aggravated sexual assault, for which harsher punishment is awarded. The implication is that non-consensual sexual activity causes greater harm to the pregnant woman than to a non-pregnant one. The Note raises the question, 'We need to be aware of how this provision could be interpreted by a judge—would s/he understand that the harm is supposed to be to the woman herself and not to the foetus . . .? Would the latter position not conflict with pro-choice arguments?'[81] The 'broader ideological significance' of making sexual assault a more serious crime in the case of pregnant women, the Note continues, is that it reinforces the 'value of women as wombs, rather than as individuals.'[82] Further, if it is assumed that pregnant women suffer a particular type of physical harm on being assaulted, then presumably, the harm could change over the course of the pregnancy. How, asks the Note, could this be worked into the legislation? 'Is it a more serious offence in the ninth month than in the first? How do we make these distinctions?'[83] The Note also points out that if a miscarriage results from the assault, it is already punishable for life under Section 313 of the IPC. However, this section seeks to protect 'the rights of the unborn child', once again a problematic assertion for feminist pro-choice arguments.

The issues raised by this Note unavoidably foreground the impossibility of simultaneously defining the 'harm of rape' so exactly that legal discourse can comprehend it and so retaining ambivalences that the ethical impulse of feminism is undamaged. Underlying the Note is the whole history of feminist discussion on the ethics of abortion, on whether the foetus and the woman are to be seen as separate 'individuals' and on the unique nature of the 'pregnant body'.

The Note attempts to resolve the dilemma by denying a unique status to pregnancy—'Wouldn't it be more appropriate to draw a line between the severity and non-severity of the harm rather than pregnant and non-pregnant women?'[84] But this kind of 'sameness' approach towards pregnant and non-pregnant women is precisely what has been applied by courts between men and women, in order to strike down special provisions for women.[85] When the law treats pregnancy as a difference between persons and not between men and women, it becomes possible to argue that discrimination against pregnant women is not sex discrimination because the distinction is being made between pregnant and non-pregnant people, and both categories can include women.[86] Catharine MacKinnon has discussed how 'women's capacity to gestate children *in utero*' is sometimes used to restrict employment for women and sometimes treated as so 'normal' a physical condition that special facilities are not required.[87]

A case in the USA involving sexual assault on a mentally retarded adult woman is illustrative of the double-edged nature of rights-talk when juxtaposed with the ambivalence of the notion of consent. The woman was sexually assaulted by a group of men known to her. She appears, from her testimony, to have 'consented' to these acts, but how capable can she be considered of 'informed' consent? Her attackers were convicted on the argument that she could not comprehend the nature of that to which she consented, but there has been considerable unease about the implications of such a judgement for the rights of the mentally handicapped. It is feared that there could be a setback in the struggle to win fair treatment for them in other areas like housing and voting rights.[88]

This discussion does not necessarily mean that feminists must reject altogether the possibility of using the language of rights. It does mean however, that we must be cautious about using this language to describe the nature of 'sexuality'.

In the next section we will look at the Draft Sexual Assault Law Reforms (referred to earlier), submitted in 2000 to the Law Commission of India. A brief survey will attempt to foreground the ways in which the draft illustrates many of the key areas of ambiguity that lie between feminist and legal discourse, that we have outlined in this chapter.

The Draft Sexual Assault Law Reforms (India) 2000

The first issue that has arisen is that of democratic procedures and the question of representation. The very process by which the draft emerged is strongly criticised by many women's groups on the ground that only three organisations were invited by the Law Commission of India (LCI) to give their recommendations: 'We are concerned how the LCI has proposed these legal reforms without adequately consulting women's organisations, child rights organisations and sexual minorities to make the process entirely representative.'[89] Currently, discussions on this document (hereafter the SALR) are independently being conducted within the women's movement in different parts of the country, with a view to bring pressure to bear on the LCI to accept substantial revisions to the draft recommendations.

The main objection is to the 'gender-neutrality' of the SALR in that it refers to 'persons', not to women specifically. According to a summary of the Delhi-level discussions prepared by Saheli, it was felt that such a major change should not be recommended without a broad national-level consultation. 'It was felt that its inclusion could damage women more than help them. Already we find a backlash from men against women on issues of domestic violence. Further in our analysis all along, sexual assault has been understood as a gendered crime and so there is specificity of men's gender power over women in all cases of sexual assault.'[90]

The 'backlash on domestic violence' refers to increasing number of cases in which men have claimed physical violence by their wives and gone to court on the issue. The framing of sexual violence in gender-neutral terms is thus resisted because it is seen to be relocating the question of sexual violence out of feminist terrain based on an understanding of the gendered nature of power, to the 'neutral' terrain of physical safety of *all* bodies. Flavia Agnes put it this way: 'Underlying this recommendation is a presumption that through the stroke of a pen, the offence of rape will become desexualised . . .'[91] The statement of the national-level consultation of thirty-three women's/sexual rights groups, recognises that 'gender-neutrality' has been necessitated in the SALR because it also addresses child sexual abuse which can include the abuse of young boys. The statement suggests therefore, that a separate law is needed against child sexual abuse. 'The addition of other socially vulnerable groups (to existing sexual assault law) increases the complexity already faced by women in rape trials and procedures, which already are biased against women.'[92]

Further, it is feared that gender neutrality in assault law would 'de facto bring into its purview the issue of lesbians, gays, bisexuals, transgendered and other sexual minorities'. Since these identities/relationships are not legally recognised, the concern is that 'gender-neutrality' could criminalise them without their ever having been recognised legally. In other words, it is pointed out that same-sex relationships would continue to be illegal, but would be recognised by the law only when there is a question of assault: 'As sexual minorities . . . [i]n the absence of recognition of our sexual identities, we are extremely cautious of any purported interest in the curbing of violence amongst us.'[93]

Flavia Agnes points out that while the 1993 Draft (discussed in an earlier section) used the term 'person' to refer to the *victim* of sexual assault, it did not 'relocate the *offence* of rape beyond the boundaries of aggressive male sexuality.' The 2000 draft however, uses gender-neutral terms everywhere, and the 172nd report of the LCI too, following upon it, recommends these changes to the rape law 'on the lines of some western countries'. Further, the 1993 Draft called for a repeal of Section 377 of the Indian Penal Code, in order to decriminalise same-sex activities. The current recommendations do repeal Section 377, but ironically, only because same-sex activity now comes directly under the provisions of the gender-neutral assault laws. Thus, the repeal of Section 377 in the LCI recommendations, far from decriminalising same sex acts of sexual intercourse, place them within an overall framework that recognises non-heterosexual behaviour only in the context of assault.[94]

The premise of gender neutrality has been defended by the three individuals who drafted the SALR in subsequent meetings of women's organisations, on the grounds that it is now widely accepted by feminists all over the world. However, Flavia Agnes points to the rethinking on the 'equality' model by feminists like Martha Fineman, and suggests that such rethinking would be even more relevant in the Indian context where there has been a marked decline in the status of women over the last two decades. 'A gender-neutral rape law would open up avenues for inflicting even greater trauma and humiliation to an already marginalised section and hence defeat the very purpose of reform.'[95]

There is also an attempt in these discussions to include the perspective of Lesbian, Gay, Bisexual, Transgender and *Kothi* (LGBTK) groups in the law reforms, including the suggestion that an anti-discriminatory clause on the basis of sexuality and sexual orientation be introduced in Article 14 of the Constitution. The discussions are at present, in process.[96] One of the issues that troubles me however, is that the questioning of stable heterosexual identity seems to be taking the form of presenting alternative sexual identities as equally stable, requiring recognition in the law, rather than leading to a radical questioning of identity as such, and the assertion of the fundamental instability of sexual identity. *Kothis*, for example, are a fairly large community in the region of South and South-East Asia generally, called by different names in different areas; these are gay men who dress and behave 'like women', and want to be penetrated in the course of sex. Many are married to 'real' women. The assumptions here about femininity and naturally female characteristics cannot but be troubling for feminists.[97]

The discussions and disagreements on the current LCI recommendations on sexual violence once again bring to the fore the complex nature of the understanding of sexuality that operates among us. We find the same questions arising that have been explored in the course of this chapter—of sameness/difference, of accommodating the rich ambiguities of feminist understanding within the law, of why it is that again and again, 'legal reforms . . . may be injurious to women and other marginalised sections, or . . . hide or relocate the fundamental problems.'[98]

Deconstructing 'Sexuality'

What is a 'sexual' act? The answer might appear to be self-evident. As an American judge said of pornography, 'I know it when I see it.'[99] So an act involving contact with the breasts or genital region would appear to be a sexual act. In that case, what of the judgement in a case in Canada which concluded that an assault on a woman's breasts was not sexual because a person's 'secondary sexual characteristics' or 'erogeneous zones' should not come under this category. The court gave as an example a man's beard, the touching of which it would be absurd to consider as a sexual assault.[100] On the other hand, what of harassment by strangers which may involve a 'non-sexual' part of the body such as arms or hands; which may not involve contact with the victim's body at all, as when men expose themselves; or which may be verbal or aural? Clearly there are circumstances in which these kind of performances could be identified as sexual attack too.

It would appear that sets of ideas, values and representations construct a mesh which trap some acts as 'sex'. Moreover this mesh is constantly shifting and sieves the material passing through it in different ways at different times. In other words, 'sex' is not a clear and specific physical phenomenon always recognisable as such.

Once identified as sexual, the significance of the event is radically transformed. One, the event, if it was physically violent, is no longer an act of violence alone, but of 'sexual' violence which radically alters the quality of the victim's terror and pain. Sexual assault has been so constructed that it is the most feared, most terrifying and humiliating form of attack. A booklet written by a feminist activist, outlining the procedures to be followed in a rape case, while discussing the tendency of courts to assume consent if the woman did not put up a struggle, points to 'the paralysing effect on a young girl' that 'the sight of an erect penis can in itself have'.[101] This sense of paralysis and horror in the face of an attack recognised as sexual is not restricted to women. A counsellor in Britain heading Survivors, the principal counselling service for male rape victims, says that even 'big guys' 'freeze' when they are victims of a sexual attack. They talk of being literally unable to move, unable to offer any resistance.[102]

Even without physical violence or even physical contact, 'sexual' performances in which people are involved against their will are traumatic in a way in which other encounters are not. Such encounters are also invariably faced more by women and children and more painful for them.

Can this explosive impact of sexual violence on its victims be explained entirely by the empirically verifiable physical acts that constitute it? Or does the impact and maybe even sexual violence itself, flow from the discourse which constructs 'sex', 'sexual violence' and 'sexuality' as aspects of the individual's 'real' and 'private' self, so that to violate the sense of wholeness in this area is to threaten one's belief in one's unique selfhood?

Feminist analyses share this in common with the misogynist and sexist assumptions they critique: both are squarely situated within the discourse that mystifies 'sexuality' as the truest, deepest expression of selfhood. Sexual violence then, is seen as having 'a unique character',[103] as the 'violation of a woman's physical and mental being',[104] as 'a serious violation of (women's) freedom and their being.'[105] 'By sexual assault, men assume power over the most private part of a woman's life: her body.'[106] Thus, at the same time as 'sexuality' is constituted as the truest expression of selfhood, it is made clearly and easily identifiable with 'the body', itself unproblematically delineated as a material object with clearly definable boundaries—hence the redefinition of rape as 'violation of bodily integrity' in feminist legislative efforts. Simultaneously it is emphasised that the harm of sexual assault lies not so much in the physical assault, but in the transgression of the victim's conceptions of selfhood and sovereignty.

The repeated feminist emphasis on recognising that rape is a crime points to the positioning of sexual violence in the realm of morality and ethics rather than in the category of definable physical acts. However, as I have argued, morality and ethics cannot be encapsulated within legality. Therefore, in order to be comprehensible within legal discourse, feminists must cast 'sexuality' and 'sexual violence' in physical terms, and catalogue as exhaustively as possible all the kinds of actions that can constitute sexual assault. Thus Section 375(2) of the 1993 Draft lists as sexual assault, gestures, sounds or words or the exhibiting of any part of the body 'for a sexual purpose'. This phrase is not explained. Similarly, Section 375 (3) (b) lists the conditions vitiating consent, and part (vi) reads, 'No consent is obtained for the purposes of Section 375 (1) when the woman is mistaken about the sexual nature of the act or mistakenly believes that the sexual activity is for medical, ritualistic, purificatory, therapeutic, psychological or spiritual purposes.'[107]

In both these instances, the physical act has been qualified in terms of the 'sexual' intention of the perpetrator as well as the intention as perceived by the victim. Under what circumstances can one establish the 'mistakenness' of the belief that a particular activity is for medical, ritualistic or spiritual purposes? What would the implications be of such a formulation for traditional practices not necessarily exploitative of women? Besides, the notions of 'intention' and 'perception of intention' will certainly lose their complexity within the binary logic of the law. My contention is not that this increases the possibility of 'innocent' men being prosecuted by women who misunderstood their intentions (although this possibility will certainly be one of the principal fears expressed in forums like Parliamentary Committees). On the contrary, the ambiguity in phrases like 'for a sexual purpose' will be concretised in familiar misogynist and/or paternalist patterns in the process of the trial. One can see then, the pressure from legal discourse to cast sexuality in terms of clearly recognisable physical boundaries. Simultaneously the impossibility of doing so is also evident.

Feminists are increasingly becoming frustrated with the law in their struggle against sexual violence on women, but we continue to leave unquestioned the assumptions our own work pushes us towards unravelling. The argument so far suggests that the harm of rape cannot only be comprehended in physical or material terms and so long as 'the body' is understood to be a physical object, prior to all discourse, the notion of 'violation of bodily integrity' would not appear to be very useful either. We have seen how 'consent' can figure and refigure 'bodily integrity' and how consent itself is refigured repeatedly in different contexts. For it is not a set of clearly discernible physical acts themselves which constitute rape but the discourse that constitutes these acts as 'sexual', and therefore as attacking the root of 'identity' itself. We have so far assumed as 'natural' the symbolic order which produces this identity, which inscribes the body as body, as separate from other bodies, as healthy/unhealthy and so on, and which constructs the gendered and heterosexual body as the norm. Can we begin to conceive of a feminist politics which radically contests the production of this identity?

It is useful to consider here Judith Butler's discussion of Freud's *The Ego and the Id* (1923) in which Freud argues that the body does not precede and give birth to the idea of the body, but rather it is the idea of 'a body' that makes the body accessible as a body. Any description of the body therefore takes place through the circulation and validation of imaginary schema. In other words, the body does not exist prior to and independent of, all ideas and definitions of it. There are two points that Butler is making here:

(a) That the boundaries of the body are defined by psychic projection. It is the psychic conception of the body which constitutes it as a unity—the very contours of the body are not merely implicated in the 'irreducible tension' between the psychic and the material but *are* that tension.

(b) At the same time, she is not positing the materiality of the body as an effect of the psyche. She affirms an array of materialities that pertain to the body, signified by the domains of biology, anatomy, illness, age and so on. Each such domain is constituted by what its boundaries exclude, and is marked by the history of its constitution. In other words, as Butler puts it, they are both 'persistent and contested regions'. We could claim, she argues, that what persists in these contested domains is the materiality of the body.[108]

If we work on the belief that it is the idea that makes the body phenomenologically accessible, feminist practice would be liberated from the stranglehold of the discourse that designates the body as the site of selfhood. The boundaries of the stable, gendered, heterosexual self would be seen to be cultural and historical constructs, and not the natural immutable 'reality' that we are apparently irrevocably faced with. [109]

Sexual Harassment in the Workplace

The feminist understanding of sexual harassment is, as one writer puts it, that it is more than simply one of two extremes—either transient, often non-physical, acts in public spaces or clear-cut cases of physical molestation. It is more like a climate, an environment. Sexual harassment is particularly endemic in the workplace, it 'permeates the very procedures' of hiring and promotion, and in a university, academic research and pedagogy as well.[110] This is a fact I will take as given, not requiring to be spelt out, explained or proved. There is sufficient awareness and information about sexual harassment in feminist circles, and an enormous volume of feminist scholarship on the subject. So my purpose in this section is to explore the extent to which feminists can hope to capture this reality of women's lives through legal codes. My analysis here is in keeping with my general argument offered in this book, and draws on the growing recognition in feminist circles that

> Sexual harassment is neither a clear cut example of force, nor a simple display of interest. More than a mere reflection of the highly contradictory nature of gendered power relations, sexual harassment is *productive* of these relations . . . Sexual harassment is a social exchange in which the very meaning and embodiment of gender identity is at stake.[111]

In 1997 in India, a landmark judgement of the Supreme Court (*Vishakha v. State of Rajasthan*) laid down guidelines for all employers to follow to protect women from sexual harassment. This judgement came in response to a petition by some NGOs and individuals following the rape of Bhanwari Devi, the case we have discussed earlier. The judgement views sexual harassment in the workplace as a violation of the rights to life and to equality guaranteed in the Constitution, as well as of the right to practise any profession.[112] The guidelines apply to all public and private sector institutions as well as to the unorganised sector; it attempts to define various dimensions of sexual harassment as unwelcome physical contact and advances, the demand or request for sexual favours, sexual remarks, display of pornography, as well as any other unwelcome physical, verbal or non-verbal conduct of a sexual nature. The Court also asks trade unions to address the issue. Employers are given the responsibility of notifying and circulating a definition of sexual harassment. The composition of complaints committees is spelt out: women should constitute at least fifty per cent, and the chair should be a woman. In addition there should be a third party representative from an NGO or other organisation familiar with the issue of sexual harassment.[113]

In the wake of the guidelines, several universities are working on, or have come out with, codes as have some NGOs and private sector employers. Committees have been constituted to look into specific cases, in some cases before an official code has been formulated. Assessing this experience, certain areas of concern emerge, which I will outline in this section. I must emphasise that my focus is not on the inevitable problems that arise in addressing sexual harassment, faced by feminists everywhere. These have been made sufficiently plain by now. Such problems include non-implementation of the guidelines; reluctance of employers to set up committees and the lack of enforcement machinery especially in the unorganised sector; loopholes that allow perpetrators to escape; committees that fail to understand the nature of the harassment, underestimate its impact, or function with sexist assumptions (even when in some cases, such assumptions—for instance, reacting favourably to a complainant's sexual innocence—act in the complainant's favour).[114] We have come across these kinds of problems while discussing rape. All these are walls against which feminists have crashed often enough, and continue to struggle to demolish, go through, or climb.

I am not taking up either, the kinds of codes that can be formulated in the absence of a feminist understanding. For instance, the National Commission for Women (NCW) has recently formulated a draft bill on Sexual Harassment at the Workplace that is causing considerable concern in feminist circles. Many women's groups have expressed grave reservations because the tabling of such a Bill in the absence of extensive consultations can have 'serious and negative implications for working conditions for women all over the country.' Some of the points that have been raised in a letter to the Chairperson of the NCW by eight women's groups who have been working on the issue for several years are (a) the preventive aspect is not highlighted as in the Vishakha judgement; (b) the Bill does not set out in a preamble the position on sexual harassment at the workplace and the purpose that this law seeks to serve; (c) the Bill addresses only the organised sector; (d) the definition of sexual harassment is unacceptable—for instance, the Bill uses the term 'avoidable' where it should say 'unwanted' physical contacts and advances; (e) the functioning of complaints committees has not been clearly laid out; (f) there is no mechanism of appeal; (g) there is no provision to take care of the situation where the employer himself is the accused.[115]

The NCW is a government organisation and has all too often demonstrated its lack of feminist understanding.[116] It is not necessary for my purpose therefore, to go further into the problems with the draft bill that it has formulated. *My concern in this section is rather, with the difficulties of evolving a code even when the exercise is being carried out by a group of feminists with a shared understanding, and with what can go wrong despite the most feminist of committees.* It seems to me that we need to try to understand this latter set of problems if we are to go anywhere with our struggle against sexual violence in all its forms.

One kind of concern has been consistently expressed by Ratna Kapur. This has to do with her commitment to the feminist project of 'recuperating and theorising desire and pleasure . . . particularly against the backdrop of the rise to power of the Hindu Right.'[117] Kapur's fear is that in attempting to translate the Supreme Court's ruling into operative codes, feminists are unwittingly participating in a policing of sexuality that is part of the 'increasing assertion of a cultural nationalism that regards sex and sexuality, their current representations and practices, as external contaminants which are eroding "Indian cultural values and ethos" '.[118] Sexual harassment law and policy as it is developing in India, she argues, is reinforcing a conservative sexual morality, compromising women's sexual rights and inviting protectionist responses to women's experience of subordination and discrimination.[119] She points out that in the USA, where sexual harassment was first developed as part of sex-discrimination law, there is considerable rethinking among feminists and legal practitioners over two decades of experience. The main areas of concern about the functioning of sexual harassment law in the USA have been its encroachment on freedom of speech and expression, and the extent to which it has denied women and sexual minorities the space for sexual expression, while not having much controlled the actual occurrence of sexual harassment in the workplace. Further, such law has been exposed as being unavailable to women who belong to sexual, racial or religious minorities.[120] Kapur feels that this experience has not been taken seriously in India, and at a time when women have finally succeeded in creating the public space to discuss sexual wrongs, sexual harassment policies work towards closing off spaces in which sex can be discussed publicly. Thus, there is a silence on, and erosion of space for, 'the expression, assertion and enforcement of women's sexual rights'.[121]

I think Kapur's concern must be taken seriously. Talking about 'sex' has only recently acquired a tenuous legitimacy in India, and this is due in larger part to the current concern about the need for AIDS awareness. However, this latter concern need not be in tune with feminist notions of bodily integrity, and indeed, is often framed in the conservative language of disapproval of sexual activity outside socially legitimised frameworks. This kind of attitude to sexuality is pervasive in our culture. The Saheli Report mentions as an example of sexual harassment, a student in Delhi University who found 'uncomfortable', during a Pali language class she was attending, some of the examples the teacher used—they were not in 'good taste', she felt.[122] The exact instances are not mentioned, but it is worth remembering that feminist teachers have often made classes uncomfortable by open mention of body parts during discussions on sexuality, or even simply by discussing sexuality or prostitution as a part of say, political theory classes. A student once told me that she found 'insulting', the classes of a particular male professor of anthropology in which he discussed menstrual taboos and practices. The point is that such 'uncomfortable' discussions can further intellectual inquiry, be empowering and challenge dominant world-views, or they can equally, be intimidating to women and sexual minorities, and vitiate the atmosphere. No code can capture the exact meaning of such encounters in a way that the feminist project is always furthered, for the 'meaning' is not contained *inside* the encounter, but is produced by the context in which the encounter takes place.

For instance, one of the codes that has emerged after extensive research and discussion within the university community, with substantial input from the feminist Gender Studies Forum is that of Jawaharlal Nehru University, Delhi. The definition of sexual harassment there is partly, '. . . visual, verbal or physical conduct of a sexual nature . . . (when it) has the purpose or effect of unreasonably interfering with an individual's academic or work performance or creating an intimidating or hostile . . . environment.' Once again the context is crucial, for such a definition can well be made to work against feminist attempts to challenge heterosexist common sense and sexual double standards.

I would like to raise a further set of issues here.

(a) The first has to do with the difficulties faced in actually formulating codes to try and encompass the range of behaviour women experience as sexual harassment. Here a critical issue is the distinction that the Saheli Report poses between 'gender discrimination' and 'sexual harassment'.[123] The first phrase is used to refer to the general gender bias in society as a result of which women's work is not taken seriously, women are denied opportunities in typically male-dominated fields, are not paid equal wages as men for the same work, despite a law prohibiting such discrimination,[124] and so on. In other words, this phrase refers to the anti-woman discriminatory atmosphere in most workplaces, which does not necessarily constitute sexual harassment. The Saheli Report's understanding is that there is a close relationship between the two—'when gender discrimination is so rampant in almost every area of work, sexual harassment finds an easy ground.'[125] However, it is of critical importance to maintain this distinction while formulating codes to combat sexual harassment, for gender bias is too amorphous to be legally delimited. On the other hand, women do find intimidating and debilitating a range of behaviour that cannot be classified as 'sexual' harassment, but which affects their productivity and work satisfaction. It is tempting therefore, to try to capture this experience in a code. For instance, during the discussions over evolving a code for Delhi University, the Forum Against Sexual Harassment, a body of teachers and students that has long been active on this issue, made the following point while commenting on the Draft Report produced by the Committee to Frame Guidelines Against Sexual Harassment:

> Not all forms of sexual harassment are specifically sexual in nature, these are *sexualised* in that they are derogatory of a person on the basis of *gender* . . . These are equally derogatory and require legislation. Therefore it is crucial to state that all forms of unwelcome behaviour that discriminates people [*sic*] on the basis of their gender that may be explicitly sexual or not be explicitly sexual could amount to sexist behaviour.[126]

In the course of discussions this suggestion was not incorporated, precisely because many felt that 'sexual harassment' must be precisely defined, and should not try to encompass sexism as a whole. The issue is not resolved by this, however, and the distinction between 'gender discrimination' (or sexism) and 'sexual harassment' will continue to be a troubling one.

It is also the experience of the Jawaharlal Nehru University's Gender Sensitisation Committee Against Sexual Harassment (GSCASH), as one of its founders and active teacher members Ayesha Kidwai points out, that there is an anxiety to make the committees responsible for the redressal of every type of gender injustice, such as domestic violence and violence within a relationship. GSCASH has had to refer two such complaints to other disciplinary bodies in the University, 'with the painful awareness that these complaints may not be proceeded with in a duly responsible manner.' Kidwai makes the further insightful comment that 'This fact illustrates to me the particularity of the problem of constituting a broadly progressive institution (GSCASH) within a larger structure not informed by similar concerns.'[127]

The point has been made that while no 'watertight "definition" can be given', a policy becomes 'a means for consciousness-raising . . . deterring potential harassers and empowering victims to speak out. In that sense, the Supreme Court guidelines mark a step towards gender sensitisation, and not just legislation.'[128] However, I would reiterate my general argument here, that once put in place, legal codes have their own dynamic, and more often than not, tend to reinforce prevalent structures and relations of power.

(b) Another issue has to do with the setting up of committees. Here the question arises as to whether members should be nominated or elected to committees. Since the Supreme Court guidelines place the responsibility of forming committees on the employer, nominations cannot but reflect the interests of those in power. However, elected membership by no means solves the problem, as many of us felt during the process. Since sexual harassment arises in a context of widely prevalent misogyny, sexism and patriarchal attitudes, election can return candidates who reflect that value system.[129] Some balance needs to be maintained between elected and nominated members. In this context, it is significant that the feminist lawyer who played a crucial role in the petition that led to the Supreme Court guidelines, Naina Kapur, said in response to a question during a workshop assessing two years of the Vishakha judgement, that she was not interested in bringing about legislation on the issue. 'It is easier to convince three judges than five hundred legislators,' she said.[130] The undemocratic implications of this are clear, for the process of 'convincing' legislators is precisely what a long-drawn-out political campaign could be, with all its attendant drawbacks. On the other hand, we have seen that 'democracy' does not necessarily always have positive implications from our point of view.

The other problem with constituting committees attempting to represent all sections of the particular institution is that, in our experience, they often consider themselves responsible for representing the interests of the section they represent, rather than for combating sexual harassment. For instance, in a case where a teacher may have been accused of harassing a student, the teacher representative may try to ensure that the accused is not convicted.

Thus the formation of committees is only the beginning of a long and uncertain process of making them serve feminist interests, in the course of which, undesirable trends may be reinforced despite our best intentions.

(c) The responsibility of formulating codes of conduct and setting up a committee has been placed on the employer, as we have seen. This raises a further set of problems. In the absence of trade union rights, the existence of a committee set up by the employer is not necessarily what feminists might want. For instance, at the meeting referred to above, the representative from a hotel that has set up a committee against sexual harassment reported that instances of sexual harassment no longer occur since everyone knows that if an employee is found guilty, 'he is out'. Upon being asked what the process of dismissal was, and how the hotel's employees' trade union reacted to this, the response was that there is no trade union in that hotel.[131] Employers can be expected to frame guidelines that could reflect not only an anti-women, but also an anti-working class bias. For instance in Delhi University, the Committee set up to frame guidelines suggested that 'No hawkers or shops/*dhabas* or rickshawalas/autos should be allowed within one hundred yards of colleges, libraries and hostels.'[132] The memorandum by the Forum Against Sexual Harassment pointed out that the assumptions behind that recommendation were extremely problematic, suggesting that all danger to students came from poor and working class men, and referred to the Delhi University Gender Studies Group's report on sexual harassment of 1996, for statistics to prove the contrary.[133] The clause was deleted after this protest, but the situation in a university is very different from other institutions, where employees would not have the space to intervene in this manner. In fact, by entrusting employers with the responsibility, the Supreme Court guidelines have prevented the emergence of employees' initiatives. Saheli members have also pointed out that the mere presence of women and NGO representatives on committees does not ensure justice to complainants. The women members would be vulnerable to the power of the employer, and NGOs themselves are not free from sexual harassment and labour disputes.[134]

(d) Finally, my experience of serving on committees has shown that committees are expected by local supporters of the complainant to take into account internal political struggles, when one of the difficult tasks of a committee is precisely to extricate the issue of sexual harassment from other power configurations in the local context. It has had to be reiterated on several

> occasions that we cannot expect to use the committees against sexual harassment to work out our broader political agendas—combating caste discrimination say, or authoritarianism of institutional heads. It may be that the incident of sexual harassment in question is implicated in these relations, but often enough, it is not. Feminists in committees may have to work carefully to unravel the different strands involved, because the insertion of sexual harassment cases within such broader agendas often works against feminist goals.

Another complication is that, as Ayesha Kidwai points out, sometimes complaints 'in bad faith' are often made in the interest of 'groups larger than an individual, and the individual is to some extent instrumentalised by the group. As these interests remain in the shadows, foregrounding only the individual as the false complainant . . . the committee can only deal with it as the perjury of an individual. In general, the question is how to deal with group interests.'[135] Once again this kind of situation can bring together local politics and the issue of sexual harassment in a manner inimical to feminist goals.

The Saheli Report referred to above reflects the feminist struggle to express the complexity of women's experience of oppression while negotiating the narrow, inflexible corridors of the law. The Report reiterates its 'healthy scepticism about law and legal procedures' even while recognising that the Supreme Court guidelines have lent visibility to the issue of sexual harassment at the workplace.[136] As we have seen, the visibility and legitimacy that legal recognition is seen to give an issue, is one of the reasons why despite every negative experience, the women's movement continues to use legal reform as strategy. Nevertheless, I would emphasise here the general argument I make, that concretising through legal codes what constitutes 'sexual' harassment, cannot address the overall climate of sexism. Further, in the context of such a climate, our efforts to pin down categories of offensive behaviour can act against a broader feminist ethic and feminist understanding of sexuality. Saheli points out that if a woman wants to pursue a case of sexual harassment, existing criminal law has to be referred to, with all its limitations and sexist assumptions.[137] And in this chapter I have been concerned to demonstrate how drafting new law is an exercise fraught with danger from a feminist point of view. Saheli's own understanding is that 'Women's long experience with the law has shown that rigid and specific usages have been counterproductive in seeking justice. Most often, the legal domain has been used to reinforce the domination of male, upper class, upper caste and other powerful interests.' Nevertheless, it is in the arena of law that 'we seek to define and assert the realities women face in all their complexity.' One of the tasks Saheli envisages therefore, is to actively implement the guidelines to test out their efficacy and loopholes.[138] At the same time, Saheli asserts that

> the creation of a non-threatening atmosphere is an intangible no law can achieve . . . The culture of the workplace needs to be entirely changed. We need to pressurise authorities and management to the extent we can, in an organised manner, to act upon this issue. The fight against such harassment in the workplace is also a challenge to the dominant notions of women's sexuality.[139]

Am I pushing Saheli's analysis if I suggest that they might after all, be in agreement with Nandita Haksar's observation in another context, that continual recourse to the law is 'a substitute for the other harder option of building a movement for an alternative vision'?[140]

Ayesha Kidwai suggests that in her experience, when sexual harassment committee members have had some long-term association with the women's movement or other progressive political movements, such committees have performed better. 'In the absence of such expertise, procedures are simply applied bureaucratically, and are therefore, frequently discriminatory.'[141] It is doubtful that all or even most committees would have members with such political experience, and once again, the ethical ambitions of feminist politics come up against the impossibility of embodying these ambitions in legal codes.

Conclusion

What can this kind of analysis mean for us in our very real struggle against constant dehumanisation and humiliation through sexual violence of different kinds? The discussion in this chapter seems to point to the recognition that the possibility of realising the emancipatory impulse of feminism lies, not in concretising and more fully defining the boundaries of 'our bodies' through law, but in accepting 'the self' as something that is negotiable and contestable. The indeterminacy of identity need not lead to political paralysis—on the contrary, it could dislocate feminist practice productively, from sterile engagement with legal discourse and hegemonic cultural productions of selfhood, to a realm of radical doubt and constant negotiation of what constitutes 'me' as a 'woman' in some contexts. Emancipation itself must be recognised as disaggregated, split along different axes, just as identity is not just a positive conglomerate of different subject positions, but an ever-temporary construction, forming anew at the intersections of shifting subject positions.

It might be possible then, in the case of sexual violence, to see the feminist project, not as one of 'justice' but of 'emancipation'. It is a characteristic of the discourse of justice that it leaves unproblematised the harm that is sought to be redressed—that the harm is a 'harm' does not have to be proved within its terms, only whether the harm actually was perpetrated. Thus in the case of sexual violence, once 'rape' can be proved in legal terms, its harm is not in question. It is assumed by all the discourses that circulate around and produce 'sexual violence' as a category (including feminist discourses), that women can always be raped, and that rape is an attack on the very selfhood of woman. The issue then becomes one of 'proving' that rape did in fact take place, and ensuring justice through securing conviction by law. This leaves the ever-open possibility of other (all) women continuing to get raped.

What if our struggle were rather, to emancipate ourselves from the very *meaning* of rape? Does the ever-present threat of sexual violence flow from the locating of the 'female' self inside the sexually defined body of woman? The attempt then should be to redraw the map of our body to make it accessible to new codes, to new senses of the self, so that at least some of these selves would be free of the limits set by the body.

Such a project does not, as some critiques of what is termed 'post-modern feminism' suggest, 'reduce anti-rape politics to a psychic dimension', nor is it a 'general (re)turn to interiority'.[142] What is being suggested in such an argument is not that *individual* women must retreat inward into themselves and learn to reimagine their bodies, as the writer quoted above seems to think, but rather, that the feminist *movement*, feminist politics, must shift its focus from the law and the discourse of 'rape as violation', to work towards transforming common sense understandings of rape and of sexual violence in general. After all, 'rape as violation' is not only a feminist understanding, it is perfectly compatible with patriarchal and sexist notions of women's bodies and our sexuality. For instance, in India the Hindu right-wing-led government has been suggesting capital punishment for rape for some time now, and in the USA too, 'victims' rights' movements originate from and survive on right-wing patronage, pushing for longer prison sentences and increased executions.[143]

What this brings us to is a point this book has made again and again—the need to move from law-driven understandings of social transformation to a more long-term and continuous struggle to hegemonise common sense in our terms. The final chapter will address more fully the implications of such a redefined feminist project.

Notes

1. Flavia Agnes, 'Protecting Women Against Violence?'.
2. Ibid., p. WS 21.
3. Jennifer Temkin, 'Women, Rape and Law Reform', in Sylvana Tomaselli and Roy Porter, eds, *Rape*, Oxford, Basil Blackwell, 1986.

4. Ibid., p. 31.
5. 'Draft Amendments to Sexual Assault Law', 1993. (Committee consisting of Abha Bhaiya, Asha Ramesh, Elizabeth Vatsyayan, Enakshi Ganguli Thukral, Indu Prakash, Jasjit Purewal, Kirti Singh, Naina Kapur, Ratna Kapur, Ritu Menon, Seema Misra. Report available with the National Commission for Women, New Delhi.)
6. Naina Kapur, Jasjit Purewal and Kirti Singh, *Sexual Assault Law Reforms: A Process Document*, Delhi, 2000.
7. 1993 Draft, p. 11.
8. Ibid., p. 1.
9. Ibid., p. 12.
10. Ibid., p. 2.
11. Ibid., p. 4.
12. Susan Brownmiller, *Against Our Will: Men, Women and Rape*, New York, Bantam, 1976.
13. Carol Smart, *Feminism and the Power of Law*, p. 44.
14. 1993 Draft, p. 10. Emphasis added.
15. Ibid., p. 12.
16. Catharine MacKinnon, *Feminism Unmodified*, p. 3.
17. Ibid., p. 89.
18. Ibid., p. 86. Emphasis in original.
19. Catharine MacKinnon, 'Feminism, Marxism, Method and the State. Towards Feminist Jurisprudence', *Signs*, vol. 8, no. 4, Summer, 1983, p. 647.
20. Catharine MacKinnon, *Feminism Unmodified*, p. 87.
21. For a critique along these lines, see Drucilla Cornell, *Beyond Accommodation, Ethical Feminism, Deconstruction and the Law*, New York and London, Routledge 1991, pp. 124–5; Carole S. Vance, 'Pleasure and Danger: Towards a Politics of Sexuality', in Carole S. Vance, ed., *Pleasure and Danger*, Boston, Routledge and Kegan Paul, 1984, pp. 1–28.
22. This legislation has come under attack from the Feminist Anti-Censorship Taskforce for its potential to be used by the right-wing and by conservative governments to stifle a wide range of sexual expression.
23. Drucilla Cornell, *Beyond Accommodation*, p. 120.
24. Sharon Johnson, 'Rape: The Conservative Backlash', *Ms.*, March–April 1992.
25. Jasjit Purewal and Naina Kapur, 'Have You Been Sexually Assaulted'? New Delhi, undated, p. 3.

26. Ibid., p. 5.
27. 1993 Draft, p. 1.
28. Catharine MacKinnon, *Feminism Unmodified*, p. 103.
29. Mick Brown, 'Male Rape is Not Even Recognised as a Crime', *The Pioneer*, 16 December 1992.
30. Adrian Howe, 'The Problem of Privatised Injuries: Feminist Strategies for Litigation', in Martha Albertson Fineman and Nancy Sweet Thomadsen, eds, *At the Boundaries of Law*, New York and London, Routledge, 1991, pp. 148–9.
31. Kristin Bumiller, 'Fallen Angels: The Representation of Violence Against Women in Legal Culture', in Martha Albertson Fineman and Nancy Sweet Thomadsen, eds, *At the Boundaries of Law*, p. 96.
32. Michel Foucault, *Discipline and Punish: The Birth of the Prison*, New York, Vantage Books, 1977, p. 17.
33. *Nattu v. State of Madhya Pradesh*, Cri. L.J. 1990: 1567.
34. Ibid., at Para 16.
35. Hindu law as codified through Acts passed between 1955 and 1956 were based on inegalitarian Victorian English patterns of marriage and inheritance and on the customary practices of some of the dominant communities in North-West India, among whom women's rights have been seriously eroded. The practices of the Nairs in Kerala, Meitei in Manipur, Meenas in Rajasthan and Jains, which provided better rights to women in many respects, were presumed to be non-existent or non-Indian. Thus the Hindu codified law is in many ways a step backward for some communities. See Bina Agarwal, 'Rural Women, Poverty and Natural Resources', *Economic and Political Weekly*, 28 October 1989: WS-54; Madhu Kishwar, 'Codified Hindu Law. Myth and Reality', *Economic and Political Weekly*, vol. 20, no. 33, 13 August 1994; G. Arunima, *There Comes Papa: Colonialism and the Transformation of Matriliny in Malabar*, New Delhi, Orient Longman, 2003.
36. Upendra Baxi, *The Crisis in the Indian Legal System*, New Delhi, Vikas, 1982, pp. 36–7.
37. Flavia Agnes, *Journey to Justice*, Bombay, Majlis, 1990, p. 68.
38. Ibid., p. 7.
39. Ibid., pp. 10–11.
40. Ibid., pp. 35–6.
41. Jasjit Purewal and Naina Kapur, p. 11.
42. Catharine MacKinnon, *Feminism Unmodified*, p. 5.

43. 1993 Draft, p. 1.
44. Flavia Agnes, 'Protecting Women Against Violence?', p. WS-20.
45. AIR 1952, SC 54, Paras 46–7.
46. Flavia Agnes, 'Protecting Women Against Violence?'.
47. Ibid.
48. Carole Golberg-Ambrose, 'Unfinished Business in Rape Law Reform', *Journal of Social Issues*, vol. 48, no. 1, 1992, p. 175.
49. Flavia Agnes, 'Protecting Women Against Violence?'
50. Carol Smart, *Feminism and the Power of Law*, p. 33.
51. Ibid., pp. 33–4.
52. *Jayanti Rani Panda v. State of West Bengal*, Cr. L.J. 1984: 1535.
53. Flavia Agnes, 'Protecting Women Against Violence?', p. WS-21.
54. *Moti Ram v. State of Maharashtra*, AIR 1955, Nag. 121.
55. *Queen v. Clarence 22 QBD 23 at 2.*
56. This anomaly can also be interpreted in a startlingly different way. In his evidence to the Joint Committee of Parliament considering the Criminal Law Amendment Bill passed in 1983, a DIG of police argued that since the legal minimum age of marriage is eighteen years, the law must assume a 'wife' to be eighteen. Once married, a woman must be considered to be eighteen, and therefore he held that the exception should read 'sexual intercourse by a man with his wife is not rape'. See J.P. Atray, *Crimes Against Women*, Delhi, Vikas Publishing House, 1988, p. 144.
57. 1993 Draft, p. 4.
58. See Tanika Sarkar on the Age of Consent debate in India in the nineteenth century. She demonstrates how all strands of opinion, whether colonial, reivalist-nationalist or medical-reformist, defined consent in terms of a purely biological category, that is, the stage when the female body was ready to accept sexual penetration without serious harm. They only differed, she points out, in assessing when this stage was reached. Tanika Sarkar, 'Rhetoric Against Age of Consent: Resisting Colonial Reason and Death of a Child-Wife', *Economic and Political Weekly*, vol. 28, no. 36, 4 September 1993, p. 1875.
59. *Kanchan Das v. the State, 1991*, Cri. L.J. 2036, Delhi High Court.
60. *1978, Sachindranath Mazumder v. Bistupada Das.*
61. 1993 Draft, p. 13.
62. Ibid., p. 13, emphasis added.
63. Ibid., p. 4.

64. Ibid., p. 4.
65. For a discussion of feminism and nationalism in former Yugoslavia, see Jill Benderly, 'Rape, Feminism and Nationalism in the War in Yugoslav Successor States', in Lois A. West, ed., *Feminist Nationalism,* New York and London, Routledge, 1997, pp. 59–72. For a significant feminist critique of nationalism in post-socialist Yugoslavia, see two papers by Rada Ivecovic (translated into English), 'The Bosnian Paradigm', *Dialogue,* Sarajevo, 1998 and 'Nation and Identity in Post-Socialist Transition', *Die Erweiterung Europas,* Vienna, 25–7 September 1998, pp. 229–43.
66. Kristin Bumiller, 'Fallen Angels', p. 110.
67. Flavia Agnes, *Journey to Justice,* p. 8.
68. *Bhoginbhai Hirjibhai v. State of Gujarat,* AIR 1983, SC 753, Para 10.
69. *National Law School Journal* (the journal of the National Law School, Bangalore), vol 1, 1993, p. 170. The article cited does not carry an author's name.
70. *National Law School Journal,* vol. 1, 1993, pp. 170–1.
71. AIR 1992 SC 2007, Note 1 at Para 5, Quoted in *National Law School Journal,* vol. 1, 1993, p. 167.
72. Ibid.
73. *Lok Sabha Debates, 1983,* vol. 42.
74. Ibid., p. 431, translated from Hindi.
75. Ibid, p. 456.
76. Ibid., pp. 366–9.
77. Ibid., pp. 375–6.
78. Ibid., p. 413.
79. Naina Kapur, 'CBI's Approach Discouraging for Rape Victims', *The Pioneer,* 21 September 1993.
80. *National Law School Journal,* p. 171.
81. 1993 Draft, p. 8.
82. Ibid., p. 8.
83. Ibid., p. 9.
84. Ibid., p. 8.
85. The writer of the Note has herself co-authored an incisive and comprehensive critique of this approach to equality as demonstrated by Indian courts (Ratna Kapur and Brenda Cossman, 'On Women, Equality and the Constitution': Through the Looking Glass of Feminism', *National Law School Journal,* vol. 1, 1993.

86. Mary Joe Frug, *Postmodern Legal Feminism*, p. xii.
87. Catharine MacKinnon, *Feminism Unmodified*, pp. 36–8.
88. Catherine S. Manegold, 'A Rape Case Worries Advocates for the Retarded', *The New York Times*, 14 March 1993.
89. Statement issued at national-level meeting on LCI Recommendations, Mumbai, 17–18 January 2002, published in *Saheli Newsletter,* Delhi, January–April 2002, p. 18.
90. Saheli letter by email dated 9 November 2001.
91. Flavia Agnes, 'Law, Ideology and Female Sexuality: Gender Neutrality in Rape Law', *Economic and Political Weekly*, 2 March 2002, p. 844.
92. Statement of national-level meeting, pp. 18–19.
93. Ibid., p. 18.
94. Flavia Agnes, 'Law, Ideology and Female Sexuality', p. 846. She points out that the one area where the LCI found it necessary to disagree with the SALR is on the matter of marital rape, holding that 'this may amount to excessive interference with marital relationships.'
95. Ibid., p. 847.
96. See Statement of national-level meeting, p. 18.
97. I learnt about the existence of *kothis* and the issues that circulate around this identity through a term-paper by a student, Geetika Bapna. I would like to thank her for some illuminating discussions. I would also like to note here an interesting response to the concern expressed above, by Manohar, an activist with Sangama, a group in Bangalore, working with LGBTK people. According to Manohar, in the course of being involved with Sangama, and through the discussions and political campaigns, these identities tend gradually to shift and realign in terms of their own self-identification.
98. Flavia Agnes, 'Law, Ideology and Female Sexuality', p. 844.
99. Catharine MacKinnon, *Feminism Unmodified*, p. 163.
100. Christine Boyle, 'Sexual Assault and the Feminist Judge', *Canadian Journal of Women and the Law*, 1985.
101. Flavia Agnes. *Journey to Justice*, p. 10.
102. Mick Brown, 'Male Rape is Not Even Recognised as a Crime'.
103. 1993 Draft, p. 10.
104. Flavia Agnes, *Journey to Justice*, p. 8.
105. Jasjit Purewal and Naina Kapur, p. 3.
106. Ibid., p. 8.
107. 1993 Draft, p. 13.

108. Judith Butler, 'The Lesbian Phallus and the Morphological Imaginary', *Differences: A Journal of Feminist Cultural Studies*, vol. 4, Spring 1992, pp. 135–43.

109. I would like to use this opportunity to respond to Gayatri Spivak's patronising comments on the arguments in this section, an earlier version of which was published as a paper, 'Embodying the Self: Feminism, Sexual Violence and the Law', in Partha Chatterjee and Pradeep Jeganathan, eds, *Community, Gender and Violence: Subaltern Studies XI*, Delhi, Permanent Black, 2000 (In 'Discussion: An Afterword on the New Subalterns', in the same volume, pp. 317–18). Since those comments were published in the same volume but without my having seen them first, this is the first opportunity to respond that presents itself. Spivak clearly believes that it is presumptuous on my part to have attempted to make Derrida and Foucault work for us in the Indian context. 'If there is anything to be known about deconstruction,' she says, 'it is that you cannot will yourself to perform it.' Further, 'We can make Derrida and Foucault work for us only if we have learnt the ground well enough to lose our conviction of their superiority . . .' The enormous condescension of these remarks, suggesting that only Spivak can 'do deconstruction' without being overwhelmed by the superiority of European thinkers leaves me baffled. As a political activist and scholar, I insist that deconstruction does not happen *despite* ourselves, but that the insights that are produced by that method can and must be brought to bear on our political practice and our scholarship. Of course, I do not need to be reminded by Spivak that this process is always necessarily fraught and incomplete. Indeed, that is precisely the point I make about any project of radical politics, that we need to think of our goal as one involving a receding horizon, not as one apocalyptic moment of fullness and achievement. Spivak's astonishing comment that 'we cannot take Foucault and Derrida's side *against* the feminists who work on the ground' tempts me to move into an equally patronising mode, and remind her that 'theory' and 'practice' constitute, not binary opposites, but constitutive parts of each other. Also, that her 'we' in that sentence, in so far as it occupies the highly privileged realms of First World universities, certainly does not include me, for in the binary she posits, I am right here with the 'feminists on the ground'. Finally, a last comment on her absolute incomprehension of my argument about the slogan used by the women's movement during the protests about the rape of Bhanwari Devi, '*Izzat gayi kiski, Bhateri ki*'. Spivak scornfully suggests that I read

this slogan as 'self-evident proof of a radical deconstruction that displaces honour or *izzat*' and tells me off for my 'hopelessly romantic' belief that 'the subaltern produces high theory'. However, it does not take a very careful reading of my argument to see that I use the slogan simply as an illustration of the different directions that the *women's movement* in India (not 'the subaltern') is trying to take public discussions on rape. I do not offer the instance as 'proof' that Butler is being translated into grassroots politics. The oversimplifications and bad faith of Spivak's comments on my essay are particularly remarkable from one who has often been attacked for obfuscatory high theory herself. Perhaps I can be forgiven for wondering if Spivak believes that the gods of deconstruction may only be approached through their high priestess?

110. Ania Loomba, 'Let's Talk About Lex', *The India Magazine*, April–May 1998, p. 24.
111. Laura Ring, 'Sexual Harassment and the Production of Gender', *Differences: A Journal of Feminist Cultural Studies*, 6.1, 1994, pp. 129, 130.
112. Articles 21, 15 and 19(g) of the Constitution respectively.
113. See *Another Occupational Hazard: Sexual Harassment and the Working Woman*, A Report by Saheli, Delhi, October 1998; Ratna Kapur and Shomona Khanna, 'Women's Right to Law', *The Hindu*, 26 April 1998, p. iv; and Ania Loomba, pp. 22–3, 27.
114. For a discussion of such problems, see Bina Srinivasan, 'Dealing with Sexual Harassment at the Workplace: Impasse Continues', *Economic and Political Weekly*, 11 September 1999, pp. 2638–9; the Saheli Report, *Another Occupational Hazard*; and Ratna Kapur, 'Sexcapades and the Law', *Seminar* 505, September 2001, p. 44.
115. Letter to the NCW by Saheli, Gujarat Forum for Women Studies and Action Groups, Jagori, Sama, Nirantar, Lawyers Collective, Women's Rights Initiative, Human Rights Law Network, Partners in Law and Development, November 2001.
116. The most notorious of NCW's achievements was its report on rape by Poornima Advani, Lina Gonsalves and J.K. Mittal, *Rape: A Legal Study*, National Commission for Women, 2000. This report was widely criticised for its patriarchal and Hindu right-wing assumptions. Kumkum Roy prepared a comprehensive critique of this document which she presented at a women's groups meeting at the office of the National Federation of Indian Women, Delhi, on 31 July 2000. Roy's critique is on file with this author.

117. Ratna Kapur, ' "A Love Song to Our Mongrel Selves": Hybridity, Sexuality and the Law', *Social and Legal Studies*, vol. 8, no. 3, 1999, p. 353.
118. Ratna Kapur, and Shomona Khanna, 'Women's Right to Law'.
119. Ratna Kapur, 'Sexcapades and the Law', p. 41.
120. Ibid., pp. 42–3.
121. Ibid., p. 45.
122. Saheli Report, p. 8.
123. Saheli Report, p. 15.
124. The Equal Remuneration Act, 1975.
125. Saheli Report, p. 15.
126. *Memorandum*, Forum Against Sexual Harassment in Delhi University, 29 September 1999, p. 3.
127. Ayesha Kidwai, personal communication, 26 November 2001.
128. Ania Loomba, 'Let's Talk About Sex', p. 23.
129. For instance, in 1999, in Jawaharlal Nehru University (Delhi), a male candidate who contested elections to the Gender Sensitisation Committee Against Sexual Harassment campaigned, and won, on the platform that he would protect the rights of 'falsely accused' men.
130. Workshop on 'Supreme Court Guidelines Against Sexual Harassment: A Review', organised by Radhika Chopra at India International Centre, Delhi, 11 August 1999.
131. Ibid.
132. *A Draft Report on Guidelines Against Sexual Harassment in Delhi University,* Committee to Frame Guidelines Against Sexual Harassment in Delhi University, May 1999, p. 13.
133. *Memorandum*, by Forum Against Sexual Harassment, p. 12.
134. See Note 127.
135. Ayesha Kidwai, personal communication.
136. Saheli Report, p. 35.
137. Ibid., p. 34.
138. Ibid, p. 35.
139. Ibid., p. 36.
140. Nandita Haksar, 'Human Rights Layering: A Feminist Perspective', in Amita Dhanda and Archana Parasher, eds, *Engendering Law: Essays in Honour of Lotika Sarkar*, Lucknow, Eastern Book Company, 1999, p. 80. This argument is discussed in more detail in the Introduction.
141. Ayesha Kidwai, personal communication.

142. Carine M Mardorossian, offering a critique of Judith Butler and Sharon Marcus, among others, in 'Towards a New Feminist Theory of Rape', *Signs*, vol. 27, no. 3, Spring 2002, p. 747.
143. See ibid., pp. 759–60.

CHAPTER FOUR

Reservations for Women: 'Am I That Name'?[1]

When the Women's Reservation Bill first appeared as the 81st Amendment Bill in 1996, proposing to reserve 33 per cent of seats in Parliament for women, it burst into public discourse full-blown as a 'women's' (indeed, a feminist) issue, and continues to be debated largely in terms of women's rights. It is becoming increasingly clear however, that the questions thrown up by the timing of the Bill and the responses to it cannot be understood solely within the framework of women's rights. This chapter attempts to relocate these questions in a complex matrix of political identities in order to understand their full significance. I also argue that the debates around the Bill reveal a more fundamental set of questions about the issues of *citizenship, representation*, and *the subject of feminist politics.*

Historical Background

The question of reservations for women in representative institutions has long been debated in India. The issue of reservations for women had come up in the Constituent Assembly but had been rejected by women representatives as it was felt to be unnecessary, since the working of democracy in the normal course would ensure the representation of all sections of Indian society. The suggestion was also seen to underestimate the strength of women to compete as equals. Over twenty-five years later, the Committee on the Status of Women (CSWI) in India considered the same question. It was agreed that rural women's experience and problems had remained undervalued and invisible. The CSWI therefore unanimously recommended the establishment of statutory women's panchayats. Prior to this, the Panchayat Acts of most states had reserved one or two seats for women, to be filled by nomination if no woman was returned by election. But this had remained a token gesture and the CSWI recommended instead that the reserved seats be occupied by elected office-bearers of the proposed women's panchayats. On the question of reservations for women in Parliament and state legislatures, the debate took a shape familiar to us today. The arguments made in favour of reservation were mainly that

(a) political parties because of their generally patriarchal character were reluctant to sponsor women candidates, and therefore reservations were necessary;
(b) reservations would increase the number of women in Parliament all at once and they would be able to act as a strong lobby. At present, their being in a small minority inhibits their effective participation in the interests of women;
(c) the presence of more women in Parliament would lead to a change in the direction of debates and policy.

Arguments made against reservations were mainly that

(a) this would run counter to the principle of equality in the Constitution;
(b) women cannot be equated to socially backward communities as women are not a socially homogeneous group;
(c) women's interests cannot be isolated from those of other economic, social and political strata;
(d) such a system would lead to similar demands from other groups and communities, thus posing a threat to national integration.

Finally the CSWI by a majority decided to uphold the position taken in the Constituent Assembly and rejected the reservation of seats for women in Parliament and state assemblies.

The latest phase of the debate began with the National Perspective Plan (1988–2000) recommending a 30 per cent reservation of seats for women at panchayat and zilla parishad levels. Subsequently states like Karnataka and Gujarat implemented some form of reservation for women in panchayati raj institutions. In 1993, the 73rd and 74th Constitutional Amendments provided for one-third reservation for women nation-wide in these bodies. By the general elections of 1996, women's organisations put forward a joint demand to all political parties for reservations for women in state assemblies and Parliament.[2] The major parties supported the demand although they themselves gave less than 15 per cent of their total number of tickets to women. The Reservations Bill was included in the Common Minimum Programme of the United Front which assumed office, and the 81st Amendment Bill was introduced in 1996, proposing 33 per cent reservation for women in Parliament. It could not be passed and was referred to a Joint Select Committee. In 1998 the Bill (now the 84th Amendment Bill) was introduced again by the BJP government to strong opposition, and once again was derailed. Its most recent incarnation is as the 85th Amendment Bill, introduced in December 1999, and its fate continues to be as uncertain as it ever was.

Gender and Caste since the 1980s

What were the developments between 1974, when women's movement activists in the CSWI rejected reservations for women in Parliament, and 1996, when almost the same representatives of the women's movement demanded such reservations? What were the shifts in the two intervening decades that would explain this change? In the years that passed, there were two significant developments in Indian politics. One had to do with challenges to the legitimacy of the national integrity argument. By the mid-1970s the legitimacy of the post-independence elites had begun to erode with the economic and political crisis precipitated by the failure of development planning. There was a resurgence of militancy in every section of society. Critical questions were arising as to whose interests were being protected by the 'integrity' of the nation-state. By the mid-1980s various regional movements were challenging the inherited idea of Indian nationhood, and backward caste assertion had begun to transform the nature of the political arena and the composition of the Lok Sabha. Yogendra Yadav points out that 'The influx of lower orders into the field of democratic contestation has . . . (made) it respectable to talk of caste in the public-political domain. The emergence of social justice as a rubric to talk about caste equity (and) *political representation of castes and communities* . . . is a distinct achievement of this period.' [3]

The other development was that women had emerged as a significant force in politics. Women had been at the forefront of the movements against corruption and price-rise that preceded the imposition of Emergency. The 1980s saw the emergence of the vocal and visible autonomous women's groups which placed feminist issues firmly on the public agenda—dowry, rape, violence against women. At the same time it was clear that women were underrepresented on representative bodies. By the time of the National Perspective Plan therefore, there was both an acknowledgement of women's militant participation in politics as well as of their absence in decision-making bodies. Vina Mazumdar, who had been Member Secretary of the CSWI, points out how as 'daughters of Independence', her generation had been critical of special representation, but gradually 'we have found our understanding of nation-building changing radically'.[4] By 1996 then, the 'daughters of Independence' had come to acknowledge that abstract citizenship was only a cover for privilege, and that difference had to be acknowledged.

However, the point I would emphasise here is that the emergence of women as a significant grouping in Indian politics is only one of two factors shifting the consensus on women's reservations. The other, the transformation of the caste composition of Parliament and the growing presence of backward castes through successive elections is an equally significant development. I will argue that these processes produced two very different (even opposed) sets of concerns—feminist and upper caste—that tied in at this particular conjuncture to produce the sudden general acceptability of women's reservations.

Is the WRB Only About 'Women'?

The career of the Women's Reservation Bill in Parliament is striking for the high drama and rhetoric of women's rights that has accompanied it, the passionate opposition to the Bill being generally characterised by its supporters as anti-women and patriarchal. Some of the comments and phrases decrying the derailing of the Bill are illustrative: 'a predominantly male parliament developed cold feet';[5] '*sansad par kabiz purush satta*'; [6] 'Parliament was divided into men and women, the former all opposed to the Women's Reservations Bill';[7] 'Parliament is like an all-male club and I feel like an unwanted intruder';[8] 'On caste-based arguments in defence of male domination.'[9] Similarly, speculating about the reasons why political parties who supported the reservation of seats for women in local bodies are reluctant regarding similar legislation at the parliamentary level, Shirin Rai and Kumud Sharma wonder, 'Could it be that enhanced representation of women in the national parliament spells a far greater and immediate challenge to the gendered status quo within the party political system?' Or conversely, 'Is it that the pattern of quota systems in India has shown that elite-based strategies of empowerment are less helpful to groups seeking greater recognition than those based on grassroots institutions?'[10] In other words, is it the case that political parties resist the Bill because they fear it will empower women too much or too little? However, as Rai and Sharma unravel the actual arguments of the protagonists and antagonists of the Bill, it becomes clear that while the protagonists make their arguments in terms of gender justice, the arguments against the Bill come from two opposed positions—they stem either from opposition to reservations in general or from a belief that reservations for women should be extended to other disempowered groups (the quotas within quotas position).[11] The arguments against, in other words, are not 'anti-feminist'. In spite of their own evidence however, the writers continue to frame their discussion in terms of whether mainstream political bodies have 'embraced the gender justice agenda' or not.

It is now evident that to continue to understand the Bill in terms only of attitudes to women would be a partial exercise at best. Rather, I would argue that when we tease out the strands in the debate, we find two sets of arguments for and against. There are feminist (or at least, pro-women) arguments for and against reservations for women, and (implicitly or explicitly) caste-based arguments for and against.

A *feminist case for reservations* is made in terms of the need for affirmative action to redress the situation of women. This argument comes from Left parties and women's groups. A characteristic statement of this kind is that made by Vasanth and Kalpana Kannabiran, long-time activists of the women's movement. 'Women's participation in the political process is critical both to the strengthening of democratic traditions and to their struggle against oppression.' But they are obstructed in such participation by 'power relations that . . . operate at many levels of society from the most personal to the highly public.' It is necessary therefore to appropriate 'spaces in mainstream political arenas and reshape them'.[12] A CPI(M) MP expresses another facet of this strand when she argues that while reservations policy *per se* is not democratic, it is nevertheless necessary to rectify existing imbalances. Thus, it is a partial measure, but one that is unavoidable if women are to participate effectively in politics.[13] Similarly, an editorial of *ML Update*, the weekly bulletin of CPI (ML)-Liberation, states that while 'formal equality in law hardly brings equality in society', the Bill is important as 'The moot point at this stage is to recognise women in their entirety as an oppressed category in an otherwise male-dominated society.' More importantly, the Bill 'may prove catalytic to the larger entry of women from backward and dalit castes in the political arena'.[14] The feminist argument for reservations is thus made in terms of creating equality of opportunity in order to make real the formal equality given by the Constitution.

What could be called a *pro-women case against reservations* is made by Madhu Kishwar, the editor of *Manushi* (which calls itself 'a journal about women and society'), and by the Shetkari Mahila Aghadi (SMA), a peasant women's organisation founded in 1986. Their broad argument has to do with the concern that reservations will only bring to the fore the 'biwi–beti brigade'. The SMA in an 'Open Letter to MPs', signed by Gail Omvedt among others, said that quotas for women 'is being pushed by women in the creamy layer'. Omvedt too, opposes the Women's Reservation Bill, terming one of the most disturbing aspects of the debate around it, 'the way it seemed to set (mainly upper caste) feminists against (mainly male) OBC leaders'.[15] The SMA prefers to put up all-women panels for panchayat elections as the experience of reservations in panchayats in Maharashtra has not been favourable—relatives of established male leaders are fielded, and there has been no impact at all on inefficiency and corruption. It suggests a more fundamental transformation in the election system, the introduction of three-seat constituencies. Each voter would have three votes, at least one of which must be cast for a woman candidate. Two seats would then be filled by the candidates male or female with the highest number of votes, and one by the woman with the highest votes among women candidates.[16]

Kishwar too originally backed the proposal of the SMA although now she has come up with a separate proposal (endorsed by Omvedt in a different form) which we will look at later in this chapter. Kishwar believes that reservations are unnecessary because 'our country has a well-entrenched tradition whereby any party, politician or public figure who tries to bad mouth women in public or oppose moves in favour of women's equality is strongly disapproved of . . . Hence, compared to many other parts of the world, it is relatively easy to get legislation favouring women passed in India.'[17] This is an amazing statement—a cursory look at newspapers would reveal that extremely patriarchal and sexist, at best protectionist, views of women are routinely publicly expressed in the course of rape trials and election campaigns, in police statements on violence against women, and the like. These are contested only by women's groups and women's wings of political parties, usually of the Left. As for legislation favouring women, Kishwar's is a surprisingly naïve understanding of Indian politics, and of how and why laws get passed. Take for instance, the right to abortion which she cites as an example. As we saw in Chapter Two, the Medical Termination of Pregnancy Bill was introduced as a population control measure in 1971 and the debate in Parliament was entirely within those terms. It is not surprising therefore that only two MPs opposed it. Abortion was not being discussed as a question of women's rights over their bodies, but on the contrary, as a measure necessitated in order to achieve lower population growth. In the context of countries of the global South where 'overpopulation' is presented as the reason for poverty, state control of fertility is the problem for feminists, not the illegality of abortion. Therefore, the fact that this right took 'decades of struggle in the West' while it was 'enacted in India without a fight', as Kishwar puts it,[18] has to be understood very differently. In other words, the passing of apparently 'feminist' legislation has to be located also in the context of the compulsions of ruling elites in order to understand the complex dynamics involved.[19] Eventually however, Kishwar concedes that 'our democracy has failed to include women in its purview', partly due to the Gandhian legacy which saw women's role in politics as self-sacrifice rather than as a bid for power, and more recently, because of the increasing corruption and criminalisation associated with politics.[20]

I term the SMA and Kishwar's position as a 'pro-women' critique of reservations because their objections arise from focusing on women's interests, which they believe would be better served by other measures. The next set of arguments, which I term 'caste-based', take positions for and against reservations explicitly or implicitly, in terms of caste. The most reviled, explicitly *caste-based opposition to women's reservations* has been the derogatory reference of Sharad Yadav to the 'short-haired' women who would overrun Parliament. While this has been understood as a misogynist statement, we must see it also as expressing a legitimate fear that reservations for women would radically alter the composition of Parliament in favour of upper classes and upper castes—the term *'parkati mahilaen'* in this context drawing upon a common stereotype of westernised and elite women. Of course this stereotype is sexist and misogynist, but that is not really the point here, because surely we are under no illusion that all the support for women's reservations comes from those who actively contest and reject such stereotypes. Rather, this kind of opposition to the Bill in its present form has to be recognised as arising from the politics of caste identity.

The idea of reservation for an undifferentiated category of 'women' has been uniformly denounced by politicians and writers speaking for backward castes and dalits. At its most explicit, such an argument attacks the Bill as an upper-caste ploy to stem the rising tide of lower-caste men in politics.[21] In this context, we must take into account the experience of women's reservations in panchayati raj institutions. Studies in Gujarat and Karnataka have confirmed that the entrenched power of the dominant castes has been strengthened by women's reservations.[22] It is not surprising then, that OBC and Dalit leaders are highly suspicious of the WRB. In an interview, Mayawati, the Bahujan Samaj Party leader, demanded that there should be 50 per cent reservations for women, and within this, separate reservations for backward castes and minorities.[23] Mulayam Singh Yadav of the Samajwadi Party has consistently opposed the Bill, saying that in its present form it is anti-minority and anti-dalit.[24]

Most interestingly, Uma Bharati of the BJP, herself from a backward caste, has taken a position opposed to that of her party's. Unlike Sushma Swaraj, the upper-caste BJP leader most vocal in support of the Bill, Uma Bharati makes a clear feminist argument for reservations, while asserting that a backward caste or dalit woman is doubly oppressed, and so should have a place within the quota. Characteristically, Uma Bharati does not grant a quota for Muslim women, even while conceding that they are among the most oppressed, for 'In a secular constitution, there can be no place for reservations based on religion.' This could push the country towards theocracy. She does not however, reject the idea of reservations for Muslims altogether.

Her solution is instead, to give reservations to Muslim caste-groups already included in the OBCs as outlined in the Mandal Commission Report, for example, *julahe, bunkar, ansari.* Thus, in a move which challenges BJP's nationalist Hindutva perspective, she decisively privileges caste identity over a monolithic religious community identity.[25] It is this split within the party that keeps the BJP from pushing through the Bill, rather than mere 'hypocrisy' about gender justice, as many commentators have suggested. 'Hypocrisy' is in my opinion, insufficient as an explanatory device.

Within the caste-based opposition to the Bill I would place another strand—a defence of abstract citizenship against any kind of affirmative action. That is, an anti-reservation position in general. It is significant that this position is not taken by any political party, and is expressed only by individual commentators in the media. Thus for example we have an editorial in *The Indian Express* which says that the pandemonium in Parliament over the Bill 'is a sorry vindication of this newspaper's traditional position that affirmative action is a wrong-headed idea . . . Once unleashed, it perpetuates and propagates itself in the most divisive ways . . . Is Parliament to be parcelled into lots of the historically oppressed, leaving the rest of mainstream India to its own devices?'[26] Chandan Mitra bemoans the fact that 'Already the vicious spectre of casteism has begun haunting the party system' and feared the degeneration of Parliament to a 'caste panchayats' union'. Reservations for women would lead to demands for reservations for other groups, and 'instead of moving towards the twenty-first century and age of virtual reality, we have been dragged back into medievalism'.[27]

This last anti-reservation position *opposing* the Bill is an interesting counterpoint to the final position I present—the (implicitly) *caste-based* support *for women's reservations.* These two apparently contradictory positions, one rejecting reservations *in toto* and the other supporting women's reservations while rejecting caste-based reservations, represent similar interests. It is when we examine the latter that we move more directly towards the suggestion I made earlier, that upper-caste concerns and feminist concerns happen to tie in at this historical moment on this question. This position pushes for the passing of the Bill and flatly rejects the demand for further quotas within the 33 per cent. Within this last position I would place the BJP and the Congress. While within the BJP there is considerable contestation of the official party line rejecting 'quotas within quotas', as we have seen, any debate within the Congress is muted. The party seems reconciled to the loss of its earlier dalit and Muslim base, and is pushing for the Bill in its present form.

Madhu Kishwar takes heart from the fact that the very same people who opposed the Mandal reservations for OBCs have accepted the reservations for women 'with apparent grace and enthusiasm'. For her this is further proof of the great women-friendly traditions of India.[28] As a political analyst one cannot help but note, however, that the fearsome future that Chandan Mitra and *The Indian Express* editorial outline is precisely what a blanket 33 per cent reservation for women hopes to prevent. That is, an immediate filling of 33 per cent of seats with women would certainly change the class and caste composition of Parliament back in the short term, to one more comfortable for our elites, which clearly considers itself to be 'the mainstream', as opposed to the 'historically oppressed', as the editorial quoted above unabashedly declares. As Vasanthi Raman points out, OBCs and Muslims, given their numerical strength as well as their social location, pose a greater threat to upper castes than SC/STs, about whom some complacency was still possible.[29]

Within the broad feminist camp, the suggestion of 'quotas within quotas' has received mixed responses. As Gail Omvedt points out, by now the stark antagonism between OBC and feminist leaders is easing.[30] Most women's groups accept the principle of quotas within quotas, but while some groups are prepared for a redrafting of the present Bill to include such quotas, others, like the Left groups, continue to insist that the Bill must be passed first, and further quotas can be worked out later.[31]

This survey of positions on the WRB throws into relief a set of interrelated questions about (a) 'women' as the subject of feminist politics, (b) citizenship in postcolonial democracies and (c) the idea of political representation. That is, about women and the women's movement on the one hand and women and the nation-state on the other, with representation as the category mediating both relationships.

Feminism and Citizenship

A good question to begin with here could be this: Why are 'women' acceptable to the ruling elites as a counter-measure to deal with rising backward caste presence in Parliament? Why are women and the women's movement not only *not* perceived as a threat to social order, but even as a force that can restore the control of upper castes and classes? One possible explanation could have to do with the co-optation and domestication of gender issues by the state and NGOs since the late 1980s. The emergence of autonomous women's groups at the beginning of that decade marked a new and militant, highly visible phase of the women's movement, but by the end of the 1990s, almost all of these groups were running on funding from government and international bodies. That is, these groups which began as an attempt to create spaces outside the orthodoxies of party women's wings, are now far from autonomous of the compulsions of getting and retaining funding.

Further, while the 'empowerment of women' is a slogan much in use by government agencies, it has been argued that this kind of government programme aims at empowering women only to the extent of harnessing women's contribution to 'growth'—a goal which government is under considerable external pressure to attain. Thus, drives against child marriage serve the purposes of population control. Or to take another example, the growth of grassroots women's movements centring on the disastrous impact of development policies, like the Chipko Andolan, have posed a challenge to the state. By providing space to women in the planning and implementation of government programmes, such as forest management programmes, protest movements are sought to be led into non-confrontationist channels.[32]

Writing on the increasing circulation of the term 'empowerment' in the context of World Bank-directed new economic policies in India in the 1990s, Manoranjan Mohanty argues that empowerment, particularly of women, is understood in international documents not as a goal but a prerequisite for productive investment. Terms like empowerment, civil society and democratisation, which form part of the new liberalisation discourse therefore, are not a response to the struggles that have marked Indian politics, but have been given a restricted meaning and oriented in order to 'serve the present global drive of western capitalism'. Since market development is a key feature defining the stage of development of 'civil society' in this understanding, those who are weak or unorganised, or who reject the prevailing system are excluded from 'civil society'. Thus, he concludes, 'the agenda of globalisation promotes democracy for those who can participate in the bargaining process.'[33] The growing statism and NGO-isation of the women's movement are a cause for concern in this sense.

This is a feature of which the movement is very aware. A report by six women's organisations from Delhi and Bombay, investigating the dismissal of some employees of the Rajasthan government's Women's Development Programme, came to the conclusion that the Programme, designed with the active cooperation of feminist activists, had been successful in reducing people's distrust of the state by appropriating the legitimacy garnered by the women's movement. The report urged a serious consideration of the implications of this.[34] So a harsh conclusion that we seem to be forced to confront is that as far as the ruling elites are concerned, 'women' are something they can deal with.

A more complicated reason for 'women' being acceptable while 'OBCs' are not, has to do with the way in which identities emerge in politics. Indian politics has shown often enough that class, religious, caste (or any other) identity has tended to prevail over gender identification. On issues like the Uniform Civil Code, the anti-Mandal upper-caste agitations, or in Hindu right-wing mobilisation, 'women' have tended to rally as upper/lower caste or Muslim/Hindu.[35] The women's movement has been as much attacked by dalit women for being *savarna* (upper caste) as the dalit movement has been attacked for being patriarchal, and feminists of minority communities have challenged the women's movement for being Hindu by default, in its claim to being secular.[36] Thus, by the late 1980s, the women's movement had to accept that 'women' as the subject of feminist politics, and gender justice as an issue, would have to be inflected through the lens of other identities. On the Uniform Civil Code for instance therefore, from a straightforward demand for a state-legislated Uniform Civil Code, other positions have emerged within the women's movement, which seek in different ways to support initiatives for reform within communities, or to provide alternative, differentiated legal spaces for women.

In other words, feminist politics has been coming to the difficult recognition that 'women' do not simply exist as a category that is available for feminist mobilisation—the question then remains, *who is the subject of feminist politics*? If 'women' must be located within the grid of other identities that circulate, then what a 'feminist' position would be, on questions like the Uniform Civil Code and women's reservations, is not so self-evident. For what we are talking about here is more than simply the truism that 'women have many identities'. We must go much further than saying that 'women' mobilise as upper caste/dalit and so on. Rather, we need to come to the more complex recognition that under different circumstances, and given different kinds of political mobilisation, 'people' identify and come together as 'dalits', 'Muslims', 'working class', or much less often, as 'women'. This is the difficult political fact to face—that women coming together as upper caste/dalit may not necessarily be coming together as upper caste/dalit *women*. We are forced to see the creation of 'women-as-subject' as the end or goal of feminist politics, not the starting point.

What this means in the context of the Women's Reservation Bill is that when confronted with upper-caste concerns that seem to tie in with feminist concerns at this conjuncture, the women's movement must make the moves necessary to undercut the upper-caste project—and quotas within quotas seems to offer that possibility. But this is only the minimum required of us.

We need to push the question much further. Have we taken seriously the ways in which the core operating principle of bourgeois democracy—universal suffrage—is reshaped by the principle of reservations for groups in representative institutions? And have we confronted how the very understanding of 'democracy' can take different forms over space and time? For western liberal democracies, as Anne Phillips points out, the institutionalisation of group representation seems to conflict with the historical movement of democracy away from group representation and group privilege and towards the ideal where every individual vote counts equally as one. The question of group identity in those societies has therefore been at the centre of heated debate, the most well-known form of which has been the liberal individualist/communitarian debate.[37] Will Kymlicka points out that the acceptance of group identity and group rights is usually on the understanding that they are 'a temporary measure on the way to a society where the need for special representation no longer exists'. It is assumed that ideally, society should seek to remove the oppression thereby eliminating the need for these rights.[38]

In postcolonial societies of Asia and Africa on the other hand, as Sudipta Kaviraj has argued, the fact that democracy entered be fore the notion of the individual took root means that our democracy takes very different shapes than it does in the societies of its origin.[39] As a large body of scholarship in our societies shows, liberal individualism never became the uncontested core of anti-imperialist struggles or of post-independence politics. Whether Gandhi and Ambedkar in India or African socialists like Nyerere or Nkrumah, most nationalist leaders constructed national identities, not through the idea of individual citizenship but through that of communities: caste, religious, ethnic groups. Their language of politics remained non-individualistic, although ultimately there remained a tension between two notions of the bearer of rights—the community defined in various ways and the individual—a tension we know to be reflected in the Indian Constitution.

In this context the movement for *parite* (parity) in France offers an instructive comparison. The parity movement, which emerged in the 1990s, is a demand for complete equality, that is, numerically equal representation for women and men in decision-making bodies, especially elected assemblies. However, the debates over the issue play out very differently in France. The centrality occupied by the category of the Universal in France is in stark contrast to India, where both the demand for reservations as well as the opposition to it, is posed in a way that challenges the universal abstract citizen. The demand itself introduces the difference of 'women' into the category of 'citizen' while the opposition to it poses further differences (caste/community) against that of 'women' (the 'quotas within quotas' position). But in the case of France, all arguments on the issue of parity—both feminist pro- and anti-parity positions as well as anti-feminist denunciations of parity—are largely in terms of different kinds of reassertion of the Universal. In other words, in France, parity is both demanded on the grounds that it would make the Universal more meaningful, and rejected because it threatens with fragmentation the universal unmarked citizen. In India, on the other hand as we have already seen, the opposition to the demand of reservations for women comes from a position that would *push further* the critique of the abstract unmarked citizen.

The distinctive historical trajectories of the two democracies—the one having undergone a 'classic' bourgeois democratic revolution in the eighteenth century, the other a postcolonial democracy that came into being two hundred years later—have created different sets of concerns about citizenship and representation. The next section will explore some of the questions that arise for feminist politics from such a recognition of the significance of differential 'locations', both temporal and geographical.

The Movement for Parity in France

The universalism of the French Republic is a hardy notion that has survived despite every evidence of exclusion. When 'universal suffrage' was declared in 1848 there was no written law prohibiting women from voting. So it has been possible for French history books to proclaim to this day that 'universal suffrage' was achieved when all men were allowed to vote, without property qualifications, in 1848.[40] Joan Scott argues that the granting of the vote to women in 1944 (through an ordinance) was seen as signifying the dissolution of all difference. The inclusion of women as citizens 'was a gesture of national reconciliation, ending divisions among Radicals, Socialists, Communists and Catholics . . . even between colonial subjects and their rulers, as well as between men and women. All were declared the same, and their sameness lay in their membership of the nation.'[41] So five decades later when the parity movement was launched (in 1992) with a tract authored by three women calling for equal representation for women and men in all French elected assemblies, it was met with general hostility.[42]

The point of the demand was to correct a situation where, in 1992, fewer women were elected to national public office (4.3 per cent) than in 1946, the first year they voted, when 6 per cent of the Chamber of Deputies was female. Later, in 1993, a full-page advertisement appeared in the newspaper *Le Monde* entitled 'The Manifesto of the 577 for a Parity-Democracy', signed by 289 women and 288 men (representing the total number of deputies in the National Assembly), asking that a law be voted or a constitutional amendment be brought about to ensure that as many women as men hold elected office in France. In 1996 a new manifesto was published, signed by ten women from different political parties ranging from centrist to socialist, calling for parity on electoral lists, but not making the demand for a law. Many of the problems faced by pro-parity groups centred around a decision by the Conseil Constitutionnel, which rules on whether laws passed by the legislature are constitutional. In 1982 it had struck down as unconstitutional a law passed unanimously by the

National Assembly and the Senate, stipulating that no more than 75 per cent of candidates running for office should be of the same sex. This law would have ensured that at least 25 per cent of the candidates running for office would be female. After this setback, two pro-parity strategies emerged—one targeting the Constitution since the 'quota law', as it was called, was deemed to be unconstitutional under the present one, and the other submitting to the National Assembly and the Senate a new law for parity, arguing that 'parity', unlike 'quotas', was not unconstitutional. We will look more closely at this intriguing distinction later in this section.

After intense lobbying with political parties, in 1998, a motion was submitted to vote in the National Assembly. This was an amendment of Article 3 of the Constitution which read: 'The law determines the means to ensure equal access to women and men to all elected bodies.' An overwhelming majority passed it in the National Assembly, but in 1999 the Senate turned it down and proposed instead an amendment to Article 4 that would have made political parties responsible for equal representation on electoral lists. The National Assembly voted again reaffirming that the legislature, not political parties should be responsible for parity. The Senate capitulated, but insisted on one change to the original amendment suggested—the law would 'encourage' rather than 'determine' equal access for men and women. This is the diluted form in which both houses have now passed the amendment.[43] Further, there is no enforcing machinery, and many pro-parity feminists feel that the constitutional amendment has no teeth. Eliane Viennot for example, holds that the amendment has achieved nothing, and that there should be electoral laws that will ensure that all elected bodies will be composed of 50 per cent women. Such laws would force political parties to field as many women candidates as men.[44] In the last municipal elections, the first to be held after the amendment, there has been a substantial increase in the number of women elected—from 25 per cent to 47 per cent. However, since these were only local elections, in which a substantial number of women contest as Independents, this is not being seen as an accurate indicator of the success of the parity amendment.[45]

When we look at the debates swirling around the issue, what is interesting from the Indian perspective is that at the heart of it all lie competing claims to the universal. First, let us consider the crucial distinction (referred to above) made by pro-parity feminists, between 'parity' and 'affirmative action' (or quotas). To Haase-Dubosc for instance,

> Parity is not affirmative action. It is not a series of aggregative and pragmatic measures such as quotas or 'reservation' by which women can be 'added' to political life, the way one can include a particular into the general or add it to another particular. It is about universal rights . . . [C]alling for sexual parity . . . postulates a bi-gendered universal.[46]

In this understanding, parity is a more fundamental, radical demand than merely asking for quotas. More importantly, as we saw with the second pro-parity strategy discussed earlier, it is conceded that quotas may be unconstitutional since they present a 'difference' to be accommodated, while 'parity' is presented as simply an attempt to fully realise the universal.

Anti-parity feminist Eleni Varikas on the other hand, prefers affirmative action strategies as a more limited, practical method to deal with the problem of underrepresentation of women. The amendment of the Constitution to bring about parity, Varikas feels, splits the category of 'citizen' into male and female and then homogenises the two new categories produced—it erases the power relations *among* women. Parity does not make 'women' visible, rather, in her understanding, it produces an essentialised category of 'Woman'. Thus it goes beyond challenging the non-fulfilment of the universal (which can be done by using corrective strategies to remedy the exclusion of non-whites, women and so on), and inserts a homogenised and essentialised sexual difference at the heart of citizenship.[47] This is not seen as a problem by all feminists of course—pro-parity feminist Monique Dental for instance, asserts this as precisely the significant contribution of the parity amendment. Parity recognises that the Universal is made up of two sexes, while affirmative action is an uncertain strategy, and makes women into merely another category like other categories in society. Dental pointed out that in France the term for affirmative action is 'positive *discrimination*', throwing up the spectre of American-style 'multiculturalism', which is seen as the ultimate threat to the Republic.[48]

An argument similar to that of Varikas against parity is made by Christine Delphy when she says, 'Parity wants to inscribe the duality of the human species in the Constitution; on the contrary, the philosophy of affirmative action wants to affirm the oneness (unicity) of the species and translate it into facts.'[49] Delphy argues for affirmative action projects, for according to her, 'Affirmative action is a universalist philosophy that unlike false universalism, does not *start* from the premise of equality between all human beings. It wants to *achieve* this equality.'[50] On the other hand, Francoise Gaspard considers quotas to be 'demeaning', a merely 'cosmetic' method that would prove to be an insurmountable ceiling unless pursued as part of a broader plan for equality, while parity is 'quite simply an application of the principle of equality among the people who make up the human race.'[51] Or as Janine Mossuz-Lavau put it, quotas are only 'a small part', but parity is 'perfect equality'.[52]

What is striking about this exchange is that all the arguments are set out from a universalist position to criticise the strategies they reject, whether it is 'parity' that is being rejected or 'affirmative action'.[53]

The anti-parity arguments from feminists on the Left too, can come from a universalist position. Christine Delphy, for example, argues that 'difference' expresses not only sexual but also class positions, and parity 'puts them both in the same box'. She is worried that social conflicts are 'becoming increasingly culturalised'.[54] Eleni Varikas develops a post-Marxist critique of parity on the grounds that it cannot transform the practices of power, it will only benefit privileged women, and will not bring in 'authentic' democracy.[55] This understanding replicates the long-standing tension between liberal notions of formal political rights and the socialist understanding of substantive economic and social rights. Parity is problematic, from her point of view, for two reasons—one, parity brings in the idea of a fixed self-definition, which is never settled once and for all, since identities change, and we have multiple identities. Two, parity obscures power relations among women. It is dangerous, she said, to argue that 'women have better things to bring to politics', for it essentialises an idea of the moral superiority of women.[56] This understanding seems to reject parity as an attempt to split the universal permanently, on the basis of some assumed natural difference, and Varikas believes that more limited strategies are sufficient to deal with the non-fulfilment of the universal with regard to categories that have hitherto been excluded. This is an interesting anti-essentialising move in defence of the universal.

There are other arguments that reject both parity and affirmative action on universalist grounds. Elisabeth Badinter, for example, dismisses parity as nothing more than a call for quotas. Parity claims to be positive discrimination, but discrimination can never be positive, she argues, for discrimination of any sort carries 'carries mortal implications for our secular and universalist Republic'. Once sexual difference is granted representation in the Assembly, all manner of groups will come forward to claim this right, undermining the greatest achievement of French republicanism, national integration. Joan Scott, who is sympathetic to the parity movement, points out that in this understanding, unlike race and ethnicity which are understood to resist assimilation into the republican culture, women are seen as 'already French, already integrated'—their challenge is therefore more threatening.[57]

It is clear then, as Rada Ivecovic demonstrates, that parity is both advocated and opposed in the name of universalism—the criticism of parity (accommodating difference within the universal) is that it 'breaks the rationality of the legal system'. On the other hand, 'the claim for parity is also made *in the name of a completion of universality*' (emphasis in original). However, Ivecovic believes that the former, those who oppose parity in the name of protecting universalism, are mistaken, because there is no universality that is not historically mediated.[58]

This last contention is strongly made by pro-parity feminists arguing in the name of the universal. Francoise Collin puts it this way:

> . . . we ought first to consider whether the citizenship of the individual citizen is as neutral as 'universalism' presupposes it to be, and whether to accede to representation as a human individual is not and has not always been marked by gender. It seems to me in fact that the neutrality of the citizen, which determines its potential universalism, is a decoy both in its foundation and in its actual functioning.[59]

It is universalism itself, she suggests, that ensures the 'sexualisation of power'. Parity attempts to desexualise power by extending it to both sexes, 'therefore the true universalism (not a monoversalist universalism but a pluriversalist universalism) is parity'.[60] Indeed, Janine Mossuz-Lavau sees a contradiction in the position of anti-parity feminists who resist the differentiation of the universal citizen on the basis of sex. She argues that in that case, these feminists should not see it as problematic that Parliament is almost entirely composed of men, for from the point of view of abstract citizenship, men can represent women. But even feminists who reject parity do see it as a problem, and suggest instead, some form of affirmative action to remedy the situation. Thus, according to Mossuz-Lavau, it is not possible to sustain a critique of the male domination of Parliament along with an assertion of the indispensability of abstract citizenship.[61] Eliane Viennot makes a similar point when she says that while she understands the anti-parity argument against essentialising 'man' and 'woman', nevertheless in real life people are recognised as such, even legally, as in identity cards, for example. So the difference between 'man' and 'woman' already exists in law, and is not a creation of the parity movement.[62]

Joan Scott has pointed out the paradoxical way in which notions of French national character depend on an intertwining of sexual difference and republicanism, so that a critique of one is taken as an assault on the other. Scott takes up a particular kind of anti-feminist critique of parity that valorises sexual difference and which attacks parity as influenced by 'American feminism' that supposedly destroys the 'natural' erotic difference in sexual relationships. Thus, she shows that 'The insistence that sex and sexual seductiveness are traits of French culture is tied to the belief that universalism of the abstract individual is the key to equality in the French republic.' As she demands indignantly, 'Why are French critics of feminism so eager to defend sexual difference as a social practice and so quick to denounce it as a political demand?'[63]

These pro-parity feminists argue, in opposition to critiques of parity from the universalist position, that the Universal has never been unmarked. From this point of view therefore, parity is simply an attempt to realise the true universal.

Thus, both pro-parity as well as anti-parity feminists in France bring into play different kinds of universalist arguments, while anti-parity non-feminists too, mobilise the universal to present it as being under threat. This is remarkable for us, because, as this chapter has shown, in the Indian debate on reservations for women the notion of the universal has not come into play in any significant way. Rather, different kinds of 'difference' have been posited against the identity of 'women'.[64] As I have shown, there was a point up to the 1970s when some notion of the universal did operate, in arguments such as that reservations for women would (a) open up the possibility of other groups making similar demands, thus posing a threat to national integration, and (b) run counter to the provision of equality in the Constitution. However, even at that time, not only did such arguments *not* operate in the case of caste-based reservations, but there has been a remarkable shift in the women's movement's position on reservations since the late 1980s, when the idea of the nation itself came into question. It would seem that citizenship has from the beginning been understood in a relatively non-individualist and group-differentiated way in our postcolonial context, and the decades after independence have only strengthened that trend.

Representation: The Identity-or-Ideology Dichotomy

The phenomenon of groups seeking recognition in representative bodies on the basis of ethnic, religious or gender identity has been understood by many scholars as the shift from 'ideology' (in which people are willing for their 'ideas' to be represented rather than their 'self') to 'identity' (where the representative must actually 'mirror'[65] the characteristics of the people represented.) Anne Phillips for instance, terms this the shift from a politics of ideas to a politics of presence.[66] The politics of ideas suggests 'a broadly secular understanding of politics as a matter of judgement and debate, and expects political loyalties to develop around policies rather than people'.[67] A politics of presence on the other hand, privileges the question of 'who' rather than 'what' and demands equal representation of women, ethnic minorities, and other groups that see themselves as excluded.[68]

In this section, I will problematise the very framing of the relationship between ideas/presence (or what/who) as a dichotomy. I must emphasise that I am not concerned with finding arguments to justify the legitimacy of the demand for recognition of 'identity' over 'ideology'. Such arguments that justify the need for group representation over abstract citizenship (or identity over ideology) may have relevance in the liberal democracies of the West, which have traced a different route to democracy. However, the experience of societies that came to democracy and modernity through the encounter with colonialism has been such that group identity has always been the axis upon which democratic institutions turn. So it is not necessary in our context to rehearse the arguments justifying recognition of difference.[69]

To return to the main argument of this section then, in my opinion the distinction made between presence and ideas is unsustainable. The distinction can be maintained only if we assume that 'identity' is natural, pre-political—that is, pre-ideology; that 'presence' is pre-'ideas'. However, as I have argued in an earlier section, identities are created and mobilised in and through politics, they do not pre-exist politics. When we make this argument about caste or religious identity in India it is by now generally accepted, for these are no longer seen as natural or primordial identities, but as identities that have taken their present forms over the course of certain historical developments. The huge body of writing and debate over the Uniform Civil Code bears witness to this assertion. However, when it comes to 'women', there continues to be a tendency to view the category as self-evident, when in fact the painful recognition that the women's movement has had to come to terms with is precisely that 'women' as the subject of feminist politics has to be brought into being by political practice.

It is interesting in this context to note that Anne Phillips makes only a minimalist case for 'quotas' while rejecting the idea of 'representation'. Phillips makes a limited argument for a politics of presence—since half the population is female and there is a substantial non-white presence, bodies of elected representatives should reflect this distribution. 'When the composition of decision-making assemblies is so markedly at odds with the gender and ethnic makeup of the society they represent, this is clear evidence that certain voices are being silenced or suppressed.'[70] However, she is very clear that the argument is not strengthened, is even weakened, by claims that this quota would *represent* a constituency. 'Accountability is always the other side of representation, and, in the absence of procedures for establishing what any group wants, or thinks, we cannot usefully talk of their political representation.' This is why 'we should detach the arguments, for example . . . for parity between men and women, from the arguments for representing women as a group. The case still stands whether the women "represent" women or not.'[71] From Phillips's point of view, the political views of the women entering legislatures are irrelevant, they may or may not be feminist, right-wing or socialist. The point she makes is that women's presence in legislatures is justified by their presence in the population.

The problem with this argument is that Phillips sees 'women' as a category existing in society independently of their politics, when the dilemma for feminist politics arises precisely from the fact that different political configurations produce different identities. Identity does not exist independently of ideology, or, to put it differently, 'presence' is already constituted by a number of identifications, of which gender is only one. To reiterate a point I have made earlier, there are not 'women' who may be right wing or left wing, white or black—there are people who may respond in different kinds of political mobilisation as 'white', 'left wing' or as 'women'. Phillips can see this point when it comes to race:

> In the case of Britain, for example, the all-embracing concept of 'black' people rapidly dissolved into a distinction between Asian and Afro-Caribbean communities, and then subsequently into finer distinctions . . . What in this context then counts as 'adequate' ethnic representation? Such questions can hardly be answered in isolation from politics and political mobilisations . . .

However, she uses this understanding to cast doubt on the legitimacy of demands for ethnic quotas, as opposed to 'more 'permanently' relevant categories' such as women.[72] The apparent intractability of the biological category of 'women' blinds Phillips to the implications of her own argument. If 'women' too is recognised as produced by political mobilisation, then quotas for women cannot be promoted in isolation from quotas for other marginalised groups in society.

Here her position is similar to some feminist Muslim voices in the Indian debate (individuals, not groups), which continue to make a feminist defence of women's reservations while totally rejecting the idea of other quotas within the women's quota.[73] The demand for quotas within quotas is seen as an attempt to 'divide' women into categories like Muslim and OBC.[74] The argument here is that quotas for Muslim women, for instance, will segregate them from the mainstream—surely something that can be said for reservations for women in general? Or that the demand for quotas for Muslim women is suspect because it comes from the same patriarchal quarters within the Muslim leadership that pushed for the Muslim Women's Bill.[75] But again, this argument does not stand, because one of the strongest supporters of the Women's Reservation Bill is the Hindu right-wing BJP, which was opposed to the Muslim Women's Bill for entirely communal reasons while it supports the Women's Reservation Bill to preserve upper-caste power. This is precisely the point, that 'women' have proved to be remarkably difficult to demarcate within the matrix of other identities in which they are embedded. On the question of gender-discriminatory personal laws as we know, feminist demands for a Uniform Civil Code seemed indistinguishable from the Hindu Right's programme. 'Speaking for women' has been demonstrated to arise from very different kinds of concerns. It is impossible to sustain an argument defending reservations for 'women' on the basis of an assumed shared experience while at the same time rejecting any notion of a shared experience that is 'Muslim' or 'dalit'.

Phillips of course, does not make 'shared experience' a criterion for quotas—as we saw, she considers 'presence' a sufficient condition to justify them. What she shares with the positions discussed above though, is the assumption that the *presence* of 'women' can be clearly demarcated from that of 'race', 'caste' or 'religious' identity—the belief that while these are politically produced categories, 'women' pre-exist politics.

A recent alternative proposal to the Women's Reservation Bill makes the same assumption. Since the Bill ran into such rough waters, the Election Commission proposed that all political parties should mutually agree on the percentage of seats where they will mandatorily field women candidates in parliamentary and assembly elections. Failure to do so would result in punitive action to be taken by the Election Commission, even up to derecognition.[76] Left parties have criticised this formula, but the opposition is on the grounds that this is a 'compromise formula' that will only ensure tickets for women, not guarantee their victory.[77] However, this seems to me to be the weakest argument against the proposal. The more serious objection to it should be on the grounds of the anti-democratic nature of this kind of policing by the Election Commission, a body not accountable to the people in any way. The principle of parties ensuring female representation internally has worked elsewhere, in the Nordic countries, and in the African National Congress, for example. But in these cases it has been a self-regulating move. In 1980, parties in Norway and Sweden proposed legislation that would commit all political parties to a minimum of 40 per cent women on their electoral lists, but failing the success of this bid, various parties introduced the practice unilaterally.[78] There has been no attempt to police the practice except through the sheer pressure of democratic politics.

It is one thing to say that Parliament as an institution of state should at least formally serve as a forum representing all interests and identities, but quite another to insist that political parties as part of political society, should also be modelled on the same pattern. Parties exist in a democracy precisely in order to represent sectional interests. The absurdity of this proposal, that the Election Commission should have the right to regulate the internal matters of political parties, would be immediately evident if the suggestion had been that all parties would be forced to give a percentage of their seats to dalits or upper castes, to Muslims or Hindus, or to working class people. Why does it not seem absurd when the category here is women? The suggestion can seem reasonable only if 'women' is evacuated of all political content, as if it is a neutral category that exists independently of all political considerations. And the burden of this chapter has been to show that this is most definitely not so.[79]

Gail Omvedt also supports the alternative proposal that parties should reserve a proportion of their tickets for women, which she sees as an advance on the original Women's Reservation Bill. However, she does not explicitly appear to endorse any role for the Election Commission in ensuring that parties do so. Rather, she concedes that the alternative proposal does not guarantee 33 per cent reservation, but it is nevertheless 'a move towards real empowerment—and in a way that brings about the total welfare of society.'[80] It is clear that the only 'guarantee' she assumes is that of political commitment, which gives the proposal a different shape altogether. Omvedt's rejection of the Bill and support for the alternative proposal then falls into place within the context of her general preference for mass politics over legal reform. In 1990, for example, she saw the government proposals for 30 per cent reservation for women that were then circulating, as a response to the collective challenge offered by different 'drives of women for local political power' all over India. That is, she sees legal reforms as a *consequence* of the pressure created by mass politics, not as the *precondition* for social transformation.[81] This puts her support for the proposal in a very different category from the form in which it is cast, both by the Election Commission and the Forum for Democratic Reforms.[82]

Conclusion

This final section brings us to a set of questions that is by no means amenable to easy resolution. If we accept that it is not the individual but the group, defined in whatever way, that is the basis of representation, then we need to evolve a way of leaving open the potential for any group to choose in the future to define itself as one which requires reservation in Parliament. If identities emerge in and through political mobilisation, then we need to guard against the possibility that some identities may freeze into new formations of power, thus blocking the emergence of new identities and new alignments. Cautioning against the possibility of collective rights 'overtaxing' the theory of rights 'tailored to individual persons', Habermas fears that group rights could represent 'a kind of preservation of species by administrative means':

> For to guarantee survival would necessarily rob the members of the very freedom to say yes or no if they are to appropriate and preserve their cultural heritage.[83]

Although Habermas uses this critique to limit the recognition of group rights, a debate we have already seen to be framed very differently in postcolonial societies, nevertheless this point must be taken seriously. We would however, need to take it in the opposite direction to the one taken by Habermas. That is, rather than reasserting the need as Habermas does, for 'political integration of citizens',[84] we would need to push the possibilities of continuing 'pluralisation'. Here I refer to the distinction made by William Connolly, '*pluralism* is often presented as an achievement to be protected, while the eruption of new drives to *pluralization* are often represented as perils to this achievement.'[85] If democracy remains unresponsive to the emergence of new configurations of identity, then once-emancipatory identities can entrench themselves into formations blocking further democratisation.

What kinds of transformations of democratic institutions and practices would ensure an 'ethos of critical responsiveness'? [86] Serious debate on radical alternatives is necessary. One of the suggestions doing the rounds is the advocacy of proportional representation.[87] But to conceptualise Proportional Representation in the context only of currently existing parties that would get seats in proportion to their votes, is not sufficient. We would have to think of a re-visioned system that would have room (and continue to make room) for newer kinds of political configurations—the anti-big dam movements, anti-nuclear energy movements, alternative sexualities/gay and lesbian rights movements, to name but a few. A public debate on the potential and limitations of proportional representation is certainly worthwhile, although that too would only be a beginning. We would also need to keep in mind the fact that in a globalised world, as Canadian feminist Maude Barlowe puts it, 'Power has shifted elsewhere. It has been sucked away by an elite group of global capitalists who dictate to national governments . . .' Almost every political party in Canada has affirmative action programmes to ensure women candidates. But like Barlowe, many feminists in Canada feel that when they finally got there, as in the nursery rhyme, 'the cupboard was bare'—the national government is under the control of global capital.[88]

David Scott, discussing the impasse that constitutional negotiations on ethnic politics in Sri Lanka seems to have reached, suggests a more radical reformulation of democracy. He makes a case for the need to re-examine 'the inscription of liberalism and democracy into the colonial and postcolonial state', arguing that this has created a 'whole new game of politics' of which one crucial aspect is its reliance on 'number'. In his view, modern liberal democracy is inseparable from the 'statistical principle'. Therefore,

> [t]he task rather is to find the institutional arrangements in which to embody the forms of life of historical communities and then determining what kinds of mediating frameworks can be established in which these groups can negotiate their claims. What this means in effect, is the establishment of intersecting public spaces—spaces that practice different forms of belonging, in which different self-governing practices can be cultivated, in the different languages of identity.[89]

The discussion has only begun. For now I would conclude by suggesting that if reservation politics is not to solidify into different forms of elite control over state institutions, if it is to act, as indeed it must, as merely one of the strategies in a radical politics of subversion, then the debate cannot remain limited to the quotas question.

NOTES

1. Denise Riley famously asked 'Am I that name?' referring to the label 'Woman'. *Am I That Name? Feminism and the Category of 'Women' in History*, Minneapolis, University of Minnesota Press, 1988.
2. Vina Mazumdar, 'Historical Soundings', *Seminar* 457, September 1997, p. 16.
3. 'Electoral Politics in the Time of Change. India's Third Electoral System, 1989-99', *Economic and Political Weekly*, 21–28 August 1999, pp. 2393–9 (emphasis added). Yadav concludes that from the 1989 election onwards, the electoral political arena has seen greater participation and more intense politicisation, particularly among marginal social groups. The odds that a dalit will vote are much higher today than that of an upper caste. The dominant peasant proprietor OBCs were already politicised, but now the lower OBCs are equally militant.
4. Vina Mazumdar, 'Historical Soundings', p. 15.

5. Shirin Rai and Kumud Sharma, 'Democratising the Indian Parliament: The "Reservation for Women" Debate', in Shirin Rai, ed., *International Perspectives on Gender and Development*, London, Macmillan, 2000, p. 159.
6. Translatable as 'the patriarchal forces controlling parliament'. Yogendra Yadav, 'Swarth Aur Moh ke Beech Fansa Mahila Arakshan Bill', *Dainik Bhaskar*, 26 August 2000.
7. Seema Mustafa, 'Forget Footing, Men can't even Stomach the Bill', *Asian Age*, 18 July 1998.
8. Krishna Bose, Trinamool Congress MP, in Parliament. Reported in *The Times of India*, 9 March 1999.
9. Title of article by Brinda Karat, in *People's Democracy*, 15 June 1997.
10. Shirin Rai and Kumud Sharma, 'Democratising the Indian Parliament', p. 159.
11. Ibid., pp. 159–62.
12. 'From Social Action to Political Action: Women and the 81st Amendment', *Economic and Political Weekly*, vol. 32, no. 5, 1 February 1997, p. 196.
13. Malini Bhattacharya, 'Democracy and Reservation', *Seminar* 457, September 1997, pp. 23–4.
14. *ML Update*, vol. 1, no. 9, 15 July 1998.
15. Gail Omvedt, 'Women and PR', *The Hindu*, 12 September 2000.
16. Statement of the Shetkari Mahila Aghadi, 'Reservations on Reservation', *Communalism Combat*, June 1997, p. 6.
17. Madhu Kishwar, 'Women and Politics: Beyond Quotas', *Economic and Political Weekly*, vol. 31, no. 43, 26 October 1996, p. 2867.
18. Ibid.
19. See Chapter Two for a fuller discussion.
20. Madhu Kishwar, 'Women and Politics', p. 2869.
21. P.T. Rajshekhar, 'The Voice of the Persecuted Nationalities Denied Human Rights', *Dalit Voice*, vol. 17, no. 18, 1–15 August 1999, pp. 3–5. Cited by Meena Dhanda, 'Representation for Women: Should Feminists Support Quotas?', *Economic and Political Weekly*, 12 August 2000, p. 2971.
22. Indira Hirway, 'Panchayati Raj at the Crossroads', *Economic and Political Weekly*, vol. 24, no. 29, 1989 and Utsahi Mahila Abhyudaya, in *UMA Prachar*, April–June 1996. Cited by Janaki Nair, 'An Important Springboard', *Seminar* 457, September 1997.

23. Press Conference, *The Hindu*, 28 November 1999.
24. News report in *The Times of India*, 9 March 1999.
25. Uma Bharati, 'Not a Woman's World: Case for OBC Reservation', *The Times of India*, 17 July 1998, p. 12. As told to Vidya Subramaniam.
26. Editorial, *The Indian Express*, 15 July 1998.
27. Chandan Mitra, 'Parliament as Caste Panchayats' Union', *The Pioneer*, 31 August 1997.
28. Madhu Kishwar, 'Women and Politics', p. 2867.
29. Vasanthi Raman. 'Women's Reservations and Democratisation: An Alternative Perspective', *Economic and Political Weekly*, vol. 34, no. 50, 11 December 1999, pp. 3494–5.
30. Gail Omvedt, 'Women and PR', *The Hindu*, 12 September 2000.
31. There is now recognition on the Left, although it is grudging, that caste is a reality of Indian politics, and has to be dealt with. The CPI(M)'s *Draft of Updated Party Programme* (May 2000) acknowledges that 'The assertion by dalits has a democratic content reflecting the aspirations of the most oppressed sections of society. The backward castes have also asserted their rights in a caste-ridden society.' However, this is qualified by the following: 'At the same time, a purely caste appeal which seeks to perpetuate caste divisions for the narrow aim of consolidating vote banks and detaching these downtrodden sections from the common democratic movement has also been at work' (p. 25). The Left engagement with caste is still very uneasy.
32. Anonymous, 'Women. Invisible Constituency', Commentary in *Economic and Political Weekly*, 18 May 1996, p. 1173.
33. Manoranjan Mohanty, 'On the Concept of Empowerment', *Economic and Political Weekly*, 17 June 1995, pp. 1434–6.
34. Saheli, Sabla Sangh, Action India, Disha, Women's Centre, Forum Against Oppression of Women and Awaz-e-Nizwan, *Development for Whom: A Critique of Women's Development Programmes*, 1991. For a fuller discussion of this issue, see Nivedita Menon, ed., *Gender and Politics in India*, Introduction, pp. 20–1.
35. Gabriele Dietrich, 'Women and Religious Identities in India after Ayodhya', in Kamla Bhasin, Ritu Menon and Nighat Said Khan, eds, *Against All Odds*, Delhi, Kali for Women, 1994, p. 43.
36. Flavia Agnes, 'Women's Movement within a Secular Framework: Redefining the Agenda', *Economic and Political Weekly*, vol. 29, no. 19, 1994, p. 1123; Gail Omvedt, *Violence Against Women: New Movements and New Theories in India*, Delhi, Kali for Women, 1990, p. 39.

37. Anne Phillips, 'Democracy and Difference: Some Problems for Feminist Theory', in Will Kymlicka, ed., *The Rights of Minority Cultures*, Oxford, Oxford University Press, 1995, pp. 290–3.
38. Will Kymlicka, 'Three Forms of Group-differentiated Citizenship in Canada', in Seyla Benhabib, ed., *Democracy and Difference: Contesting the Boundaries of the Political*, Princeton, Princeton University Press, 1996, p. 158.
39. Sudipta Kaviraj, 'Dilemmas of Democratic Development in India', in Adrian Leftwich, ed., *Democracy and Development*, Cambridge, Polity Press, 1996, p. 132.
40. Danielle Haase-Dubosc, 'Sexual Difference and Politics in France Today', *Feminist Studies*, vol. 25, no. 1, Spring 1999, p. 184.
41. Joan W. Scott, *Only Paradoxes to Offer*, p. 163.
42. Francoise Gaspard, Claude Servan-Schreiber and Anne Le Galle, *Au Pouvoir, Citoyennes: Liberte, Egalite, Parite*, Paris, Le Seuil, 1991. Cited in Francoise Gaspard, 'Parity—Why Not?', *Differences: A Journal of Feminist Cultural Studies* 9(2), Summer 1997.
43. This account has been taken from Danielle Haase-Dubosc, 'Sexual Difference and Politics', and from Joan Scott, 'La Querelle des Femmes', in the Late Twentieth Century', *Differences: A Journal of Feminist Cultural Studies* 9(2), Summer 1997, 70–81.
44. Interview with Eliane Viennot, 14 June 2001.
45. Interview with Sandrine Dauphin, 29 June 2001 and Monique Dental, 22 June 2001. (The interview with Monique Dental was simultaneously translated by Danielle Haase-Dubosc.)
46. Danielle Haase-Dubosc, 'Sexual Difference and Politics', p. 187.
47. Interview with Eleni Varikas, 13 June 2001.
48. Interview, 22 June 2001.
49. Christine Delphy in *Le Monde Diplomatique*, March 1997, pp. 7–8. Cited in Haase-Dubosc, 'Sexual Difference, and Politics', p. 199.
50. Cited in Haase-Dubosc, 'Sexual Difference, and Politics', p. 199.
51. Francoise Gaspard, 'Parity—Why Not?', p. 96.
52. Interview with Janine Mossuz-Lavau, 22 June 2001.
53. I also spoke to two feminists who felt that the distinction between parity and affirmative action was being drawn too sharply, and that in fact, parity *is* a form of affirmative action. Interviews with Eliane Viennot, 14 June 2001 and Sandrine Dauphin, 29 June 2001.
54. Christine Delphy in 'Parity and Universalism', translated transcript of a discussion held at Maison des Sciences Humaine, Paris. Published in

Differences: A Journal of Feminist Cultural Studies 9(2), Summer 1997, p. 131.

55. Discussion in Haase-Dubosc, 'Sexual Difference, and Politics', p. 194.
56. A pro-parity feminist Sandrine Dauphin, however, seemed to suggest that the point is not that women would bring something different to politics. Their political positions are irrelevant, what is important is that they need to be in Parliament because they are half the population. (Interview, 29 June 2001). This is also the position taken by Anne Phillips, discussed in the next section.
57. Scott discusses Badinter's position in Joan Scott, ' "La Querelle des Femmes", in the Late Twentieth Century'.
58. Rada Ivecovic, 'A Feminist Philosophical Approach to Nationalism', unpublished lecture delivered at Copenhagen University, 7 April 2000.
59. Francoise Collin in 'Parity and Universalism', p. 117.
60. Ibid., pp. 118–19.
61. Interview.
62. Interview.
63. Joan Scott, ' "La Querelle des Femmes" in the Late Twentieth Century', p. 79.
64. I found it significant that in French, the word often used in the context of recognising difference is 'stigmatisation'. The very recognition of difference in the French context has negative connotations, suggestive of being 'branded'.
65. A term used by Hanna Fenichel Pitkin in *The Concept of Representation*, Berkeley, University of California Press, 1967. Cited by Anne Phillips in 'Democracy and Difference', p. 297. Pitkin was critical of the idea of mirror representation, but Phillips develops the idea more positively.
66. Anne Phillips, *The Politics of Presence: The Political Representation of Gender, Ethnicity and Race*, Oxford, Clarendon Press, 1995. Reissued in paperback, 1998. All references to the book here are to the 1998 edition.
67. Ibid., p. 1.
68. Ibid., p. 5.
69. We may note that feminist/pro-women arguments against reservations in India do not reject identity politics as such. That is, Madhu Kishwar and the SMA, for example, or Gail Omvedt, all fully endorse the need to see women as a collectivity with shared experiences which require special strategies to be fairly represented in decision-making bodies. Their opposition to the Women's Reservation Bill is on the grounds that it is not an effective strategy. This is why Meena Dhanda's carefully argued

defence of identity politics as a counter-position to Kishwar is rather off the mark. However, Dhanda's refutation of Kishwar's consequentialist arguments against the Women's Reservation Bill is very useful. See Note 79 below.

70. Anne Phillips, 'Democracy and Difference', p. 296.
71. Ibid., pp. 296–8.
72. Anne Phillips, 'Democracy and Difference', p. 297.
73. Seema Alavi, 'Muslim Women don't Need Reservation', *The Times of India*, 15 July 1998, p. 12; Seema Mustafa, 'Forget Footing'.
74. Seema Mustafa, 'Forget Footing'.
75. Seema Alavi, 'Muslim Women'.
76. Nirmala George, 'Debate on Women's Bill is Two Years Old, It's Going Nowhere', Interview with M.S. Gill, Chief Election Commissioner, *The Indian Express*, 26 April 2000, p. 9.
77. Shahid Faridi, 'Left Criticises Gill Formula for Women's Reservation', *The Asian Age*, 25 April 2000.
78. Anne Phillips, 'Democracy and Difference', p. 296.
79. The alternate proposal to reservations in Parliament, that instead, parties should reserve a proportion of their tickets for women has a longer history. Mulayam Singh Yadav first made the suggestion in 1998 (as a self-regulating mechanism, without any role for the Election Commission) but it was not seriously considered. Then in 2000, Madhu Kishwar of *Manushi*, along with Jayaprakash Narayan of Lok Satta Hyderabad, Yogendra Yadav of the Centre for the Study of Developing Societies, Delhi and Dhirubhai Sheth of Lokayan Delhi, came out with an alternative proposal to the Women's Reservation Bill, as the Forum for Democratic Reforms. This proposal is titled 'Women's Representation in Legislatures' and is an undated publication, jointly by all four organisations/individuals. Here reservations are rejected as an effective measure, and instead, the role of the Election Commission in ensuring that parties not only give one-third of their tickets to women, but that these tickets are spread out over all constituencies, is worked out in great detail. Apart from the objection I have outlined in the text of the chapter above, to giving the Election Commission this kind of control over the political agenda of parties, there are other problems with this alternative proposal. Meena Dhanda has dealt exhaustively with the kind of argument in the proposal which envisages certain consequences of following the reservation policy. Kishwar originally laid out these supposed consequences in her article, 'Women and Politics. Beyond Quotas', cited above, and these

are outlined once again in this proposal. Dhanda, addressing the earlier article, points out that not all the relevant consequences are necessarily taken into account, and it is a matter of disputation whether some of the consequences presented as negative are indeed so. She concludes, 'Reflection on the Indian debate shows that selective emphases and different interpretations of the probable consequences of following a policy of gender quotas leads to stalemate.' See 'Representation for Women. Should Feminists Support Quotas?', pp. 2970–1.

I shall briefly lay out the other problems with this proposal —(a) Six of the fourteen points that outline the problems with the Women's Reservation Bill (pp. 3–4, points 1–5 and 9), have to do with weaknesses in the idea of the rotation of reserved constituencies. An alternative which thinks in terms of fixed reserved constituencies could perhaps be considered, rather than giving up on reservations in Parliament altogether. (b) Most of the other arguments against the Bill function on the classic assumption made by the privileged to reject reservations on principle. That is, instead of going on the assumption that it is patriarchal structures that keep women out of decision-making bodies, which is why reservations become necessary, the document makes arguments which suggest that the absence of women is because there are not enough capable candidates among them. With this underlying assumption, it becomes easy to make predictions like 'women elected in reserved constituencies will be contesting against other women only, and will lack the legitimacy . . . to prove their ability' (p. 4). Conversely, if parties can choose their female candidates, 'natural leadership' is promoted, and there will be a large pool of 'credible and serious' women candidates. As they will be elected in competition, they will have legitimacy and not be seen as 'beneficiaries of charitable measures' and will not be 'mere proxy or lightweight' (p. 5). Clearly, the assumption is that this would be the case with reservations. Such assumptions are elitist and even offensive. (c) The concern of the proposal is weighted in favour of the interests of the male candidates, rather than those of the electorate or of the women candidates. Thus, an assumption of 'resentment' against women by 'men who get pushed out of their constituencies' is one of the problems outlined, if reservations are enforced (p. 4).

80. Gail Omvedt, 'Women and PR'.
81. Gail Omvedt, *Violence against Women*, pp. 39–41.
82. See Note 79.

83. Jurgen Habermas, 'Struggles for Recognition in the Democratic Constitutional State' (translated by Shierry Weber Nicholsen), in Amy Gutman, ed., *Multiculturalism*, Princeton, Princeton University Press, 1994, p. 130.
84. Ibid., pp. 134–5.
85. William Connolly, *The Ethos of Pluralization*, Minnesota and London, University of Minnesota Press, 1995, p. xvi.
86. Ibid.
87. See Gail Omvedt, 'Women and PR'.
88. Rama Lakshmi, 'Having a Say in Policy', *The Hindu*, 15 April 2001.
89. David Scott, 'Community, Number, Ethos of Democracy', in *Refashioning Futures: Criticism After Postcoloniality*, Princeton, Princeton University Press, 1999, pp. 162, 188–9.

CHAPTER FIVE

Recovering Subversion*

In this concluding chapter I will draw out some of the main themes that have emerged in the course of this study, and try to trace their contours more fully. In the process we may be able to see more clearly the implications of the argument made here for a radical politics—that is, for the kind of political critique that seeks to bring about fundamental social transformation.

Law and Justice

It is generally assumed that law should be the institutionalised pursuit of justice, or to put it another way, that 'law ought to try to imitate justice.'[1] Thus, while it is accepted that there would be an excess of justice that cannot be captured by the law, counter-hegemonic political practices reflect the belief that the processes of the law can be forced to reflect the ideal of justice, however imperfectly, incompletely or unwillingly.

In this context, I urge instead the serious consideration of the following set of propositions:

(a) That at this historical moment law has limited capacity to pursue justice. That is, social movements may have exhausted

*This chapter emerged out of a presentation prepared for the Neelan Thiruchelvam Commemoration Conference organised by the International Centre for Ethnic Studies, Colombo, January 2000.

the emancipatory potential of law. If injustice is understood as constituted by the unequal dynamics of power, then the law can touch injustice only to the extent that power is juridically derived. However, Foucault's comment on modern forms of power is telling. He points out that while many of the juridical forms of power continue to persist, these have

> gradually been penetrated by quite new mechanisms of power that are probably irreducible to the representation of law . . . [T]hese power mechanisms are . . . those that, beginning in the eighteenth century, took charge of men's existence, men as living bodies . . . [T]he juridical system . . . is utterly incongruent with the new methods of power whose operation is not ensured by right but by technique, not by law but by normalisation, not by punishment but by control, methods that are employed on all levels and in forms that go beyond the state and its apparatus. We have been engaged for centuries in a type of society in which the juridical is increasingly incapable of coding power, of serving as its system of representation.[2]

In Foucault's understanding then, modern forms of power do not simply oppress, they produce and regulate identity. Law is an important technique by which this is achieved. Law cannot therefore, be expected to 'emancipate' in any straightforward way—legal recognition simultaneously involves regulation and normalisation of identity.

(b) That the very dynamic of the law tends towards the fixing and universalising of identity. Indeed, the emancipatory potential of the law, emerging as a tool of the bourgeois democratic revolutions in Europe, lay precisely in this dynamic. Law was the tool which fought the unequal treatment of individuals, henceforward assumed to be equal. However, 'democracy' has now been dislocated both in time and space. The central argument of this study is that today democratic aspirations are articulated in far more complex ways, particularly in postcolonial societies,[3] and are no longer simply posed in opposition to an absolutist state. Under these circumstances, the force of the law functions, not to emancipate, but to disable the ethical vision of feminism and other social movements that seek to bring about 'justice'. More starkly put, our attempts to transform power relations through the law tend rather to resediment them and to reassert dominant values.

(c) That there are serious problems in conceiving of 'justice' in a universal sense as suggested for example, by the term 'social justice'.

If, as this study seeks to establish, rights are constituted by the values derived from specific moral universes, justice can no longer be conceived of as a metanarrative, representing self-evident and universal values, although in the self-representation of 'justice', these are precisely the values it attributes to itself. Today however, in the era of late capitalism, multiple visions of justice have come to coexist, all laying claim to universality. In other words, there is a distinct lack of identification between the multivalence of 'justice' and the force of law that must tend towards eradicating multiplicity.

I should emphasise that I am aware that the legal campaign as a strategy has thrown up many doubts and questions and such campaigns have not been resorted to in an unthinking manner. In fact, as I have emphasised at other places in this study, the questions raised here spring precisely from two decades of feminist legal campaigns and the growing unease within the movement about the consequences of engaging with the law. For instance, Nandita Gandhi and Nandita Shah hold that no part of the women's movement is under any illusions that the law is a genuinely transformative instrument. At most, women's groups see legal reform as a broad strategy to achieve legitimacy and social recognition, and some short-term legal redress. Most women's groups, they feel, would agree with the group Pennuramai Iyakkam of Tamil Nadu, which says, 'Laws are basically against women but there should be a struggle to amend them because we believe that women should be involved in all decision-making processes and at all levels, in their homes, neighbourhoods and at the national level.'[4]

The introductory chapter outlined the main lines of criticism of the legal strategy from within the movement as (a) that the law is not enough, it can only be part of a wider struggle; (b) that more legislation often means only increasing state control; and (c) that legal reform offers no challenge to the social and systemic basis of the oppression of women.

And yet, in Gandhi and Shah's words, 'Why is it that every campaign in the movement has demanded legal reforms despite its severe criticism of the legal system, the hopelessness of achieving legal redress, and the endless squabbles with law makers and implementers?'[5] Gandhi and Shah themselves conclude their discussion of the disillusionment of women's groups with the law by suggesting that 'a special and specific set of laws which recognise the secondary status of women, the unequal relations between men and women and the strength of the overriding patriarchal ideology in society, will grant a distinctive status to women . . .' They envisage something along the lines of the separate labour laws and courts.[6] However, the experience of labour laws has been far from encouraging. What can lead us to expect 'a special set of laws' to 'recognise overriding patriarchal ideologies' or to 'eliminate the conditions that breed violence' against women? So powerful is the hold on our imaginations of the perception of the law as an instrument of transformation that every critique seems to land back on its terrain.

This study suggests that we need to recognise that we (feminists as well as other social movements) may have reached the limits of the emancipatory potential of the language of rights which gives us an entry point into the realm of law. As we have seen in the case of the issues of abortion and sexual violence, law may no longer offer us even the short-term legal redress which Gandhi and Shah hold is all that most women's groups expect. On the contrary, the functioning of legal discourse tends to subvert the ethical impulse of subordinate groups, and to reassert dominant values. This is because, I argue, the 'rights' on the basis of which we claim legal action are informed by moral and ethical values which are specific to our particular worldview. Rights are not inherent in human beings, they are not natural and universal, but are constituted by different kinds of political practice. Law, on the other hand, is a realm in which diverse conceptions of rights compete, and since the law seeks uniformity and concrete identities, it tends to flatten all ambiguity and multiplicity to fit dominant norms.

It was in recognition of the ways in which legal discourse hijacks feminist politics that a feminist legal activist said that she would rather lose a rape case if in the process the right kind of debate were made possible.[7] But are these two eventualities compatible with each other? If the case were conducted in such a way that the 'right' issues were raised from a feminist perspective, but conviction was not secured, that is, if the feminist argument lost the case, would it not 'prove' to society that these values are not 'right' but 'wrong'? The overwhelming legitimacy accorded to legal discourse makes it impossible to engage with it except on its own terms.

Democracy and Radical Politics

At this point I would like to lead the discussion to a related paradox of our times—the emerging *contradiction* between the functioning of democracy and the ethical ambitions of feminist politics. We have already had a sense of this contradiction in our discussion in earlier chapters, in the debate over women's decision to abort female foetuses, over election-versus-nomination of sexual harassment committees, and in the debate over reservations for women. In each of these cases, the issue is of democratic functioning versus a greater value in our terms. In each case 'we' take the side of state regulation or regulation by authority over 'freedom to choose'. I suggest that the reason why we tend to turn to the law so insistently is precisely because democracy, with its assumption of the rights-bearing citizen endowed with 'free will', poses a problem for us until the values we hold to be crucial are hegemonic in society. Until then, the state and law are expected to override democracy and bring about social transformation from above.

I will expand on this assertion in what follows, by examining the circulation of the notion of 'free will': in three issues—abortion, sati and religious conversions—in order to illustrate the paradox as it emerges from the central argument made in this book.

Simply put, the problem that democracy poses for 'our' kind of politics—feminist, secular, or any other—is that what 'we' consider to be the correct values are not hegemonic in society. The functioning of democracy therefore can produce results that are opposed to our ethical vision. This contradiction revolves around the notion of the autonomous rights-bearing citizen who embodies 'free will'—the subject of a democratic constitution. Constitutions must assume a subject who is rational and freely choosing—precisely in this recognition lies the democratic potential of constitutionalism. This subject could be the individual or, in postcolonial nation-states, also the community. Given the trajectories followed by our histories of colonialism, constitutions in societies such as ours attempt to maintain the delicate balance between liberal expectations of individual rights and the particular space that communities have come to occupy in our polities. Whatever the balance struck, the very premise of constitutionalism is that of autonomy, the possibility of agency. Within this framework, the role of the state and the law is central in ensuring that individual and community can exercise the optimum autonomy compatible with social stability and social justice.

However, when we turn to feminist/Left/secular politics, we are faced with a subject who is yet to be made into an autonomous agent. The objective of this kind of politics is precisely to uncover the ways in which agency is both constituted and subverted by existing structures of power, to disclose the autonomous subject obscured by ideological, cultural and economic practices. From this perspective, its subject (the peasant, the worker, the woman) is affected by various oppressive practices in such a way that when she acts, she does not in fact, exercise her autonomy or free will. This is so in two senses. At one, more obvious, level, free will is actively *constrained* by coercion. At another, more subtle level, what appears to be free will is *produced* by the operation of structures of power that hegemonise notions of right and wrong, of common sense, and of permissible solidarities. A typical statement addressing this complex location is the following: 'Women's positioning in the social moment of sexual harassment is . . . contradictory. While imbued with agency and the capacity for creative responses, we are also constrained by cultural discourses of gender which frame our very desire.'[8] In other words, we are both free and unfree simultaneously. The task of feminist politics then, is both to enable the subject to act—to exercise that will constrained by power structures—as well as to demonstrate that the will is truly free only when the structures that 'frame our desire' are exposed and dismantled. In other words, the final objective of feminist politics is the freely acting subject, but the present subject of such politics is produced by oppressive power relations, so that even when she apparently acts freely, she is in fact constrained, because she is constituted by power.[9]

The crucial factor which 'our' kind of politics assumes that legal discourse cannot, is the operation of hegemony. The law has no space to conceive of hegemony, which I here understand in the Gramscian sense as the production of common sense by oppressive structures of power. As a result of this incommensurability, when these two discourses—law and radical politics—intersect, a Self is generated which seems unsustainable in either discourse, unless we frame the questions that might generate new spaces. It seems to me that while we do encounter the contradiction often enough, particularly when we attempt to engage directly with the law to change social practices that we perceive to be oppressive, we have not fully confronted the implications.

Take for instance, the dilemma discussed in the chapter on abortion—that as feminists we must attribute 'free will' to women choosing to terminate a pregnancy, but not to women who choose specifically to abort a female foetus. I suggest that what we are doing here is functioning on the assumption that the subject of our politics is *already* feminist. We assume that no woman would of her own will selectively abort a female foetus, but that in all other cases, women who take the decision to abort are choosing to exercise their right to control their bodily integrity. The contradiction here is between two notions of 'unfreedom'. One, the notion of a will *constrained* by power and two, that of a will *produced* by power. The recognition of the latter aspect of 'unfree' will is central to feminist politics, for it must assume that those subjects of our politics who do not recognise their own interests and act in ways that further oppress themselves, are not really free. The operation of hegemony works to make them imagine that they are freely choosing options which go to reinforce their oppression. However, the impasse arises precisely from the fact that while the constrained will can be *freed* by constitutional practices, the will produced by the operation of hegemony can only be *affirmed* by constitutionalism and the law. In other words, as long as no coercion of a visible and explicit kind can be established, the operation of legal discourse will, indeed must, affirm an action as freely taken.

This realisation arises equally strongly in the second instance we will examine, the case of a woman, Charan Shah, burning herself on her husband's funeral pyre in a village in Uttar Pradesh.[10] Four days after the incident took place, a fact-finding team sent by the local unit of the All India Democratic Women's Association (AIDWA)[11] concluded that Charan Shah had committed 'suicide', and that it had not been 'sati'. The distinction was made in order to establish that the AIDWA team had found no evidence of force used to make Charan Shah mount her husband's pyre in a ritual act of sati. This verdict was unacceptable to some feminist groups in Delhi, who questioned the distinction between suicide and sati, arguing that it was invidious to open up the possibility of sati being accepted as 'voluntary'. As an influential article written earlier by Kumkum Sangari and Sudesh Vaid puts it, 'the specific nature of the "volition" must be ascertained according to the particular exigencies of each case and should be seen in relation to determining social, cultural and religious factors existing in the region.'[12] This means that the family cannot escape responsibility for not preventing the act even if it was 'voluntary'. This position was put even more sharply by an angry feminist activist in Jaipur interviewed on television at the time of an earlier incident of sati, that of Roop Kanwar in 1987. She said that in a situation where women have absolutely no choice in how they are to live their lives, when and if they are to marry or whom they will marry (Roop Kanwar's husband had been an ailing man very much older to her), how is it that their freedom of choice is respected so absolutely only when they want to kill themselves?

The same troubled notion of free will arose in the case of Charan Shah. A second fact-finding team of women's groups from Delhi urged in their statement that whether or not the use of force could be established, the incident should not be 'relegated to mere suicide'. In any case, the statement continued, 'it is our conviction that force is not merely direct physical force, but also collective pressure in other forms, and religious beliefs and ideologies that legitimise such practices as widow immolation.'[13]

It is evident that this document and the report that accompanies it are aware that so long after the event, it was impossible to prove the use of physical force. As the report that accompanies the statement puts it, 'what needs discussion is whether anyone will be able to sift out the truth after the event. The logic of the eye-witness accounts, the need for miracles and of attributing the power of sati to the woman, creates its own narrative that permeates the entire chain of events to make it difficult to separate fact from fiction.'[14] The final statement is as follows, 'Events such as this must be condemned. The manner in which reactionary patriarchal values combine with the desire to commercialise religion, and strengthen orthodox notions of womanhood make this a particularly dangerous trend.'[15]

What feminists are grappling with here is of course precisely the circumscription of 'free will' by the operation of hegemonic patriarchal values.[16] However, can this kind of oppression involved in fashioning the will of people to the needs of existing structures of power, can this process of 'manufacturing consent',[17] actually be captured in the language of the law? Of course religious practices are in the main, misogynist and oppressive of women and the powerless. Of course patriarchy operates to deny subjecthood to women. But what I am arguing is that we can capture only one aspect of the unfree will through constitutionalism—that is, the *suppression of autonomy.* The other aspect of unfreedom, the *production of oppression* as natural, fulfilling, and so on, escapes constitutional and legal logic. When we try to address this second aspect through the language of constitutionalism, we are in effect, mobilising the coercive force of the state to *prevent* the operation of free will—a free will operating in a manner we believe to be antithetical to our vision. Thus, unless we retain the limited notion of a technically free, juridical 'free will' when we work within legal discourse, we could be subverting the very essence of democracy.

It seems to me that we may not have confronted adequately the dangerous implications of bringing into the arena of the law, the idea that when people act without apparently being 'forced', they may still be acting against their best interests. Such an interpretation of unfreedom, once introduced into legal discourse, will not remain in our control. Diverse worldviews, diverse notions of rights and entitlements, converge in that sphere. We can expect political forces opposed to a radical transformative vision to interpret counter-hegemonic practices as constraining free will. At an everyday level we are familiar with accusations that 'outsiders'—feminists (or communists, or dalit activists)—are disruptive of happy, well-functioning families, factories, villages, that they seek to 'brainwash' (and control the will of) otherwise contented women/workers/lower castes. Such an understanding when translated into the language of the law acquires a power we cannot underestimate.

This is not simply a hypothetical situation conjured up to strengthen an argument. Here we come to the third issue this section will address, that of religious conversions. The Hindu right has for some time now been raising the question of conversions, alleging that 'forcible' conversions to Christianity are taking place, particularly in tribal areas. The 1996 Election Manifesto of the Bharatiya Janta Party (currently the leading party in the coalition government) wanted to make punishable by law, all 'fraudulent conversions, including those done by holding out the promise of economic and social benefits,' and to introduce 'a system of registering all conversions'.[18] Over the last few years, front organisations of this political formation have carried out physical attacks on Christians all over the country, and on missionaries in particular, leading to several deaths; churches and schools have been burnt down, and there has been a relentless campaign against missionaries as foreign-funded. Again, as with the discussion on sati, I cannot go into all the dimensions of this issue and the debates raging around it. I will focus only on the notion of 'free will' that emerges from the anti-conversion arguments of the Hindu right.

The BJP manifesto quoted above makes it clear that from their perspective the promise of social and economic benefits constitutes 'fraudulent' conversion. What is meant here is that 'innocent' tribals and lower castes are being induced to leave their religion because of the conditions in which they live. They are being attracted by the possibility that their children can go to school, that they can live with dignity. The understanding of 'fraudulent' in anti-conversion arguments assumes precisely the notion of agency that we have seen operating in our own understanding in other contexts, namely, that what appears to be 'free' will is in fact produced by a set of external factors exercising control over decisions. At this point it is instructive to go back to the debates on conversion in the Constituent Assembly—one is struck by the feeling that the arguments at that time were not resolved but merely frozen by the flick of a switch when the Constitution came into effect. Today, after decades, they appear to have been animated at exactly the same point, and to follow the same trajectories.

The Interim Report on Fundamental Rights contained a clause which was intensely debated: 'Conversion from one religion to another brought about by coercion or undue influence shall not be recognised by law.'[19] K.M. Munshi moved an amendment to this clause which would include in it first, conversion of minors below eighteen years of age but more significantly from our point of view, he wanted to include the word 'fraud'.[20] From the deeply fraught debate that followed, I will pick up briefly only the threads that concern us in the development of the argument I am making, although it is tempting to track it fully to reveal the amazing resonances with fears and anxieties being expressed publicly today.

A speaker, P.R. Thakur, identifying himself as a member of the Depressed Classes argued that 'fraud' should cover circumstances in which 'preachers of other religions approach these classes of people, take advantage of their ignorance, extend all sorts of temptations and ultimately convert them.'[21] Algu Rai Shastri too, supported the amendment moved by Munshi, saying that conversions often happened out of 'greed', 'temptation and allurement', or inducement of 'prospects of financial gain'.[22]

On the question of minors, Purushottam Das Tandon, Ramnath Goenka and Algu Rai Shastri argued that children below eighteen should not be considered capable of taking such a serious decision, nor should the decision be taken on their behalf by families. On this, Rev. J.J.M. Nichols-Roy and Rev. Jerome D'Souza (the latter regretting that the discussion should suggest that this was almost exclusively a minority problem) urged that for the preservation of family life and the authority of the father, minor children of a family that changed its religion would have to convert too. In addition, Nichols-Roy argued that conscience and spiritual understanding existed in the youngest of children, and must be respected.[23] In other words, 'free will' here is being attributed both to individuals as well as to the family as a 'unit'.

On the other hand, in a later letter written by Maulana Azad as Education Minister to Cardinal Gracias, Azad explicitly denies agency to 'large groups of people' in the context of mass conversions. 'On most occasions, such groups are composed of people who have no education, people who are singularly incapable of making up their minds on issues that inform a matter as serious as religious belief.'[24] His argument here is not dissimilar to that of radical critics of dominant structures of power—even when it appears that people are acting freely, their action is in fact constrained by lack of information and of real autonomy.

I have merely touched on selected parts of the debate on conversions in the 1940s and 1950s in the context of my argument that the conception of 'free will' and its 'unfreedom' circulates in similar ways in many—otherwise mutually opposed—discourses. In the context of conversions, it is quite clear that the task of democratic politics is to protect the notion of a juridical free will so that the right to proselytise and to convert is preserved, whatever our critique of religious patriarchies may be. The closure of such an option would in essence, freeze identity at birth. For a constitution to forbid citizens the option of assuming a legal persona other than that conferred on them by accident of birth, is fundamentally undemocratic.

This particular issue outlines most starkly how problematic it is to invoke the self produced by the operation of hegemony within the limits set by the law. It is not only 'we' who can invoke that self. I am suggesting that we have to give up on the belief that we can address the operation of hegemony in the language of legal discourse. We need to look to other kinds of political practice to develop the idiom that we need in order to address the production of the myth of free will. That is, in order to produce counter-hegemonic values, we need the kind of political practice that I have termed here 'radical politics': long-term struggles to reclaim meaning at the level of common sense, work within communities to challenge local structures of power, the building up of alternative structures in opposition to the family and other hegemonising institutions. This kind of practice would have to work in tandem with other kinds of transformative strategies, including the law, but the latter is not the appropriate arena to address the second, and more crucial aspect of the unfree will that we have discussed. It is necessary therefore, that within the constraints posed by liberal democracies, radical politics retains the limited notion of 'free will' when it comes to the law, and that we struggle elsewhere to combat hegemonised productions of the self.

Civil Society *versus* Political Society

I find suggestive here the distinction that Partha Chatterjee makes between civil society and political society in postcolonial democracies.[25] 'Civil society' according to Chatterjee is constituted by the institutions of modern associational life, and is marked by *modernity*, while 'political society' is a domain of mediating institutions between civil society and state, and is the sphere of *democracy*. There is a contradiction between 'modernity' and 'democracy' in his terms; what characterises non-western modernity (that which marks postcolonial societies) is precisely the hiatus between the two, that is, between civil society, composed of a small section of 'citizens', and political society, composed of 'population'. Population groups, unlike citizens, are not the product of rational contractual association, but rather, are the target of the 'policy' of the legal bureaucratic apparatus of the state. The civil society of citizens, on the other hand, shaped by the normative ideals of western modernity, excludes the vast mass of the population, towards which it assumes a 'pedagogical mission' of enlightenment.[26] Political society—parties, movements, non-party political formations—channellises popular demands on the state through a form of mobilisation we call democracy. 'The point is that the practices that activate the forms and methods of mobilisation and participation in political society are not always consistent with the principles of association in civil society.'[27] Democratic aspirations in other words, often violate institutional norms of liberal civil society. However, precisely *because* this is so, if we accept this understanding, then it is clear that the struggle to reclaim and produce meaning will have to be waged in this uncomfortable realm, that of political society.

In reading 'political society' in this way, I unhitch Chatterjee's notion of 'political society' from its link in his argument to the 'welfare' function of government, and relocate it as the realm of struggles to produce an alternative common sense—alternative that is, to the common sense of civil society. It seems to me that the kind of political practice with the capacity to challenge the hegemonised will—*radical politics* in short—can be carried out only in political society understood in this sense, not in civil society, the domain of constitutionalism.

Of course, the problem with 'political society' understood in this way is that the activities here would not necessarily conform to our understanding of what is 'progressive' or 'emancipatory'. They could be struggles of squatters on government land to claim residence rights (which would include illegally tapping electricity lines, for example), but they could as easily be the effort of a religious sect to preserve the corpse of their leader in the belief of its resurrection[28] or the decision of a village panchayat to kill a woman accused of adultery. The point is that any project of radical democratic transformation would have to engage and collide with the ideas, beliefs and practices in *this* sphere. It cannot remain in the rarefied realms of 'civil society' where in fact both the struggles of the 'unauthorised' squatters as well as those of the religious sects would be dismissed as uncivilised. From the point of view of constitutional norms, the large grey realm of survival strategies of the urban poor can only be dismissed as simply 'illegal'.

It is from the point of view of 'civil society' that it seems necessary and 'progressive' to dislocate labouring communities not only for development projects, but also paradoxically, to mitigate the long-term ecological consequences of unbridled capitalist development. The creation of National Parks, for example, for the protection of forests and wildlife, treats forest communities living there for centuries rather than the depredations of contractors in wood and encroaching urbanisation, as responsible for the destruction of forest cover. The boundaries of these Parks administered by government therefore treat them as trespassers and they are dispossessed from their lives and livelihoods.[29] Similarly, the continuous process of dispossessing the urban poor in order to build the modern city is impeccably couched in the language of rights and has increasingly, since the 1990s, been initiated by the courts. The spate of judgements by the 'Green' bench of the Supreme Court through the 1990s ordering the closure of 'polluting' industries have simply thrown out of work without any attempt to rehabilitate, thousands of workers, some of whom have been in secure employment for over three decades. When there were mass protests over the court orders, the Supreme Court justified its decision by asserting that 'health is more important than livelihoods.'[30] Does this not boil down to health in civil society versus livelihoods in political society? These kind of moves are attempts by 'civil society' to transform India in the image of a 'developed' country, and within this framework, the values that are cited are the right of 'citizens'—defined generally, but in practice, delimited strictly—to clean air and protection of the environment. The lives and practices of the labouring poor cannot but fail the tests of legality and constitutionality set by civil society.

The point is that there is nothing inherently 'progressive' in the realm of 'civil society' or in the language of rights. Feminist politics then, will have to surrender its reliance on the certainties offered by civil society, and acknowledge the uncertainties and unpredictability of attempts to wage a struggle in political society.

The Institutionalisation of Feminism

What does this mean for feminist practice? Perhaps we must try to recover what was truly 'political' about feminism, its potential to subvert, to destabilise, not just dominant values and structures, but ourselves.

In many ways, an institutionalisation of feminism has taken place over the last decade in India. In the 1980s what came to be called 'autonomous' women's groups came into being in many cities, in order to address patriarchy more directly than was possible within large party structures. These groups were responsible for the foregrounding of issues around sexual violence and the family through the 1980s. From the 1990s however, most of such groups were transformed into NGOs, that is, they started receiving funding from government and/or foreign funding agencies. Very few of the autonomous women's groups of the 1980s remain non-funded. Thus, feminism need not be a political practice any longer, it can be a profession. There is considerable debate within the movement on the issue of funding, often acrimonious, but the danger is usually seen to be that of co-optation. While this is certainly a possibility, it is one most groups are quite conscious of and try to deal with. The greater harm that has resulted is what I call the professionalisation of feminism. The positive fallout of professionalisation is that many committed and political women are enabled to make a living being full-time activists. But as feminists themselves are aware, freely available funds also attract people with no great political commitment, for whom feminism is an often temporary profession.[31] However, the implications of 'professionalisation' are deeper than simply that some activists have no clear feminist perspective. The compulsions of taking up and 'successfully' completing specific projects has meant that there is hardly any fresh thinking on what constitutes 'feminism'. We no longer seem to think it necessary to challenge our own notions of 'self' and 'identity'. It is as if we know what 'feminism' is, and only need to apply it unproblematically to specific instances. Thus, autonomous women's groups, which began in the 1980s as an attempt to construct a creative space outside the orthodoxies of party women's wings, appear increasingly to lack autonomy from the compulsions of getting and retaining funding.

Moreover, the very character of what can be called 'the women's movement' is affected by this transformation. Although non-funded grassroots political organisations of women continue to be active, many important legal initiatives are unilaterally taken by individual NGOs (often consisting only of one or two feminists and a paid support staff with no political orientation), supposedly representing the women's movement. For instance, the Vishakha judgement of the Supreme Court was brought about primarily by the intervention of the NGO Sakshi. While the judgement has been generally welcomed by other women's groups, it did not come about as a result of prior discussions within the movement. Similarly, the current controversial draft Bill on sexual violence discussed in Chapter Three has been submitted to the Law Commission of India (LCI) by three individuals, two from NGOs and one from a non-funded political organisation. The published version of the draft Bill acknowledges three funders, The MacArthur Foundation, Ford Foundation and UNIFEM 'for supporting the printing' of the document.[32] Other women's groups which have serious problems with many of the core provisions of the Bill have now to deal with the LCI directly, since the three individuals in whose names the report has been submitted consider the ball to be now in the LCI's court. The NGO-isation of the women's movement thus has the potential to break up the movement into separate groups with their own organisational, funder-driven, agendas.

It should be clear, I hope, that the critique I offer here of funded politics is quite different from the attack on NGOs that we have seen since the late 1990s in India, Pakistan and Bangladesh on the grounds that such organisations are foreign-funded and anti-national, and that by raising questions about the oppression of women they are fulfilling a 'Western' agenda of dividing the country. On the contrary, I am pointing rather, to the ways in which the original political thrust of autonomous women's organisations has been blunted by what I have called 'professionalisation'—that is, by corporatisation and careerism promoted by the availability of easy funding for 'gender issues' and more recently for 'sexuality' because of the AIDS scare. I do not share therefore, the understanding of Raka Ray that with 'the quickening pace of India's economic liberalisation and India's increased openness to the world economy', the increase in the money available to NGOs and decrease in state regulation will create 'resource-rich NGOs' that 'can create an alternative political culture, one that will perhaps offer more space for a diversity of interests and voices.'[33] Ray makes this prognosis in the context of Calcutta and the control that the Communist Party of India (Marxist) exercises in the state. While I agree that the CPI(M)'s overwhelming presence in West Bengal inhibits feminist initiatives, I do not think that an effective alternative can be posed by funded organisations alone. Such an alternative can only come from political initiatives that are not driven by the compulsions of funding.

Gandhi and Shah, discussing alternatives to formal legal systems, mention that some women's groups have set up people's courts. They caution, however, that these are effective only where there are strong movements.[34] Is it possible that our tendency to turn to the law to deal with every new instance of devaluation and oppression of women in the realm of 'the body' and sexuality is precisely an indication of the lack of a 'strong movement' in this area?

Legal campaigns are usually understood to have succeeded at least in this, that they put 'private' issues on the public agenda. However, our discussion in this study seems to indicate that 'making public' in the sense of demanding legislative action not only has not achieved the purpose of ending or controlling social practices inimical to women, but rather, have tended to reinforce existing stereotypes and beliefs.

Human Rights and International Norms

A further level of complexity attends the process of treating human rights as universal norms that are to be globally institutionalised by international intervention. A significant instance is the campaign to include gender within the notion of Human Rights as it is understood in international forums. Take for example, the following statement: 'The state already has devoted vast resources to the maintenance of injustice in the private sphere; the state must be pressured to mobilise these resources to more productive ends.' This pressure is to be brought to bear by 'international consensus and backing.'[35] Another similar statement is, 'Nation states should enforce or create new measures to prevent and respond to gender-specific violence in both public and private spheres, including affirmative measures to eliminate the conditions that breed this violence.'[36]

The reformulation of 'rights' as 'capabilities', as in Martha Nussbaum's work, still requires that nations which adopt the list of human capabilities she provides, should 'commend this norm strongly to other nations' using whenever necessary, 'economic and other strategies to secure compliance'.[37]

Surely we can no longer be innocent of the implications of 'international consensus and pressure' in the context of the prevailing global balance of power? International pressure in the present context can only mean pressure on the states of the South by those of the North, particularly the USA, which now dominates—even controls—the United Nations. 'Human Rights' is increasingly being used as a lever to pressurise the South to accept structural adjustment programmes and trade practices which in the long run will impoverish and disempower the weakest groups in these societies, including women. Feminists cannot in such a context, unproblematically call for 'international' pressure to protect the rights of women.

Thus I do not find useful Habermas's conception of world citizenship which, while posed in opposition to the agenda of the USA—'enforcing the global implementation of human rights as part of the national mission of a world super-power'—affirms instead a European vision of 'enforcement of a politics of human rights . . . aimed at establishing the rule of law in international relations.'[38] From our location in what used to be called the Third World, Europe does not seem to occupy so distinctly different a position from the USA in an unequally structured global economy. In such an economy, 'world citizenship' can only mask the extreme exploitation by transnational capital, of race, geographical and class location.

In a significant paper suggesting that the international human rights movement may be 'part of the problem', David Kennedy writes,

> There is no question that the international human rights movement has done a great deal of good, freeing individuals from great harm, providing an emancipatory vocabulary . . . raising the standards by which governments judge one another, and by which they are judged, both by their own people and by the elites we refer to collectively as the 'international community'.

He adds tongue-in-cheek, 'A career in the human rights movement has provided thousands of professionals, many of them lawyers, with a sense of dignity and the confidence that one can sometimes do well while doing good.'[39] Having made this caveat, he then goes on to compile what he terms 'a short list of pragmatic worries and polemical charges.' The list is fairly extensive and covers most of the critiques that have been made by a variety of sources, but I would like to mention a few of the most sharply posed charges.[40]

One is that human rights 'occupies the field of emancipatory possibility'. The claim here is that the hegemony that human rights discourses wield, makes other, often more valuable emancipatory strategies, less available. There may be something to the claim, Kennedy suggests, that human rights has 'so dominated the imaginative space of emancipation that alternatives can now only be thought, perhaps unhelpfully, as negations of what human rights asserts—passion to its reason, local to its global, etc.' Further, to the extent that emancipatory projects must be expressed in the vocabulary of rights to be heard, good policies which are not framed in that way go unattended.

Some of the other charges that Kennedy discusses are that:

(a) human rights discourses strengthen the state, and end up equating the state with the structure of freedom—so that it seems that 'to be free is . . . to have an appropriately organised state';
(b) human rights expresses the ideology and political practice of Western eighteenth–twentieth-century liberalism, but disguised as a universal value;
(c) The human rights vocabulary promises Western constituencies a politics-neutral and universalist mode of intervention elsewhere in the world. This leads these constituencies to 'unwarranted innocence about the range of their ongoing interventions and unwarranted faith in the neutral nature of a human rights presence';
(d) The human rights bureaucracy is itself part of the problem.

> Kennedy argues that professionalisation of the human rights movement has meant a kind of depoliticisation, the sudden emergence of 'an elaborate presence pulling local elites away from their base, or consigning them to the status of local informants, attention turning like sunflowers to Geneva, New York, to the Center, to the Commission. To the work of resolutions and reports.' And away from political practice on the ground?

Kennedy's succinct presentation captures the suspicion in some quarters towards universal discourses of human rights today, but I do not share his faith that a more open conversation may lead to changes. Rather, I would reiterate here that human rights discourses may have reached their limits at this historical moment.

At the same time, it is important to recognise that the space that a feminist politics has to work out for itself, while moving beyond the 'global', cannot return to the space of the 'national'. It is certainly not my intention to endorse the traditionalist, nationalist, anti-West critiques of human rights offered for instance, by the authoritarian regimes of Singapore, Malaysia, Taiwan and China in the Bangkok declaration of 1993.[41] The objection made there to the individualistic character of human rights is merely a strategic attempt to legitimise authoritarian regimes. Rather, I would draw our attention to the kinds of critiques that insist that today we are dealing with *different forms of modernity.* Partha Chatterjee, for example, points out that it is in the context of the latest phase of globalisation of capital, that a transnational public sphere has emerged whose moral claims proceed from the assumption of the existence of a universal civil society. Chatterjee includes in this domain 'many United Nations agencies, non-governmental organisations, peace-keeping missions, human rights groups, women's organisations.'[42] These act as an external check on the sovereign powers of the nation-state, 'assessing the incomplete modernity of particular national political formations.' This framework of global modernity can only structure the world in 'a pattern that is profoundly colonial.' The framework of democracy, (located in Chatterjee's 'political society', as we have seen) on the other hand, will 'pronounce modernity itself as inappropriate and deeply flawed.' [43] However, the domain of political society cannot simply be understood to be 'traditional' as opposed to the 'modernity' of civil society. Both together occupy a space that embodies a different modernity—'our' modernity.[44] 'Our' modernity is marked by the fact that modernity here, was encountered through colonialism. While modernity was equally disruptive in Europe, the way these other societies entered into modernity involved a double violence—that of an alien structure of power, embodying in addition to the disruption of modernity itself, the violence of imperialism. There is a specificity to the relationship to modernity in such societies.

The point about historically specific relationships to modernity is what Habermas misses when, in 'the apologetic role of a Western participant in a cross-cultural discussion of human rights', he proffers the 'working hypothesis' that 'standards of human rights stem less from the particular cultural background of Western civilisation than from the attempt to answer specific challenges posed by a social modernity that has in the meantime covered the globe.'[45] It is true that modernity has covered the globe, but this modernity has not simply been replicated uniformly from seventeenth-century Europe and nor has its spread been free of coercion. It has worked within and been transformed (distorted, it might seem to Habermas) by specific socio-political, cultural and economic conditions. Habermas is unable to see that when he identifies the 'individualism and secular character of human rights that are centered in the concept of autonomy' as the core of the controversy, this character cannot be simply assumed to be culture-free and simply 'modern'.[46] Indeed it is deeply marked by the Western conception—or at least the hegemonic, dominant conception in the West—of modernity.

This notion of individuals recognised and valued as separate persons is itself a modern conception available to the Judaeo-Christian tradition; this is certainly not an intuitive or easy assumption for a Hindu or Buddhist to make. The core idea of modern democracy as it evolved in the West is that 'I' am this body and that my 'self' stops at the boundaries of my skin. Although this seems an entirely natural identification to the modern mind, it is, as we know, only about four hundred years old and has specific cultural moorings in the experience of the West. In non-Western societies this notion of the individual, separate from all other individuals, as the unit of society, is still not an uncontested one. It is relevant here to remind ourselves of Sudipta Kaviraj's argument referred to in the last chapter, that because democracy entered these societies before the notion of the individual took root, our democracy—in Asian and African countries—takes very different shapes than it does in the societies of its origin.[47]

Habermas's response to this kind of argument is telling, and it is here that we come to the heart of the matter: 'Asiatic societies cannot participate in capitalistic modernisation without taking advantage of the achievements of an individualistic legal order. One cannot desire the one and reject the other. From the perspective of Asian countries, the question is not whether human rights, as part of an individualistic legal order, are compatible with the transmission of one's own culture. Rather, the question is whether the traditional forms of political and societal integration can be reasserted against—or must instead be adapted to—the hard-to-resist imperatives of an economic modernisation that has won approval on the whole.'[48]

This statement is certainly applicable to the critiques of rights made by the authoritarian states already mentioned above. But that is an easy enemy to demolish. What about the other critique I have outlined, which resists precisely that 'economic modernisation' which Habermas characterises as 'hard-to-resist'? How is it possible for Habermas to state unproblematically in a book published in 2001, that the model of capitalistic modernisation has 'won approval on the whole'? This is a model of 'development' that has been deeply discredited, is utterly unsustainable, and is being challenged across the globe by movements of environmental groups, labour, women's and indigenous people's movements. It appears from Habermas's frank assertion that we were right after all, in associating human rights conditionalities with the requirements of global capital.[49]

As I have already suggested, feminist critiques of 'globalisation' and 'US imperialism' will simultaneously have to offer a critique of 'community' and of the nation-state, the last designated problematically by Frederic Jameson as 'the only concrete terrain and framework for political struggle'.[50] Similarly, one kind of dalit voice in India still believes that only the state can protect the interests of the oppressed. This opinion holds that anti-state voices can only come from the elite who no longer need the state.[51] On the contrary, we need to recognise that 'the nation' can only represent dominant majoritarian values; minorities asserting 'their' culture can never claim the legitimacy of representing the nation. We cannot be unreflexive of the founding moment of discursive violence that both presupposed and produced 'the nation', nor of the repressions and marginalisations on which hegemonic nationalist discourse was predicated. In the classic case of France, Eugen Weber has suggested that the process of 'acculturation' in the nineteenth century, by which the inhabitants of the area that became France were made 'French', was 'akin to colonialism'.[52] The modern nation can come into being only by positing a previous unbroken history, centuries old, and a homogeneous national culture. Thus history and this culture can be asserted only by incorporating 'other' histories and cultures that exist in its demarcated territory, or by delegitimising and destroying them.

At the same time, 'community' too, often denies to women and other marginalised groups within it, the rights it claims vis-à-vis the nation-state—autonomy, selfhood, access to resources.

Feminist critiques of the universalism of international human rights discourses must therefore, equally strongly attack the particularism of the nation-state and of the community (both of which in turn set up their own universalism internally). 'Our' space will have to be the terrain of solidarities that are simultaneously anti-imperialist, counter-globalisation[53] and post-nationalist.

Breaking through Universalism/Particularity

There has been since the 1970s a feminist critique of the Universal installed by the Enlightenment, that it was a false universal, a universal that was appropriated for the white male propertied subject. The task then, was to make the Universal more inclusive. According to Naomi Schor, in the next stage the Enlightenment itself came under intense scrutiny. Writing in 1995, she saw the third stage as 'looming on the horizon'—a feminism that situates itself beyond the Enlightenment and its universalism.[54] The question that usually arises at this point is, does the problematisation of a universal notion of justice and rights simply reject it and install in its place multiple, particularistic notions? Let us look more closely at the two assumptions underlying this question: *first*, that despite all the critiques of universalism, it still offers the strongest possible defence against discrimination and oppression, and *second*, that to problematise universalism is to lose this strength.

To address the first assumption—there is nothing in the very nature of universalism that makes it self-evidently a language of emancipation alone. It can in fact be demonstrated that discriminatory discourses too, use universalist language. Etienne Balibar points out that racism and sexism for example, may appear as particularisms, because they divide the human species and claim that the hierarchies they produce are natural, 'but racism and sexism . . . produce *ideals* of humanity, *types of ideal humanity* if you like, which cannot but be called universal.'[55] In other words, racism uses the language of universality, and so, we could argue, do other discriminatory discourses. He argues therefore, that we cannot face racism effectively with 'the abstract motto of universality. Racism has already (always already) occupied this place. So the struggle is *inside this place*, to transform universalism . . .'[56] In a similar vein I have argued elsewhere that the arguments of the Hindu Right in India, though they are generally understood to be asserting the particularity of religious identity, on closer examination are revealed as universalist. Their claim is that the Indian state, by protecting the religious identity of minority communities, has failed to protect the abstract unmarked citizen.[57]

Balibar concludes however, by asserting that he does not reject universalism, and that brings us to the second question. To problematise universalism is indeed, not to reject it altogether. The very assertion of the particular requires its differentiation from the Universal; in other words, in the process of assertion of the particular, the Universal is necessarily asserted as well. As the demands of various particularistic identities will necessarily clash with one another, we have to appeal to some more general principles to regulate these clashes. In fact all particularisms appeal to such principles in the construction of their identities. So democratic politics cannot do away with universalism altogether—the tension between the Universal and the particular must act always as the horizon, while at the same time, the necessary or permanent attachment of the Universal to any particular content must be challenged. We need to recognise that democracy is possible precisely because the Universal does not have a necessary content. Indeed, it is the continuous but always temporary appropriation of the Universal by groups representing particular identities, that constitutes political competition.[58]

This means that as feminists too, we must recognise our claim to universal values as a temporary and contingent assertion that in turn sets up new antagonisms and new oppressive possibilities. We need to remind ourselves that while the category of 'Women' emerged from the feminist positing of difference as a challenge to the abstract category of 'Citizen', the slogan 'Sisterhood is Global' set up a universal that was in its turn oppressive. As critiques *of* the feminist Universal from women of colour and other stigmatised and marginalised groups of women showed, the category 'Women' turned out to be another abstraction, which assumed the white, middle-class, heterosexual woman to be the norm. In India this kind of challenge first emerged in the 1980s from dalit women and women of minority communities, who charged that the women's movement has assumed the Hindu upper-caste woman to be the norm.[59]

More recently, the voice of lesbian women has emerged, to question the exclusion of lesbian identity from the politics of the Indian women's movement. This exclusion, it may be noted, is not limited to refusing to take on board issues that have to do with lesbianism. It extends to refusing to permit the banner of a lesbian group in March 8th rallies in Delhi. In the discussions on the issue that have been going on for over two years now, one women's organisation of a Left party made the argument that banners of lesbian groups will 'cause confusion about', and 'divert attention from', 'the issues we have agreed to highlight' (that is, demolition of slums and closure of industries). They made it clear that while they understand that a group could have as a priority, getting 'social recognition for sexual rights and preferences', this is not going to be their own priority in the 'near future.' Similarly, another such organisation expressed its support for lesbian rights as part of 'the broader ambit of the struggle for civil liberties and democratic rights' but emphasised that 'in the context of building a mass movement for women's rights, there are several *more* pressing problems.'[60] The final decision in the last two years has been that banners of lesbian groups cannot participate in the March 8th rally, even if these groups are *not* raising the issue of lesbian rights, and simply marching on whatever platform has been decided upon by the Left groups. It seems that the very acknowledgement of lesbian identity is impossible within the universalism of this kind of Left feminism.[61]

A smaller voice still, but a sharply troubling one, comes from the platform of women with disabilities. Anita Ghai, feminist academic and activist for rights of the disabled, has for some years now been insistently questioning Indian feminists on the absolute silence in the movement on this issue. It seems to me that this silence is yet another aspect of the functioning of the feminist Universal, that continually tends to obscure particularities.[62]

By taking recourse to law to legitimise our claims, we concretise and render immutable each assertion of universality, dissolving the particular in the universal, and breaking the tension between them which is essential to democracy. Recognising that categories of identity do not 'naturally' exist, but are constructed by our political practice, we need to surrender the belief that they can be given the meaning and force we desire through the validation of the law. In so far as the law exists, and is an influential force, we cannot withdraw from its orbit, but it is counterproductive at this point to seek positive changes through legislation. Not only will such changes not be brought about, we would in the process, embed ourselves further in the very values we seek to transform. This is more than simply the failure of law at a particular point in history. What this intensely engaged debate suggests is that in the four hundred years since the law emerged as an emancipatory tool, the political landscape has been irretrievably transformed, so that while the law may not have failed us, we may have outgrown the law.

If There is No 'Woman' Then Who is the Subject of Feminist Politics?

The argument so far is that we cannot unproblematically anchor our arguments to notions of 'rights', 'bodies' or even 'women'. Our examination of feminist understandings of abortion and sexual violence and the debate over women's reservations has unravelled the contingent and historically specific nature of all these categories. Of course, this theoretical recognition has been in existence in feminist circles for a long time, inaugurated in part by French feminism. Or, as Denise Riley's famous question put it, referring to the label 'Woman', 'Am I that name?' The troubling implication of this recognition too, has been energetically engaged with for over a decade: if we 'deconstruct' the category of women, then how are we to do feminist politics? Gayatri Spivak's oft-quoted answer to this is what has come to be called 'strategic essentialism'—read by Judith Butler as 'the use of impossible totalisations as terms of political analysis and mobilisation.'[63] Butler herself, in addressing the question, asserts that 'the category of women does not become useless through deconstruction, but becomes one whose uses are no longer reified as "referents" . . . Surely it must be possible both to use the term, to use it tactically even as one is, as it were, used and positioned by it, and also to subject the term to a critique which interrogates the exclusionary operations and differential power relations that construct and limit feminist invocations of "women".'[64]

The question remains a live one, and the debate unsettled till today, as is evident from the continued invocation of 'women' and 'gender' both by feminists as well as by official and state discourse all over the world. The discussion in this study too, points to the power and tenacity of the belief in the pre-given 'naturalness' of such identities, as well as of the confidence that the law is external to these, a passive tool that can be mobilised to act *upon* them in various ways. It seems worthwhile to reiterate therefore, that it is imperative now for us to recognise that the political task is not that of simply *recovering* meaning from a field of pre-existing meanings. In other words, the identities on which social movements base themselves do not represent some positive essence—there are no pre-existing 'women', 'dalits', 'sexual minorities' out there; these identities are precariously constituted by the *political* act of hegemonising meaning. We constitute identities—including our own—in and through our political practice.

Is this a 'strategic' (Spivak) or 'tactical' (Butler) move? I am uncomfortable with the vanguardist implications of this way of posing the response. Although both scholars are cautious in their formulation and no doubt aware of the danger I point to, nevertheless, the implication is that *we* can use the category of 'woman' knowing full well that it does not 'really' exist, in order to address and mobilise *others* who believe in its existence. Butler, in the passage above, talks of 'using the term even as one is used and positioned by it.' This suggests a single moment in which we simultaneously deconstruct and invoke identity. I suggest instead, that if we shift our focus to the *duality* inherent in terms naming identity, we might answer the question ('how to deconstruct while invoking') somewhat differently. That is, when we remind ourselves that 'identity' is two opposing moments—both that which is produced by discourses of power as well as that which is to be the subject of our emancipatory politics, we remember also that deconstruction-and-invocation is not a single move—we have a dual agenda.

When the agenda is to contest the naturalising of identities produced by legal codes, then we must engage in 'deconstruction': a continuous process of exposure, putting at risk our own sense of self, and pushing the limits of what both we and they (whom we address as our constituency) can take. When the agenda is that of radical politics, that is, the mobilising of identity for a politics of subversion, then we 'invoke': that is, we address both ourselves and others *as* 'women', as that already given identity, while retaining a sense that at some point we will touch the porosity of the boundaries of that identity. Here the most crucial recognition is that what we invoke is an actually experienced identity—we do in fact, exist as 'women', that is how we are produced and *interpellated*, to use Althusser's phrase.[65] It is facile and misleading to read Butler (as she often is) as suggesting that gender is 'only' performance. The identity of 'woman' is historically contingent, but it is persistent and it is certainly not 'unreal'. At different moments in our political practice, then, we must at some times 'invoke' and at other times, 'deconstruct' the category of women.

It seems to me that this foregrounding of a dual agenda might enable us to escape the implied Archimedean point 'feminists' might be assumed to occupy vis-a-vis 'women' and worse still, the suggestion of instrumentality and 'false consciousness' redolent in the terms 'strategic,' 'tactical' and 'use'. This move would also, I believe, take us beyond a helpless reassertion of the universal in the face of the explosion of 'differences', as even Derrida seems to have ended up doing. Reflecting on 'today's Europe', Derrida holds that 'the same duty' dictates that Europe both welcome foreigners and accept their alterity, as well as respect the 'universality of formal law', 'the law of the majority' and 'opposition to racism, nationalism and xenophobia.'[66] However, it seems to me that it is not in fact the 'same' duty. The task is not simply to take a step back and 'reinvent the universal'[67] after a century of critique. It is to move into the unknown and to attempt to recognise the *practical* implications of the understanding that the universal itself is oppressive. The double, and *separate*, moves of invoking and deconstructing would involve, as I have attempted to argue consistently here, letting go of the old faith that Derrida invokes above, in 'the universality of formal law'.

Towards a Radical Democratic Politics

This kind of politics does not give up on notions of equality, justice and emancipation. However, these values can no longer be considered self-evident, they become deeply contested. Nor do I suggest we can no longer talk of Woman as the subject of feminist politics, but rather, point to the continuously open-ended nature of the project of constituting the feminist subject, as I hope the previous section has made clear. It is precisely the task of hegemonising common-sense meaning around these contested notions so that they reflect 'our' understanding, that constitutes the task of politics. This kind of call to problematise the notion of Universal Truths is all too often attributed to something pejoratively termed 'postmodernism'. We need to remind ourselves that longer and very different kinds of histories are involved here.

We could, for instance, go to Antonio Gramsci, addressing, *as a materialist*, the question of 'the so-called "reality of the external world" '. Gramsci argued that to demonstrate objective reality we are forced to refer 'to history and to man'. 'Objective' for Gramsci 'always means "humanly objective" which can be held to correspond exactly to "historically subjective".'[68] Taking up the example of 'East' and

'West' as conventions or historico-cultural constructions, he refers to Bertrand Russell's statement that while without the existence of man on earth, we could not think of London or Edinburgh, we could still think of the existence of two points in space, one to the North and one to the South, where Edinburgh and London now are. Gramsci's objection to this is that without man, one cannot think of 'thinking':

> What would North–South or East–West mean without man? *They are real relationships* and yet they would not exist without man and without the development of civilisation. Obviously East and West are arbitrary and conventional, that is, historical constructions, since outside of real history every point on the earth is East and West at the same time.[69]

Through this statement, East and West are made visible not only as historically constructed conventions, but as reflecting power relations—the 'world-wide hegemony' of 'the European cultured classes', whose point of view was naturalised across the globe.[70] In this understanding, there is a materiality to East and West as points in space, but they are inaccessible to us except through ways of thinking and the organising of thought.

If this argument holds for material points in space, then it holds all the more for values like equality, justice and emancipation, none of which, we must recognise, can be grasped outside ways of thinking and organising of thought. Thus, this is *not* a call to withdraw from the arena of the state and the law. Indeed, the point precisely is that we have to accept that we cannot think in terms of such metastrategies any longer—neither that of seeing the law as the agent of transformation, nor of seceding from the realm of the law altogether, although for different reasons. The option of abdicating the law is not a viable one, for the law will not abdicate us—the only permissible identities in modern democracies are those put in place by the law. We are inextricably implicated in state and legal procedures—every aspect of my identity is legally established—as woman, as Hindu, as upper caste. But precisely for this reason, because the regulating and defining force of the law is directed towards the creating and naturalising of specific, governable identities, the law cannot be a 'subversive site'.[71] At best we may be able to use existing provisions creatively, or campaign to repeal constraining provisions—in this way, we would be able to negotiate some spaces outside and around prescribed identities. The term 'subversion' however, is too strong for such a limited exercise. Here it is useful to consider the distinction made by some feminists between *law reform strategies* and *litigation strategies.* Law reform strategies seek to bring about new legislation to give legal recognition to rights-claims, while litigation strategies use existing laws either aggressively or defensively to advance such claims. It should be clear that it is the latter strategy that I see as the only viable one. It can also only be a very partial one in the task of an emancipatory politics.

We need to distinguish between a radical political practice that seeks to redefine the very terrain of politics, and the kind of fire-fighting exercise that we find ourselves caught up in all the time. Faced, for example, with a situation like the state-sponsored carnage in Gujarat in 2002, we have no option but to call upon the constitutional provisions that will bring the perpetrators to book. Just as, faced with a rape, we may well get involved in a campaign to bring about a conviction under existing laws. For a third instance, it is useful to take up Rajeswari Sunder Rajan's argument, in the context of the issue of women's mental health, that feminist legal activists in India repeatedly call for the state to take responsibility for the condition of the institutions in which such women are housed. Sunder Rajan points out that these activists are well aware of institutionalisation as a device of normalisation and as a manifestation of state power, but in the face of the fact that Indian women 'caught in the travails of a rapidly changing society, are desperately *in need of* the services of institutions . . . that only the state can provide . . .', feminists reject a Foucauldian view of institutions as failing to meet the immediacy of the situation.[72]

The last instance contextualises the state in the contemporary moment of globalisation—the oft-cited 'retreat of the state'. Is my argument urging moving away from law and the state simply a celebration of this supposed demise of the nation-state? In response, let me state what is by now generally recognised—we have by no means witnessed the demise of the nation-state or its authority. The processes of globalisation are more complex than that. The nation-state is at once being reconstituted in all its oppressive aspects simultaneously with its retreat from development/welfare responsibilities. Whether the USA, India, or Bosnia, or Rwanda, the discourse of xenophobic and jingoistic nationalism is in full volume, and the nation-state's repressive face is very much in evidence towards the dissident and/or marginalised voices within it. The so-called 'retreat of the state' is only visible in sectors in which it previously had some responsibility for health, education and so on. This 'retreat' is in fact a proactive step towards making it easier for global capital to penetrate. All sorts of restrictive measures to control labour mobility and trade unions are very much in force, and new measures are being enacted, empowering the state to ensure a healthy climate for investment. To pose the issue more starkly—the delegitimation of the postcolonial state's authority only pertains to the positive effects (from a democratic point of view) that were generated in anti-imperialist struggles. Simultaneously the process is accompanied by the reinforcement of every negative, repressive quality we associate with the state.

This is why, I would argue, both kinds of reactions—of turning to the nation-state to reassert the old authority, as well as on the other hand, assuming its demise and celebrating globalisation—are entirely misplaced. Nevertheless, we continue, whether we like it or not, to be situated in the terrain defined by the state. So in all three cases mentioned above, I can agree that a democratic politics might well try to force the state to respond in different ways. But surely our political practice has to go beyond simply dealing with the day-to-day crises generated in a patriarchal/sexist/communal/casteist society? What is our long-term agenda to challenge the very terms set by this framework? It is in order to evolve the latter that we need to think beyond appeals to the law and the state. What I argue is that while the law-reform strategy may offer some temporary and short-term redress, especially, say, if we are dealing with discriminatory legislation, we are mistaken in turning to the law to produce new rights, or to emancipate us.

To move away from legal and state-centred conceptions of political practice is to think creatively about new forms of political engagement that are located in realms we have not seriously engaged with. We need to evolve the kind of political practice that will work at capturing the meaning of terms in *our* language. Our understanding should become the common sense—that should be our political goal. In short, the project of a radical democratic practice is nothing less than the hegemonising of common sense.

Notes

1. Andrew Sharp, *Justice and the Maori*, Melbourne, Oxford University Press, 1990, p. 28.
2. Michel Foucault, *The History of Sexuality: An Introduction*, p. 89.
3. I have explained elsewhere in this book that I use the term 'postcolonial' not in the sense of 'after' colonialism, but in the sense of having been touched by colonialism. Thus, 'postcolonialism' begins with the first moment of colonial contact, and continues till today.
4. Ibid., pp. 268–71.
5. Nandita Gandhi and Nandita Shah, *The Issues at Stake*, p. 267.
6. Ibid., p. 272.
7. Ratna Kapur, 'Workshop at Action India', Delhi, 9 December 1993.
8. Laura Ring, 'Sexual Harassment and the Production of Gender', *Differences: A Journal of Feminist Cultural Studies*, 6(1), 1994, p. 129.
9. For instance, Michele Le Doeuff, writing about legislation passed in France in 1992 making part-time employment attractive to women, says, 'This is not so-called "free choice" . . . the better to combine work and family. It is dire exploitation in the workplace and dependency on a husband at home.' 'Feminism is Back in France—Or is it?', p. 244.
10. Charan Shah, a fifty-five-year-old woman, burnt herself on her husband's funeral pyre on 11 November 1999, in Satpurva village, Uttar Pradesh.
11. The women's wing of the Communist Party of India (Marxist). AIDWA is a political organisation of proven feminist credentials generally.
12. Kumkum Sangari and Sudesh Vaid, 'Institutions, Beliefs, Ideologies:

Widow Immolation in Contemporary Rajasthan'. Reproduced in Nivedita Menon, ed., *Gender and Politics in India*, Delhi, Oxford University Press, 1999, p. 391.

13. Joint statement of women's groups on incident of sati in Uttar Pradesh, 29 November 1999, pp. 1–2.
14. *Widow Immolation, Satpurva, November 1999* (a joint report by autonomous women's groups), p. 5.
15. Ibid., p. 2.
16. Here I will not go into many other dimensions of this issue which raise significant questions about changing notions of the legitimacy of the state to bring about social reform, a legitimacy that had hitherto been assumed by the modernising elites of India, but which is increasingly being called into question. For a good sense of the large body of contemporary scholarship on sati, see Ania Loomba's review essay, 'Dead Women Tell No Tales: Issues of Female Subjectivity, Subaltern Agency and Tradition in Colonial and Postcolonial Writings on Widow Immolation in India', *History Workshop* 36, 1993, pp. 209–27. The question of community identity is also relevant here, and the recent articulations of community into modernist discourses of the nation-state. (For this aspect of the issue, see Veena Das, *Critical Events*, Chapter IV, pp. 84–117. For a discussion of this question in the context of the debate over the Uniform Civil Code in India, see my 'Women and Citizenship', in Partha Chatterjee, ed., *Wages of Freedom,* Delhi, Oxford University Press, 1998.) To the question of community identity another dimension of complexity is added by the fact that Charan Shah was dalit, and some of those interviewed in the women's groups' report expressed the belief that they were not being allowed to call her death a sati only because they were lower caste, that the upper castes and the administration were colluding in denying them the right to own a sati, hitherto a practice of the upper castes (p. 5).
17. The phrase, of course, comes from Noam Chomsky.
18. Cited in Kumkum Sangari, 'Gender Lines: Personal Laws, Uniform Laws, Conversions', *Social Scientist*, vol. 27, nos 5–6, May–June 1999, p. 59, Note 50.
19. *Constituent Assembly Debates*, vol. III, 28 April–2 May 1947, p. 442.
20. Ibid., p. 488.
21. Ibid., pp. 490–1.
22. Ibid., pp. 496–7.

23. Ibid., pp. 492–7.
24. Cited by Saeed Naqvi, 'No Mass Conversions Please', *The Indian Express*, 30 June 2000, p. 4.
25. I use three papers in which Partha Chatterjee has worked through this distinction: 'Beyond the Nation? Or Within?', *Economic and Political Weekly*, 4–11 January 1997; 'Community in the East', *Economic and Political Weekly*, 7 February 1998, p. 279; 'Introduction', in Partha Chatterjee, ed., *Wages of Freedom: Fifty Years of the Indian Nation-State,* Delhi, Oxford University Press, 1998.
26. Partha Chatterjee, 'Beyond the Nation? Or Within?', pp. 31–2.
27. Ibid., p. 32.
28. Both of these are examples used at different points by Chatterjee to illustrate his argument.
29. See Vasant Saberwal and Mahesh Rangarajan, eds, *Battles Over Nature: Science and the Politics of Conservation*, Delhi, Permanent Black, 2003.
30. See *The Order That Felled A City: A Citizens' Report on the Politics of Pollution and the Mass Displacement of Workers in Delhi*, Delhi Janwadi Adhikar Manch, February/March 1997. These instances can be multiplied: in 1996, there was a case of police firing in Delhi resulting in the death of three slum dwellers. The background to this incident is the following. Local slum dwellers had been using the park adjoining a middle-class housing society for defecation, as they had nowhere else to go. The Residents' Welfare Association of the middle-class colony filed a petition in the High Court, stating that they were prepared to maintain the park at their own cost, and the Court directed that the park should be closed off with a boundary wall to prevent it from becoming an 'open public toilet'. This closed off the park which was on public land as a thoroughfare too, restricting it for the exclusive use of the middle-class colony. The court also directed the local police to render assistance to the Delhi Development Authority in dealing with resistance from the slum-dwellers. The judgement of the High Court emphasised that the slum-dwellers are 'law-breakers, unauthorised occupants of public land'. It further observed that there was no justification for spending taxpayers' money in order to relocate the slum dwellers—this would be an 'invitation to more persons to migrate to Delhi, occupy land unauthorisedly and then be rewarded with land at state expense'. See the report of the Peoples' Union for Democratic Rights, *A Tale of Two Cities: Custodial Death and Police Firing in Ashok Vihar*, Delhi, August 1996, specially pp. 8–9.

31. 'Nine-to-Five Feminists', as a women's movement veteran referred to them disparagingly in a personal communication to me. For a fuller discussion on this issue, see Gail Omvedt, *Reinventing Revolution*, Armonk, New York, M.E. Sharpe Inc., 1993, p. 91; Nandita Gandhi and Nandita Shah, *The Issues at Stake*, pp. 297–307; Radha Kumar, *The History of Doing*, Delhi, Kali for Women, 1993, p. 157.
32. Naina Kapur (Sakshi), Jasjit Purewal (IFSHA) and Kirti Singh (AIDWA), *Sexual Assault Law Reforms: A Process Document 2000,* Delhi.
33. Raka Ray, *Fields of Protest: Women's Movements in India*, Delhi, Kali for Women, 1999, pp. 165–6.
34. Nandita Gandhi and Nandita Shah, *The Issues at Stake*, p. 269.
35. Arati Rao, 'Right in the Home', *National Law School Journal*, vol. 1, 1993, p. 81.
36. Working Group on Women's Rights of the NGO Forum at the World Conference on Human Rights, 1993.
37. Martha C. Nussbaum, *Women and Human Development: The Capabilities Approach*, Cambridge, Cambridge University Press, 2000, p. 104. For an extensive critique of Nussbaum's capabilities approach, see my review essay, 'Universalism Without Foundations?', in *Economy and Society*, vol. 31, no. 1, February 2002.
38. Jurgen Habermas, 'Bestiality and Humanity: A War on the Border between Law and Morality', translated from the German, Franz Solms-Laubach, *Die Zeit* 54, 18, 29 April 1999, pp. 1–8. English version available at Global Library, 2000, www.theglobalsite.ac.uk.
39. David Kennedy, 'The International Human Rights Movement: Part of the Problem?', *European Human Rights Law Review* (2001), pp. 245–67.
40. Ibid., pp. 250–5.
41. Discussed in Jurgen Habermas, 'Remarks on Legitimation Through Human Rights' (translated by Max Pensky), in *The Postnational Constellation: Political Essays,* Cambridge, Polity Press, 2001, p. 123.
42. Partha Chatterjee, 'Beyond the Nation? Or Within?', p. 33.
43. Ibid., pp. 33–4.
44. To use Partha Chatterjee's evocative phrase from the title of Chapter 15 of *A Possible India: Essays in Political Criticism*, Delhi, Oxford University Press, 1997.
45. Jurgen Habermas, 'Remarks on Legitimation Through Human Rights', p. 121.
46. Ibid.

47. Sudipta Kaviraj, 'Dilemmas of Democratic Development in India', in Adrian Leftwich, ed., *Democracy and Development*, Cambridge, Polity Press, 1996.
48. Jurgen Habermas, 'Remarks on Legitimation Through Human Rights', p. 124.
49. As an aside, we might also note that in the same article Habermas, while addressing the anti-state argument offered by Ashis Nandy on secularism, states that he and other 'Indian intellectuals' conflate a normative question (how one can find a shared basis for a just political life in common) with an empirical question (the public coexistence of Islamic and Hindu religious cultures). Habermas argues that 'The differentiation of a religious sphere separate from the state may in fact weaken the influence of privatised gods and demons', but this move does not attack the truth-claims of religions, rather, it enables their equally entitled co-existence within the same political community. Such a differentiation is therefore desirable from the secular point of view but does not offend the religious sensibility (pp. 127–8). But Nandy's argument is precisely that the state has lost—if it ever had—the legitimacy to offer a space of toleration (where the influence of privatised gods and demons might be weakened), nor does it have the moral and ethical resources to do so. This is because the state has acted as the agent of a harsh and oppressive modernity that has produced those pathologies of religion called 'fundamentalism'. In other words, religious fundamentalism is not a product of lingering 'tradition' but of rampant 'modernity'. But perhaps it is not surprising that Habermas misses the point so completely—he refers to Nandy's famous article ('An Anti-secularist Manifesto', *Seminar* 314, 1985, pp. 1–11), as 'anti-secularisation manifesto', does not give any references for it, and in the footnote at the end of the argument *contra* Nandy and other unnamed 'Indian intellectuals', instead gives the references of Rajeev Bhargava's 'Giving Secularism its Due' and Partha Chatterjee's 'Secularism and Toleration', both of which make arguments that are very different from those of Nandy.
50. Frederic Jameson, 'Globalisation and Political Strategy', *New Left Review* 4, July–August 2000, p. 65.
51. For a discussion of the views of dalit intellectuals Chandra Bhan Prasad and Gopal Guru, see Aditya Nigam, 'Beyond the Nationalist Imaginary: Dalit Politics in the Global Era', *The Indian Journal of Political Science*, vol. 62, no. 3, September 2001, pp. 417–32.

52. Eugen Weber, *Peasants into Frenchmen*, Stanford, Stanford University Press, 1976, p. 486.
53. I use the term 'counter' rather than 'anti' globalisation, following the self-characterisation of the movement, to suggest its difference from the kind of nationalist critiques of globalisation offered by both Right and Left in India, for example, which are in effect a defence of 'our' bourgeoisie against 'theirs'. In addition, the anti-globalisation position of the Hindu right mobilises a cultural purity argument against 'western' culture, that is directed towards policing the behaviour of women. For a useful mapping of the different kinds of anti- and counter-globalisation positions, see Aditya Nigam, 'Radical Politics in the Time of Globalisation', in Niraja Gopal Jayal and Sudha Pai, eds, *Democratic Governance in India: Challenges of Poverty, Development and Identity*, New Delhi, Sage, 2001.
54. Naomi Schor, 'French Feminism is a Universalism', *Differences: A Journal of Feminist Cultural Studies* 7(1), 1995, pp. 15–47.
55. Etienne Balibar, 'Racism as Universalism', *Masses, Classes, Ideas: Studies on Politics and Philosophy Before and After Marx*, New York and London, Routledge, 1994, p. 201.
56. Ibid, p. 204.
57. See my 'State/Gender/Community: Citizenship in Contemporary India', *Economic and Political Weekly*, 31 January 1998, pp. PE-3 to PE-10.
58. See the useful discussion on this point in Ernesto Laclau, 'Universalism, Particularism and the Question of Identity', *October*, no. 61, 1992, pp. 85–90.
59. Flavia Agnes, 'Women's Movement within a Secular Framework: Redefining the Agenda', *Economic and Political Weekly*, vol. 29, no. 19, 7 May 1994.
60. Emphasis in original. Written correspondence of Left women's organisations and Campaign for Lesbian Rights before 8 March 2001, on file with the author.
61. For an account of the beginnings of a public lesbian feminist presence in India, see Cynthia Rothschild, *Written Out: How Sexuality is Used to Attack Women's Organizing*, Report prepared by International Gay and Lesbian Human Rights Commission (San Francisco) and Centre for Women's Global Leadership (State University of New Jersey), 2000, pp. 92–105.
62. See Anita Ghai, 'Disabled Women: An Excluded Agenda of Indian Feminism', in *Hypatia*, vol. 17, no. 3, Summer 2002, pp. 49–66.

63. Judith Butler, *Bodies That Matter*, New York and London, Routledge, 1993, p. 281, Note 19.
64. Ibid., p. 29.
65. In Althusser's understanding, ideology *interpellates* individuals as subjects—it 'hails' individuals with a 'hey, you there!' and the individual turns around, recognising that the hail was 'really' addressed to her. 'By this mere one hundred-and-eighty-degree physical conversion, he becomes a subject.' See 'Ideological State Apparatuses', in Slavoj Zizek, ed., *Mapping Ideology*, London, Verso, 1994, especially, pp. 128–31. In other words, when we are hailed as 'hey there, you woman!', we do 'turn around'.
66. Jacques Derrida, *The Other Heading: Reflections on Today's Europe*, Bloomington, Indiana University Press, 1992, pp. 77–8. Cited in Naomi Schor, 'French Feminism is a Universalism', p. 41.
67. Naomi Schor's phrase, p. 40.
68. Antonio Gramsci, *Selections from the Prison Notebooks*, New York, International Publishers, 1987, p. 445.
69. Ibid., p. 447. Emphasis added.
70. Ibid.
71. The title of Ratna Kapur and Brenda Cossman's book, *Subversive Sites: Feminist Engagements with the Law in India*, Delhi, Sage, 1996.
72. Rajeswari Sunder Rajan, *Scandal of the State: Women, Law and Citizenship in Postcolonial India*, Delhi, Permanent Black, 2003.

Bibliography

Unpublished/In Private Circulation

A Draft Report on Guidelines Against Sexual Harassment in Delhi University, Committee to Frame Guidelines Against Sexual Harassment in Delhi University, May 1999.

A Tale of Two Cities: Custodial Death and Police Firing in Ashok Vihar, Delhi, Peoples' Union for Democratic Rights, Delhi, August 1996.

Another Occupational Hazard. Sexual Harassment and the Working Woman. A Report by Saheli, Delhi, October 1998.

Chattoo, Sangeeta, 'A Sociological Study of Certain Aspects of Disease and Death: A Case Study of Muslims in Kashmir', PhD Thesis, Department of Sociology, Delhi University, 1990.

Development for Whom? A Critique of Women's Development Programme. Report prepared by women's groups—Sabala Sangh, Action India and Disha (Delhi); Women's Centre, Forum Against Oppression of Women and Awaz-e-Nizwan (Bombay), 1991.

Draft Amendments to Sexual Assault Law (Committee consisted of Abha Bhaiya, Asha Ramesh, Elizabeth Vatsyayan, Enakshi Ganguli Thukral, Indu Prakash, Jasjit Purewal, Kirti Singh, Naina Kapur, Ratna Kapur, Ritu Menon, Seema Misra.) Report available with the National Commission for Women, New Delhi, 1993.

Information Sheet on Sex Determination and Sex Preselection Techniques, FASDSP and Saheli (On file with Jagori, Delhi), undated.

Joint statement of women's groups on incident of sati in Uttar Pradesh. On file with Saheli, Delhi, November 1999.

Kapur, Naina (Sakshi), Jasjit Purewal (IFSHA) and Kirti Singh (AIDWA), *Sexual Assault Law Reforms: A Process Document*, Delhi, 2000.

Kulkarni, Sanjeev, *Sex Determination Tests and Female Foeticide in the City of Bombay.* Report commissioned by the Secretary to the Government,

Department of Health and Family Welfare, Government of Maharashtra, 1996.

Letter to the National Commission for Women on NCW's draft policy on sexual harassment at the workplace. Saheli, Gujarat Forum for Women Studies and Action Groups, Jagori, Sama, Nirantar, Lawyers Collective, Women's Rights Initiative, Human Rights Law Network, Partners in Law and Development, November 2001.

Memorandum by Forum Against Sexual Harassment, Delhi University, 29 September 1999.

Note About Proposed Central Legislation to Ban Sex Determination Tests. FASDSP. (Based on workshop 'Legal Aspects of Sex Determination Tests', held in Bombay, 1988. On file with Jagori, Delhi), 1998.

Note Sent to Women's Organisations. (Regarding 'female foeticide'), FASDSP. (On file with Jagori, Delhi), undated.

Purewal, Jasjit and Naina Kapur, *Have You Been Sexually Assaulted*? New Delhi, undated.

Roundtable on Women's Perspective on Family Planning, Reproductive Rights and Reproductive Health (Based on workshop in Ottawa, Canada. On file with Jagori, Delhi), 1993.

The Order That Felled a City. A Citizens' Report on the Politics of Pollution and the Mass Displacement of Workers in Delhi, Delhi Janwadi Adhikar Manch, February–March, 1997.

Visaria, Pravin, 'A Population Policy for the Twenty-first Century: Perspectives from the Women's Movement'. (On file with Jagori.)

Women's Representation in Legislatures, Forum for Democratic Reforms, Delhi and Hyderabad, 2002.

Widow Immolation, Satpurva. (A joint report by autonomous women's groups.) On file with Saheli, Delhi, November 1999.

Government Reports

Constituent Assembly Debates, vol. III, 28 April–2 May 1947.

Lok Sabha Debates, 1971, vol. 7.7, 2 August; 1983, vol. 42, 18 November, 21 November, 1 December.

Report of the Joint Committee of Parliament on the Prenatal Diagnostic Techniques (Regulation and Prevention of Misuse) Bill, 1991. Lok Sabha Secretariat, New Delhi.

Report of the Working Group on Women's Rights of the NGO Forum at the

World Conference on Human Rights, Vienna, 10–12 June 1993, *Teaching Politics* (Delhi), vol. XIX, nos 1, 2, 1993.

Rothschild, Cynthia, *Written Out: How Sexuality is Used to Attack Women's Organizing*, Report prepared by International Gay and Lesbian Human Rights Commission (San Francisco) and Center for Women's Global Leadership (State University of New Jersey), 2000.

Books and Articles

Advani, Poornima, Lina Gonsalves and J.K. Mittal, *Rape: A Legal Study*, National Commission for Women, 2000.

Agarwal, Bina, 'Rural Women, Poverty and Natural Resources', *Economic and Political Weekly*, 28 October 1989.

Agnes, Flavia, *Journey to Justice*, Bombay, Majlis, 1990.

———, 'A Critical Review of Enactments on Violence Against Women', in Maithreyi Krishna Raj, ed., *Women and Violence: A Country Report*, Bombay, SNDT University, 1991.

———, 'Protecting Women Against Violence? Review of a Decade of Legislation 1980–89', *Economic and Political Weekly*, 25 April 1992.

———, 'Women's Movement within a Secular Framework: Redefining the Agenda', *Economic and Political Weekly*, vol. XXIX, no. 19, 1994.

———, 'Law, Ideology and Female Sexuality: Gender Neutrality in Rape Law', *Economic and Political Weekly*, 2 March 2002.

Alavi, Seema, 'Muslim Women Don't Need Reservation', *The Times of India*, 15 July 1998.

Alexander, Sally, 'Women's Work in Nineteenth-Century London: A Study of the Years 1820–50', in Juliet Mitchell and Anne Oakley, eds, *The Rights and Wrongs of Women*, Harmondsworth, Penguin, 1976.

Allen, Anita L., *Uneasy Access: Privacy for Women in a Free Society*, Totowa, NJ, Rowman and Littlefield, 1988.

Altekar, A.S., *Sources of Hindu Dharma*, Sholapur, Institute of Public Administration, 1952.

Althusser, Louis, 'Ideological State Apparatuses' (1971), Reprinted in Slavoj Zizek, ed., *Mapping Ideology*, London, Verso, 1994.

Anderson, Michael and Sumit Guha, eds, *Changing Concepts of Rights and Justice in South Asia*, Delhi, Oxford University Press, 1998.

Anonymous, 'Women. Invisible Constituency', Commentary in *Economic and Political Weekly*, 18 May 1996.

———, 'Gender Hurdles', *Economic and Political Weekly*, 3 June 2000.

Arunima, G., 'A Vindication of the Rights of Woman? Families and Legal Change in Nineteenth Century Malabar', in Michael Anderson and Sumit Guha, eds, *Changing Concepts of Rights and Justice in South Asia*, Delhi, Oxford University Press, 1998.

———, *There Comes Papa: Colonialism and the Transformation of Matriliny in Malabar 1850–1940*, New Delhi, Orient Longman, 2003.

Ashcroft, Bill, Gareth Griffiths, and Helen Tiffin, eds, *The Post-colonial Studies Reader*, London, Routledge, 1999.

Atkins, S. and B. Hoggett, *Women and the Law*, Oxford and New York, Basil Blackwell, 1994.

Atray, J.P., *Crimes Against Women*, Delhi, Vikas Publishing House, 1988.

Balasubramaniam, Vimal, 'Who's not Afraid of Family Planning', *Seminar* 331, 1987.

Balibar, Etienne, 'Racism as Universalism', *Masses, Classes, Ideas: Studies on Politics and Philosophy Before and After Marx*, New York and London, Routledge, 1994.

Bandewar, Sunita, 'Unsafe Abortion', *Seminar* 489, 2000.

Bang, Rani and Abhay Bang, 'Contraceptive Technologies: Experience of Rural Indian Women', *Manushi*, no. 70, 1992.

Barrett, Michele, 'Rethinking Women's Oppression Today: A Reply to Brenner and Ramas', *New Left Review* 146, July–August 1984.

Baxi, Upendra, 'Some Reflections on the Nature of Constituent Power', in R. Dhavan and Alice Jacob, eds, *Indian Constitution: Trends and Issues*, Bombay, Tripathi, 1978.

———, *The Crisis in the Indian Legal System*. New Delhi, Vikas, 1982.

———, *Towards a Sociology of Indian Law*, New Delhi, Satvahan, 1986.

———, 'From Human Rights to the Right to be Human', in Upendra Baxi ed., *The Right to be Human*, New Delhi, Lancer International, 1987.

———, 'The State's Emissary: The Place of Law in Subaltern Studies', in Partha Chatterjee and Gyanendra Pandey, eds, *Subaltern Studies VII*, Delhi, Oxford University Press, 1992.

———, 'Constitutionalism as a Site of State Formative Practices', *Cardozo Law Review*, vol. 21, no. 4, February 2000.

Benderly, Jill, 'Rape, Feminism and Nationalism in the War in Yugoslav Successor States', in Lois A. West, ed., *Feminist Nationalism*, NY and London, Routledge, 1997.

Benhabib, Seyla, 'The Generalized and the Concrete Other: The Kohlberg–Gilligan Controversy and Feminist Theory', in Seyla Benhabib and

Drucilla Cornell, eds, *Feminism as Critique*, Cambridge, Polity Press, 1987.

Bharati, Uma, 'Not a Woman's World: Case for OBC Reservation', as told to Vidya Subramaniam, *The Times of India*, 17 July 1998.

Bhattacharya, Malini, 'Democracy and Reservation', *Seminar* 457, 1997.

Bhattacharya, Swati (Bengali), *'Kanya bhrun hatya bishayak sabha paryabashit nari abamananaye'*, *Ananda Bazar Patrika*, 25 June 2001.

Boyle, Christine, 'Sexual Assault and the Feminist Judge', *Canadian Journal of Women and the Law*, 1985.

Boyle, James, 'The Politics of Reason: Critical Legal Theory and Local Social Thought', *University of Pennsylvania Law Review*, April 1985.

Brown, Beverley, 'Litigating Feminisms', *Economy and Society*, vol. 20, no. 4, November 1986.

Brown, Wendy, *States of Injury: Power and Freedom in Late Modernity*, Princeton, Princeton University Press, 1995.

Brown, Mick, 'Male Rape is Not Even Recognized as a Crime', *The Pioneer*, 16 December 1992.

Brownmiller, Susan, *Against Our Will: Men, Women and Rape*, New York, Bantam, 1976.

Bumiller, Kristin, 'Fallen Angels: The Representation of Violence Against Women in Legal Culture', in Martha Albertson Fineman and Nancy Sweet Thomadsen, eds, *At the Boundaries of Law*, London, Routledge, 1991.

Butalia, Urvashi, 'Community, State and Gender: On Women's Agency During Partition', *Economic and Political Weekly*, 24 April 1993.

Butler, Judith, 'The Lesbian Phallus and the Morphological Imaginary', *Differences: A Journal of Feminist Cultural Studies*, vol. 4, Spring 1992.

———, *Bodies That Matter*, New York and London, Routledge, 1993.

Chakravarty, Sukhamoy, *Development Planning: The Indian Experience*, New Delhi, Oxford University Press, 1987.

Chandrasekhar, Sripati, *Abortion in a Crowded World: The Problem of Abortion with Special Reference to India*, London, George Allen and Unwin Ltd, 1974.

Chatterjee, Partha, 'Beyond the Nation? Or Within?', *Economic and Political Weekly*, 4–11 January 1997.

———, *A Possible India: Essays in Political Criticism*, Delhi, Oxford University Press, 1997.

———, 'Community in the East', *Economic and Political Weekly*, 7 February, 1998.

———, *Wages of Freedom: Fifty Years of the Indian Nation-State*, Delhi, Oxford University Press, 1998.

Chhachhi, Amrita and C. Satyamala, 'Sex Determination Tests: A Technology Which will Eliminate Women', *Medico Friends Circle Bulletin*, New Delhi, November 1983.

Cohen, Jean, 'Democracy, Difference and the Right of Privacy', in Seyla Benhabib, ed., *Democracy and Difference: Contesting the Boundaries of the Political*, Princeton, Princeton University Press, 1996.

Connolly, William, *The Ethos of Pluralization*, Minnesota and London, University of Minnesota Press, 1995.

Cornell, Drucilla, *Beyond Accommodation. Ethical Feminism, Deconstruction and the Law*, New York and London, Routledge, 1991.

———, 'Dismembered Selves and Wandering Wombs', unpublished manuscript on file with author, 1992.

———, *The Imaginary Domain*, New York and London, Routledge, 1995.

Dahl, Tove Stang, *Women's Law: An Introduction to Feminist Jurisprudence*, Oslo, Norwegian University Press, 1987.

Das, Veena, 'Deciding on Moral Issues: The Case of Abortion', in Diana L. Eck and Devaki Jain, eds, *Speaking of Faith*, New Delhi, Kali for Women, 1986.

———, *Critical Events: An Anthropological Perspective on Contemporary India*, Delhi, Oxford University Press, 1995.

Derrida, Jacques, 'Force of Law: The Mystical Foundation of Authority' (tr. Mary Quaintance), in *Deconstruction and the Possibility of Justice*, a special issue of *Cardozo Law Review*, vol. II, nos 5–6, July–August 1990.

———, *The Other Heading: Reflections on Today's Europe*, Bloomington, Indiana University Press, 1992.

Dhagamwar, Vasudha, *Law, Power and Justice*, New Delhi, Sage, 1992.

Dhanda, Meena, 'Representation for Women. Should Feminists Support Quotas?' *Economic and Political Weekly*, 12 August 2000.

Dietrich, Gabriele, 'Women and Religious Identities in India After Ayodhya', in Kamla Bhasin, Ritu Menon, and Nighat Said Khan, eds, *Against All Odds: Essays on Women, Religion and Development from India and Pakistan*, New Delhi, Kali for Women, 1994.

Douzinas, Costas, Ronnie Warrington, Shaun Mcveigh, *Postmodern Jurisprudence: The Law of Texts in the Texts of the Law*, London, Routledge, 1991.

Duggal, Ravi, 'PNDT Act and People's Action', *Economic and Political Weekly*, 2 June 2001.

Dworkin, Ronald, *Taking Rights Seriously*, London, Duckworth, 1977.

———, 'Rights as Trumps', in Jeremy Waldron, ed., *Theories of Rights*, Oxford, Oxford University Press, 1984.

———, *Law's Empire*, Cambridge MA, Harvard University Press, 1986.

———, 'Feminism and Abortion', *The New York Review*, 10 June 1993.

Eisenstein, Zillah, *The Female Body and the Law*, Berkeley and Los Angeles, University of California Press, 1988.

Engels, F., *The Origin of the Family, Private Property and the State*, Moscow, Progress Publishers, 1977.

Faridi, Shahid, 'Left Criticises Gill Formula for Women's Reservation', *Asian Age*, 25 April 2000.

Feinberg, Joel, 'In Defence of Moral Rights', *Oxford Journal of Legal Studies*, vol. 12, no. 2, Summer 1992.

Foucault, Michel, *Discipline and Punish: The Birth of the Prison*, New York, Vantage Books, 1977.

———, *The History of Sexuality: An Introduction*, Harmondsworth, Penguin, 1978.

———, 'The Subject of Power', in Hubert L. Dreyfus and Paul Rabinow, eds, *Michel Foucault.Beyond Structuralism and Hermeneutics*, Chicago, University of Chicago Press, 1982.

———, 'Governmentality', in Graham Burchell, Colin Gordon, and Peter Miller, eds, *The Foucault Effect: Studies in Governmentality*, London, Harvester Wheatsheaf, 1991.

Fraser, Nancy, *Unruly Practices: Power, Discourse and Gender in Contemporary Social Theory*, Minneapolis, University of Minnesota Press, 1989.

———, 'The Force of Law: Metaphysical or Political?', in Manfred B. Steger and Nancy S. Lind, eds, *Violence and Its Alternatives: An Interdisciplinary Reader*, London, Macmillan Press Ltd, 1999.

Freitag, Sandria, '*Sansiahs* and the State: The Changing Nature of "Crime" and "Justice", in Nineteenth-Century India', in Michael Anderson and Sumit Guha, eds, *Changing Concepts of Rights and Justice in South Asia*, Delhi, Oxford University Press, 1998.

Friedrich, Carl, *Constitutional Government and Democracy*, Boston, Ginn, 1950.

Frug, Mary Joe, *Postmodern Legal Feminism*, New York, Routledge, 1992.

Fudge, Judy, 'The Public/Private Distinction: The Possibilities and Limits to the Use of *Charter* Litigation to Further Feminist Struggles', *Osgoode Law Journal*, vol. 25, no. 3, 1987.

Gabel, Peter and Paul Harris, 'Building Power and Breaking Images: Critical Legal Theory and the Practice of Law', *New York University Review of Law and Social Change* 11, 1982–3.

Galanter, Marc, *Competing Equalities: Law and the Backward Classes in India*, Delhi, Oxford University Press, 1984.

———, *Law and Society in Modern India*, Delhi, Oxford University Press, 1989.

Gandhi, Nandita and Nandita Shah, *The Issues at Stakes*, New Delhi, Kali for Women, 1992.

Gaspard, Francoise, 'Parity—Why Not?', *Differences: A Journal of Feminist Cultural Studies* 9(2), Summer, 1997.

George, Nirmala, 'Debate on Women's Bill is Two Years Old, It's Going Nowhere', Interview with M.S. Gill, Chief Election Commissioner, *The Indian Express*, 26 April 2000.

Ghai, Anita, 'Disabled Women: An Excluded Agenda of Indian Feminism', *Hypatia*, vol. 17, no. 3, Summer 2002.

Golberg-Ambrose, Carole, 'Unfinished Business in Rape Law Reform', *Journal of Social Issues*, vol. 48, no. 1, 1992.

Gonsalves, Lina, *Women and the Law*, New Delhi, Lancer Paperbacks, 1993.

Gordon, Linda, *Woman's Body, Woman's Right*, New York, Penguin Books, 1990.

Gramsci, Antonio, *Selections from the Prison Notebooks*, New York, International Publishers, 1987.

Greenhalgh, Susan, 'Fresh Winds in Beijing: Chinese Feminists Speak Out on the One-child Policy and Womens' Lives', *Signs*, vol. 26, no. 3, Spring 2001.

Graycar, Regina and Jenny Morgan, *The Hidden Gender of Law*, New South Wales, Federation Press, 1990.

Grover, Anand, 'Legal Aspects of Amniocentesis', *Lawyers' Collective*, March 1986.

Guha, Ranajit, 'Dominance Without Hegemony and Its Historiography', in Ranajit Guha, eds, *Subaltern Studies VI*, Delhi, Oxford University Ptess, 1989.

Guha, Sumit, 'Wrongs and Rights in the Maratha Country: Antiquity, Custom and Power in Eighteenth Century India', in Michael Anderson and

Sumit Guha, eds, *Changing Concepts of Rights and Justice in South Asia*, Delhi, Oxford University Press, 1998.

Haase-Dubosc, Danielle, 'Sexual Difference and Politics in France Today', *Feminist Studies*, vol. 25, no. 1, Spring 1999.

Habermas, Jurgen, 'Struggles for Recognition in the Democratic Constitutional State' (tr. Shierry Weber Nicholsen), in Amy Gutman, ed., *Multiculturalism*, Princeton, Princeton University Press, 1994.

———, 'Bestiality and Humanity: A War on the Border between Law and Morality', tr. from the German, *Die Zeit*, vol. 54, no. 18, 29 April 1999, pp. 1–8. English version available at Global Library, 2000, www. theglobalsite. ac.uk (tr. Franz Solms-Laubach), 2000.

———, 'Remarks on Legitimation Through Human Rights', in *The Post-national Constellation. Political Essays*, Cambridge, Polity Press, 2001.

Haksar, Nandita, *Demystifying the Law for Women*, New Delhi, Lancer Press, 1986.

———, 'Dominance, Suppression and the Law', in Lotika Sarkar and B. Sivaramayya, eds, *Women and the Law: Contemporary Problems*, New Delhi, Vikas Publishing House, 1994.

———, 'Human Rights Layering: A Feminist Perspective', in Amita Dhanda and Archana Parasher, eds, *Engendering Law: Essays in Honour of Lotika Sarkar*, Lucknow, Eastern Book Company, 1999.

Hartsock, Nancy, *Money, Sex and Power: Towards a Feminist Historical Materialism*, New York, Longman, 1983.

Heller, Agnes, 'Rights, Modernity, Democracy', in *Deconstruction and the Possibility of Justice*, a special issue of *Cardozo Law Review*, 1990.

Hirway, Indira, 'Panchayati Raj at the Crossroads', *Economic and Political Weekly*, vol. 24, no. 29, 1989.

Howe, Adrian, 'The Problem of Privatized Injuries: Feminist Strategies for Litigation', in Martha Albertson Fineman and Nancy Sweet Thomadsen eds, *At the Boundaries of Law*, New York and London, Routledge, 1991.

Ivecovic, Rada, 'The Bosnian Paradigm', *Dialogue*, N.9–10, 1998, pp. 61–85.

———, 'Nation and Identity in Post-Socialist Transition', in K. Glass, R. Hettlage, R. Scartezzini, eds, *Erweiterung Europas*, Österreichische Gesellschaft für Mitteleuropäische Studien & Humaniora, Vienna, Poznan 1998, pp. 229–41.

———, 'A Feminist Philosophical Approach to Nationalism', unpublished lecture delivered at Copenhagen University, 7 April 2000.

Jacob, Alice, 'Abortion Law Reform: A Study of the Medical Termination of Pregnancy Act, 1971', *Journal of the Indian Law Institute*, vol. 16, 1974.

Jameson, Frederic, 'Globalisation and Political Strategy', *New Left Review* 4, July–August 2000.

Jesani, Amar and Aditi Iyer, 'Women and Abortion', *Economic and Political Weekly*, vol. 28, no. 48, 27 November 1993.

Johnson, Sharon, 'Rape: The Conservative Backlash', *Ms.* March–April 1992.

Kabeer, Naila, *Reversed Realities: Gender Hierarchies in Development Thought*, London, Verso, 1994.

Kala, Arvind, 'Banning Sex Tests. Unfair, Unworkable', *The Times of India*, 25 January 1991.

Kannabiran, Kalpana and Vasanth, 'From Social Action to Political Action: Women and the 81st Amendment', *Economic and Political Weekly*, vol. 32, no. 5, 1 February 1997.

Kapur, Naina, 'CBI's Approach Discouraging for Rape Victims', *The Pioneer*, 21 September 1993.

Kapur, Ratna, *Subversive Sites: Feminist Engagements with the Law in India*, Delhi, Sage, 1996.

———, ' "A Love Song to Our Mongrel Selves": Hybridity, Sexuality and the Law', *Social and Legal Studies*, vol. 8, no. 3, 1999.

———, 'Sexcapades and the Law', *Seminar* 505, September 2001.

——— and Brenda Cossman, 'On Women, Equality and the Constitution: Through the Looking Glass of Feminism', *National Law School Journal*, vol. 1, 1993.

——— and Shomona Khanna, 'Women's Right to Law', *The Hindu*, 26 April 1998.

Karat, Brinda, 'On Caste-based Arguments in Defence of Male Domination', *People's Democracy*, 15 June 1997.

Karkal, Malini, 'Indian Family Planning Programme. A Historical Perspective', on file with Jagori, New Delhi, undated.

Karr, Robin Bradley, 'Review of Roberto Unger's *What Should Legal Analysis Become? Yale Law Journal*, vol. 106, no. 8, June 1997.

Katzenstein, Mary Fainsod, 'Getting Women's Issues on the Public Agenda: Body Politics in India', *Samya Shakti*, vol. 6, 1991.

Kaviraj, Sudipta, 'A Critique of the Passive Revolution', *Economic and Political Weekly*, Annual Number, 1988.

———, 'Dilemmas of Democratic Development in India', in Adrian Leftwich, ed., *Democracy and Development*, Cambridge, Polity Press, 1996.

Kennedy, David, 'The International Human Rights Movement: Part of the Problem?', *European Human Rights Law Review 3*, 2001.

Kessler, Suzanne, J., 'The Medical Construction of Gender: Case Management of Inter-sexed Infants', in Anne C. Herrmann and Abigail J. Stewart, eds, *Theorising Feminism: Parallel Trends in the Humanities and Social Sciences*, Boulder, Westview Press, 1994.

Khan, Ayesha and Sanchita Sharma, 'When Foeticide Gets you Money from the Court', *The Indian Express*, 4 August 2001.

Kingdom, Elizabeth, *What's Wrong With Rights? Problems of Feminist Politics of Law*, Edinburgh, Edinburgh University Press, 1991.

Kishwar, Madhu, 'Codified Hindu Law: Myth and Reality', *Economic and Political Weekly*, vol. 29, no. 33, 13 August 1994.

———, 'Women and Politics: Beyond Quotas', *Economic and Political Weekly*, vol. 31, no. 43, 26 October 1996.

——— and Ruth Vanita, 'Why Can't We Report to Each Other?', *Manushi*, no. 37, 1980–1.

——— and Ruth Vanita, 'Using Women as a Pretext for Repression: The Indecent Representation of Women (Prohibition) Bill', *Manushi*, no. 37, 1987.

Kumar, Radha, *The History of Doing*, Delhi, Kali for Women, 1993.

———, 'Sex and Punishment Among Mill-Workers in Early-twentieth Century Bombay', in Michael Anderson and Sumit Guha, eds, *Changing Concepts of Rights and Justice in South Asia*, Delhi, Oxford University Press 1998.

Kurien, C.T., *Global Capitalism and the Indian Economy*, New Delhi, Orient Longman, 1994.

Kymlicka, Will, 'Three Forms of Group-differentiated Citizenship in Canada', in Seyla Benhabib, ed., *Democracy and Difference: Contesting the Boundaries of the Political*, Princeton, Princeton University Press, 1996.

Laclau, Ernesto and Chantal Mouffe, *Hegemony and Socialist Strategy: Towards a Radical Democratic Politics*, London, Verso, 1985.

Laclau, Ernesto, *New Reflections on the Revolution of Our Time*, London, Verso, 1990.

———, 'Universalism, Particularism and the Question of Identity', *October*, no. 61, 1992.

Lakshmi, Rama, 'Having a Say in Policy', *The Hindu*, 15 April 2001.

Landes, Joan, *Women and the Public Sphere in the Age of the French Revolution*, Ithaca, Cornell University Press, 1988.

Le Doeuff, Michele, 'Feminism is Back in France—Or is it?', *Hypatia*, vol. 15, no. 4, 2000.

Lingat, Robert, *The Classical Law of India* (tr. J. Duncan M. Derrett), Berkeley, University of California Press, 1973.

Loomba, Ania, 'Let's Talk About Lex', *The India Magazine*, April–May 1998.

———, 'Dead Women Tell No Tales: Issues of Female Subjectivity, Subaltern Agency and Tradition in Colonial and Postcolonial Writings on Widow Immolation in India', *History Workshop* 36, 1993.

Luker, Kristin, *Abortion and the Politics of Motherhood*, Berkeley, University of California Press, 1984.

MacKinnon Catharine, 'Feminism, Marxism, Method and the State: Towards Feminist Jurisprudence', *Signs*, vol. 8, no. 4, Summer 1983.

———, *Feminism Unmodified*, Cambridge and London, Harvard University Press, 1987.

Mahmood, Tahir, 'Custom as a Source of Law in Islam', *Journal of the Indian Law Institute*, vol. 7, 1965.

Mamdani, Mahmood, 'Africa: Democratic Theory and Democratic Struggles', *Economic and Political Weekly*, vol. 10, no. 41, October 1992.

Manegold, Catherine S., 'A Rape Case Worries Advocates for the Retarded', *The New York Times*, 14 March 1993.

Mardorossian, Carine M., 'Towards a New Feminist Theory of Rape', *Signs*, vol. 27, no. 3, Spring 2002.

Mazumdar, Vina, 'Historical Soundings', *Seminar* 457, September 1997.

———, 'Political Ideology of the Women's Movement's Engagement With Law', in Amita Dhanda and Archana Parasher, eds, *Engendering Law: Essays in Honour of Lotika Sarkar*, Lucknow, Eastern Book Company, 1999.

Menon, Nivedita, 'Women and Citizenship', in Partha Chatterjee, ed., *Wages of Freedom*, Delhi, Oxford University Press, 1998.

———, 'State/Gender/Community: Citizenship in Contemporary India', *Economic and Political Weekly*, 31 January 1998.

———, 'Universalism Without Foundations?', *Economy and Society*, vol. 31, no. 1, February 2002.

Menon, Ritu and Kamla Bhasin, 'Recovery, Rupture, Resistance: Indian State and the Abduction of Women During Partition', *Economic and Political Weekly*, 24 April 1993.

Meyers, Diana Tietjens, 'The Rush to Motherhood—Pronatalist Discourse and Women's Autonomy', *Signs*, vol. 26, no. 3, Spring 2001.

Mies, Maria, *Patriarchy and Accumulation on a World Scale: Women in the International Division of Labour*, London, Zed Books, 1991.

Minow, Martha, 'Book Review', *Harvard Education Review* 53, 1983.

———, 'Book Review', *Harvard Law Review* 98, 1985.

———, 'Book Review', *Studies in American History* 13, 1985.

Mishra, Yamini, 'Unsafe Abortions and Women's Health', *Economic and Political Weekly*, 6 October 2001.

Mitchell, Juliet, *Woman's Estate*, Harmondsworth, Penguin, 1971.

Mitra, Chandan, 'Parliament as Caste Panchayats' Union', *The Pioneer*, 31 August 1997.

Mohanty, Manoranjan, 'On the Concept of Empowerment', *Economic and Political Weekly*, 17 June 1995.

Mossman, Mary Jane, 'Feminism and Legal Method: The Difference It Makes', in Martha Albertson Fineman and Nancy Sweet Thomadsen, eds, *At the Boundaries of Law*, New York and London, Routledge, 1991.

Mouffe, Chantal, 'Citizenship and Political Identity', *October*, no. 61, 1992.

———, *The Return of the Political*, London, Verso, 1993.

———, *The Democratic Paradox*, London, Verso, 2000.

Mukhopadhyay, Maitrayee, *Legally Dispossessed: Gender, Identity and the Process of Law*, Calcutta, Stree, 1998.

Murthy, Laxmi, 'Female "Foeticide"—Should We Use this Terminology?', Letter to the Editor in response to Mohan Rao, 'Female Foeticide: Where Do We Go?', *Issues in Medical Ethics*, no. IX(4), October–December 2001.

Mustafa, Seema, 'Forget Footing, Men Can't Even Stomach the Bill', *The Asian Age*, 18 July 1998.

Nair, Janaki, 'An Important Springboard', *Seminar* 457, September 1997.

Nandy, Ashis, 'The Politics of Secularism and the Recovery of Religious Tolerance', in Veena Das, ed., *Mirrors of Violence: Communities, Riots and Survivors in South Asia*, Delhi, Oxford University Press, 1990.

Naqvi, Saeed, 'No Mass Conversions Please' *The Indian Express*, 30 June 2000.

National Law School Journal (vol. 1), 'Rape: Challenging the Pedestals of Patriarchy', 1993.

Nicholson, Linda, 'Feminism and Marx: Integrating Kinship with the Economic', in Seyla Benhabib and Drucilla Cornell, eds, *Feminism as Critique*, Cambridge, Polity Press, 1987.

Nigam, Aditya, 'Radical Politics in the Time of Globalisation', in Niraja Gopal Jayal and Sudha Pai, eds, *Democratic Governance in India: Challenges of Poverty, Development and Identity*, New Delhi, Sage, 2001.

———, 'Beyond the Nationalist Imaginary: Dalit Politics in the Global Era', *The Indian Journal of Political Science*, vol. 62, no. 3, September 2001.

Nussbaum, Martha C., *Women and Human Development: The Capabilities Approach*, Cambrıdge, Cambridge University Press, 2000.

Okin, Susan Moller, *Women in Western Political Thought*, Princeton, Princeton University Press, 1979.

———, 'Gender, the Public and the Private', in David Held, ed., *Political Theory Today*, Cambridge, Polity Press, 1991.

———, 'John Rawls: Justice as Fairness—For Whom?', in Carol Pateman and Mary L. Shanley, eds, *Feminist Interpretations of Political Thought*, Blackwell, Polity Press, 1991.

———, *Justice, Gender and the Family*, New York, Basic Books, 1993.

Olsen, Frances E., 'The Myth of State Intervention in the Family', republished in Frances E. Olsen, ed., *Feminist Legal Theory Volume II: Positioning Feminist Theory Within the Law*, Dartmouth, Aldershot, 1985.

Omvedt, Gail, *Violence Against Women: New Movements and New Theories in India*, Delhi, Kali for Women, 1990.

———, *Reinventing Revolution*, New York, M.E. Sharpe Inc., 1993.

———, 'Women and PR', *The Hindu*, 12 September 2000.

Oudshoorn, Nelly, *Beyond the Natural Body: An Archaeology of Sex Hormones*, London, Routledge, 1994.

Padmanabhan, Manjula, 'Outlawing Sex Determination No Solution', *The Pioneer*, 22 September 1993.

Parasher, Archana, *Women and Family Law Reform in India*, New Delhi, Sage, 1992.

Parikh, Bhikhu, 'The Modern Conception of Right and its Marxist Critique', in Upendra Baxi, ed., *The Right to be Human*, New Delhi, Lancer, 1987.

'Parity and Universalism', Translated transcript of a discussion held at Maison des Sciences Humaine, Paris. *Differences: A Journal of Feminist Cultural Studies* 9(2), Summer, 1997.

Petchesky, Rosalind Pollack, *Abortion and Women's Choice: The State, Sexuality and Reproductive Freedom*, New York, Longman, 1984.

Phillips, Anne, *Engendering Democracy*, Cambridge, Polity Press, 1991.

———, 'Democracy and Difference: Some Problems for Feminist Theory', in Will Kymlicka, ed., *The Rights of Minority Cultures*, Oxford, Oxford University Press, 1995.

———, *The Politics of Presence. The Political Representation of Gender, Ethnicity and Race*, Oxford, Clarendon Press, 1995. Reissued in paperback, 1998. All references to the book here are to the 1998 edition.

Pitkin, Hanna Fenichel, *The Concept of Representation*, Berkeley and Los Angeles, University of California Press, 1967.

Poulantzas, Nicos, *State, Power, Socialism* (tr. Patrick Camiller), London, New Left Books, 1978.

Rai, Shirin and Kumud Sharma, 'Democratising the Indian Parliament: The "Reservation for Women' Debate", in Shirin Rai, ed., *International Perspectives on Gender and Development*, London, Macmillan, 2000.

Rajan, Rajeswari Sunder, *The Scandal of the State: Women, Law and Citizenship in Postcolonial India*, Delhi, Permanent Black, 2003.

Rajshekhar, P.T., 'The Voice of the Persecuted Nationalities Denied Human Rights', *Dalit Voice*, vol. 17, no. 18, 1–15 August 1999.

Raman, Vasanthi, 'Women's Reservations and Democratization: An Alternative Perspective', *Economic and Political Weekly*, vol. 34, no. 50, 11 December 1991.

Rao, Arati, 'Right in the Home', *National Law School Journal*, vol. 1, 1993.

Rao, Mohan, 'Population Policies: States Approve Coercive Measures', *Economic and Political Weekly*, vol. 36, no. 29, 21 July 2001.

Rapp, Rayna, 'The Power of "Positive" Diagnosis: Medical and Maternal Discourses on Amniocentesis', in Karen Michaelson, ed., *Childbirth in America: Anthropological Perspectives*, South Hadley, Massachusetts, Bergin and Harvey, 1987.

———, 'Accounting for Amniocentesis', in Shirley Linderban and Margaret Locke, eds, *Knowledge, Power and Practice: Medical Anthropology*, California, University of California Press, 1993.

———, 'Risky Business: Genetic Counselling in a Shifting World', in Jane Schneider and Rayna Rapp, eds, *Articulating Hidden Histories: History, Anthropology and the Influence of Eric B. Wolf*, California, University of California Press, 1994.

Ravindra, R.P., 'Campaign Against Sex Determination Tests', *Lokayan Bulletin* 8, 1990.

Ray, Raka, *Fields of Protest: Women's Movements in India*, Delhi, Kali for Women, 1999.

Rendall, Jane, *The Origins of Modern Feminism*, New York, Schocken, 1984.

Riley, Denise, *Am I That Name? Feminism and the Category of 'Women' in History*, Minneapolis, University of Minnesota Press, 1988.

Ring, Laura, 'Sexual Harassment and the Production of Gender', *Differences: A Journal of Feminist Cultural Studies* 6.1, 1994.

Saberwal, Vasant and Mahesh Rangarajan, *Battles Over Nature: Science and the Politics of Conservation*, Delhi, Permanent Black, 2003.

Sachs, A. and J.H. Wilson, *Sexism and the Law: A Study of Male Beliefs and Judicial Bias*, Oxford, Martin Robertson, 1978.

Sadashivam, Bharati, 'The Silent Scream', *The Illustrated Weekly of India*, 14 September 1986.

Sandel, Michael, *Liberalism and the Limits of Justice*, Cambridge, Cambridge University Press, 1982.
———, 'Moral Argument and Liberal Toleration: Abortion and Homosexuality', in Amitai Etzione, ed., *New Communitarian Thinking*, Charlottesville, University Press of Virginia, 1995.
Sangari, Kumkum, 'Gender Lines: Personal Laws, Uniform Laws, Conversions', *Social Scientist*, vol. 27, nos 5–6, May–June 1999.
———, and Sudesh Vaid, 'Institutions, Beliefs, Ideologies: Widow Immolation in Contemporary Rajasthan', in Kumari Jayawardene and Malati de Alwis, eds, *Embodied Violence*, Delhi, Kali for Women, 1996.
Sarkar, Tanika, 'Rhetoric Against Age of Consent: Resisting Colonial Reason and Death of a Child-Wife', *Economic and Political Weekly*, vol. 28, no. 36, 4 September 1993.
Sawicki, Jana, *Disciplining Foucault*, New York and London, Routledge, 1991.
Scanlon, T.M., 'Partisan for Life', *The New York Review* 15 July 1993.
Schneider, Elizabeth H., 'The Dialectics of Rights and Politics: Perspectives from the Women's Movement', in Martha Albertson Fineman and Nancy Sweet Thomadsen, eds, *At the Boundaries of Law*, New York and London, Routledge, 1991.
Schor, Naomi, 'French Feminism is a Universalism', *Differences: A Journal of Feminist Cultural Studies* 7.1, 1995.
Scott, David, 'Colonial Governmentality', *Social Text*, no. 43, 1995.
———, 'Community, Number, Ethos of Democracy', in *Refashioning Futures: Criticism After Postcoloniality*, Princeton, Princeton University Press, 1999.
Scott, Joan W., 'Deconstructing Equality-Versus-Difference: Or, the Uses of Poststructuralist Theory for Feminism', in Frances E. Olsen, ed., *Feminist Legal Theory I: Foundations and Outlooks*, Aldershot, Dartmouth Publishing Company, 1995.
———, *Only Paradoxes to Offer: French Feminists and the Rights of Man*, Cambridge MA, Harvard University Press, 1996.
———, ' "La Querelle des Femmes", in the Late Twentieth Century', *Differences: A Journal of Feminist Cultural Studies* 9(2), Summer 1997.
Sehgal, B.P. Singh, *Women, Birth Control and the Law*, New Delhi, Deep and Deep, 1991.
Shah, Ghanshyam, 'Conversion, Reconversion and the State', *Economic and Political Weekly*, 6 February 1999.

Sharp, Andrew, *Justice and the Maori*, Melbourne, Oxford University Press, 1990.

Shetkari Mahila Aghadi, 'Reservations on Reservation', *Communalism Combat*, June 1997.

Singha, Radhika, 'Civil Authority and Due Process: Colonial Criminal Justice in the Banaras Zamindari, 1781–95', in Michael Anderson and Sumit Guha, eds, *Changing Concepts of Rights in South Asia*, Delhi, Oxford University Press, 1998.

Smart, Carol, *Feminism and the Power of Law*, London and New York, Routledge, 1989.

Snider, I., 'Legal Reform and Social Control: The Dangers of Abolishing Rape', *Interntional Journal of the Sociology of Law* 13(4), 1985.

Spivak, Gayatri, *In Other Worlds*, New York and London, Methuen, 1987.

———, 'Discussion: An Afterword on the New Subaltern', in Partha Chatterjee and Pradeep Jeganathan, eds, *Subaltern Studies XI, Community, Gender and Violence*, Delhi, Permanent Black, 2000.

Srinivasan, Bina, 'Dealing with Sexual Harassment at the Workplace: Impasse Continues', *Economic and Political Weekly*, 11 September 1999.

Sundar, Nandini, 'The Clash of Civilizations', *The Indian Express*, 24 January 1999.

Sypnowich, Christine, 'The Future of Socialist Legality: A Reply to Hunt', *New Left Review* 193, 1992.

Taylor, Charles, 'Human Rights: The Legal Culture', in *Philosophical Foundations of Human Rights*, UNESCO and International Institute of Philosophy, 1986.

Temkin, Jennifer, 'Women, Rape and Law Reform', in Sylvana Tomaselli and Roy Porter, eds, *Rape*, Oxford, Basil Blackwell, 1986.

Tharu, Susie and Tejaswini Niranjana, 'Problems for a Contemporary Theory of Gender', in Nivedita Menon, ed., *Gender and Politics in India*, Delhi, Oxford University Press, 1999,

Unger, Roberto Mangabeira, *Law in Modern Society*, New York, Free Press, 1976.

———, 'The Critical Legal Studies Movement', *Harvard Law Review*, vol. 96, 561, January 1983.

Vance, Carole S., 'Pleasure and Danger: Towards a Politics of Sexuality', in Carole Vance, ed., *Pleasure and Danger*, Boston, Routledge, 1984.

Vishwanathan, Kalpana, 'Whose Body, Whose Health?', *Seminar* 505, September 2001.

Weber, Eugen, *Peasants into Frenchman*, Stanford, Stanford University Press, 1976.

Weinreb, Lloyd L., 'What are *Civil* Rights?', *Social Philosophy and Policy*, vol. 8, Issue 2, Spring 1991.

West, Cornel, 'CLS and a Liberal Critic', *Yale Law Journal* 97, Yale L.J. 757, April 1988.

West, Robin, 'Taking Freedom Seriously', *Harvard Law Review*, vol. 104, no. 1, November 1990.

———, 'The Difference in Women's Hedonic Lives: A Phenomenological Critique of Feminist Legal Theory', in Frances E. Olsen, ed., *Feminist Legal Theory Volume I*, Aldershot, Dartmouth Publishers, 1995.

Williams, Patricia J., *The Alchemy of Race and Rights: Diary of a Law Professor*, Cambridge, MA, Harvard University Press, 1991.

Yadav, Yogendra, 'Electoral Politics in the Time of Change: India's Third Electoral System, 1989–99', *Economic and Political Weekly*, 21–28 August 1999.

——— (Hindi), 'Swarth Aur Moh ke Beech Fansa Mahila Arakshan Bill', *Dainik Bhaskar*, 26 August 2000.

Index

The University of Illinois Press
is a founding member of the
Association of American University Presses.

University of Illinois Press
1325 South Oak Street
Champaign, IL 61820-6903
www.press.uillinois.edu